F. H. (Frederic Hungerford) Bowman

The Structure of the Wool Fibre

In it´s Relation to the Use of Wool for Technical Purposes

F. H. (Frederic Hungerford) Bowman

The Structure of the Wool Fibre
In it´s Relation to the Use of Wool for Technical Purposes

ISBN/EAN: 9783743686786

Printed in Europe, USA, Canada, Australia, Japan

Cover: Foto ©Andreas Hilbeck / pixelio.de

More available books at **www.hansebooks.com**

The Structure of the Wool Fibre.

THE MERINO SHEEP.

THE STRUCTURE

OF THE

WOOL FIBRE,

IN ITS RELATION TO THE

USE OF WOOL FOR TECHNICAL PURPOSES;

Illustrated with numerous Engravings
and Coloured Plates.

BY

F. H. BOWMAN, D.Sc., F.R.S.E., F.L.S.,

*Fellow of the Chemical Society; Fellow of the Royal Microscopical Society;
Member of the Society of Arts and Manufactures; Fellow of the Society
of Chemical Industry; Vice-President of the Society of Dyers
and Colourists; Straton Prizeman and Gold Medallist
in Technology, University of Edinburgh.*

MANCHESTER:

PALMER AND HOWE, 73, 75, & 77, PRINCESS STREET.
LONDON: SIMPKIN, MARSHALL, & CO.
PHILADELPHIA: HENRY CAREY BAIRD & CO.
1885.

All Rights Reserved.

MANCHESTER:
PALMER AND HOWE, PRINTERS, PRINCESS STREET.

To the
Memory of my Father,

James Bowman, Esq., J.P.,

of
Savile Grove, Halifax,
to whose forethought and kindness
I am indebted for the
inestimable advantages of
a Liberal and Scientific Education,
This Work is Dedicated,
with every mark of affection
and esteem by
The Author.

PREFACE.

THE following pages are the full text, with additions, of five lectures delivered to the students of the Bradford Technical College and the members of the Dyers and Colourists' Society in the early part of this year. The last lecture was delivered by special request at the Huddersfield Technical College. These lectures are a continuation of the series which I delivered in 1880 on the structure of the cotton fibre, and are intended to cover the whole range required by the mixed fabric trade of Bradford. They are, of course, very far from exhaustive, and really only form the commencement of a scientific investigation of the nature and relations of the cotton and wool fibres, so far as their structure and technical applications are concerned. The work was commenced many years ago, and undertaken because at that time there was no definite knowledge on many of the subjects to be obtained anywhere. As the work proceeded, many new investigations opened up which it has been impossible, with the time at my command, to follow more than very superficially; and no one is more aware than myself of the wide field which is left untouched. At the same time, even partial knowledge is better than none, and these lectures are offered as a first systematic treatment of the technology of the wool fibre. I have published them in the original lecture form in which they were delivered, because it offers a less rigid and exacting literary setting than a more formal work would require, and serves better for a first systematic treatment than will be afterwards necessary when we can speak with greater definiteness on many parts of the subject. Defective, however, as the work is, it has been the result of much labour and experimental research, and those who know most of the tiring and often disappointing nature of this class of investigation will best appreciate the results which I have been able to deduce from these researches in regard to the structure of the fibre, the analysis of wools, the difference in the appearance of the various classes of wools when examined microscopically, the strength and elasticity of the various wools and hairs, the regularity in the finished yarns, and the degree of perfection which can at present be obtained by our best manufacturers, as well as the spectroscopic analysis of the surface of dyed fabrics. Most of the facts I have endeavoured to verify myself, and where I have not been able to do so, I give the authorities, so that reference can be made direct. I was most dependent in this respect in regard to the various breeds of sheep, and I gratefully acknowledge the assistance derived from Youatt and Spooner's works, and also the kind assistance of several friends in giving information on this part of the subject.

If I had waited until I was satisfied with the results of my investigations, the work would probably never have been published; but the fact that I am practically acquainted with the manufacture of worsted yarns as well as cotton, having learned the business, and with my own hands erected and attended all the machines used in the spinning of worsted yarns, I thought that I was perhaps better qualified than any whom I knew to undertake the matter, since few who have had the scientific training necessary for the work have also had the practical experience. The labour of the pioneer is always the most difficult, but I have endeavoured to fulfil the task with conscientiousness as my contribution to the available literature of Technology. To render the frequent use of strictly technical and scientific terms more acceptable to the general reader, I have appended to the work a copious glossary, and a good index will also, no doubt, serve to facilitate reference.

In considering the general scope of the lectures, I thought it would be best to confine myself to the same lines as I had followed in the work on cotton, not only because it would enable a comparison to be made between the two fibres, but also because it prevented me from having in any direct manner to deal with the mechanical details of either spinning, manufacturing, or dyeing. Improvements in machinery and new processes are continually rendering the details which are applicable to one year unsuited to the next; but the general principles which underlie all these processes change at a far slower rate, while those which are founded on the structure of the raw material itself remain unchanged throughout all time. Much of the work, therefore, may prove of more than passing importance, and will, I hope, form the nucleus around which will be gathered a wider knowledge both of the principles and processes employed in the textile arts.

The plates of the typical sheep have been sketched for me from the most reliable and authentic drawings of the various animals, and the other anatomical and microscopical plates are the fac-simile reproduction of original sketches made by myself from actual objects under the microscope. Most of these sketches, from the necessity of the case, are diagrams rather than portraits, and frequently represent the result of many hundreds of careful observations, and I have to acknowledge the conscientious fidelity with which the artist, Mr. Oliver, of Manchester, has done his work in reproducing them from my drawings. The last lecture necessarily covers much of the same ground as the third lecture in the series on the cotton fibre, but viewed in the relation to the difference between wool and cotton, and this opens a wide field for further chemical research.

I have to thank many friends in Bradford, Halifax, and elsewhere for their kindness in furnishing me with samples of various yarns and wool, and I think it only due to them to state that the results given in the tables of strengths and regularities in twist and count are not derived from any one spinner's yarn, but are the average result of many testings extending over hundreds of samples made in different mills. Dr. Knecht, of Bradford, deserves my special thanks for his kindness in looking over the chemical parts of the work.

In conclusion, I feel that I ought to bear testimony to the care and attention bestowed by my publishers, Messrs. Palmer and Howe, in the production of the plates and letterpress, and I sincerely hope that this volume may only be the forerunner of others, from competent men, which will enlarge our knowledge of these important questions, and thus subserve the great work of technical education.

F. H. BOWMAN.

West Mount,
   Halifax, Yorkshire,
      April, 1885.

SYLLABUS OF CONTENTS.

LECTURE I.

GENERAL INTRODUCTION.

Importance of technical knowledge—Its relation to new industrial enterprise—Defects in existing processes—Co-ordination in manufacturing—Relation to mechanical and chemical perfection.

Variety of textile materials—Difference between animal and vegetable fibres—Gelatine and cellulose—Wool and cotton—Structure of cotton—Varieties of cotton—Flax and its structure—Chemical relations of flax.

Animal Fibres.—Silk structure—Composition and chemical relations of silk—Wool.

General division and arrangement of lectures—Nature of wool—Hair—Growth of hair—Structure of skin—Structure of hair—Surface of hair—Structure of hair follicles—Distribution of hair—Development of hair—Modification of hair—Felting of fibres—Difference between hair and wool—Typical wool fibre.

LECTURE II.

Introduction—Nature of wool—Curls and curves in wool fibre—Relation between quality and curliness.

Wool-bearing animals—Zoological classification—Characteristics of true sheep—Wild sheep.

Industrial classification of sheep—The Argali—The Rocky Mountain sheep—The Musmon.

European Sheep.—Sheep of Great Britain, Classification of—Welsh and Irish sheep—Forest and mountain sheep—Upland sheep—Long-woolled sheep.

Foreign Sheep.—Spanish and German Merino sheep—French sheep—Swiss sheep—Italian sheep—German sheep—Sheep of Holland and Belgium—Russian sheep—Danubian sheep—Sheep of Turkey and Greece—Sheep of Sweden, Norway, Denmark, and Iceland.

Asiatic Sheep.—Argali—Persian sheep—Tibet sheep—Indian sheep—Cashmere goat—Chinese sheep.

African Sheep.—Sheep of Egypt, Soudan, and Abyssinia—Sheep of Morocco, Algiers, and Tunis—West Coast sheep—Cape Colony and Natal.

Australasian Sheep.—Australian, New Zealand, and Tasmanian sheep.

American Sheep.—Sheep of United States—South American sheep—River Plate sheep—Alpaca goat.

Angora goat—Its introduction into Cape Colony and America.

LECTURE III.

Introduction—Recapitulation—Difference between wool and hair.

1. WHAT IS THE TYPICAL STRUCTURE OF A WOOL FIBRE?

   (a) In regard to the mechanical arrangement of its ultimate parts.

   General structure of fibre—Structure of surface—Structure of interior—Early investigations—Cause of lustre—Effects of washing—Colour in fibre—Pigment cells—Structure of cortical substance.

Strength of wool fibres—Experiments on strength of various hairs and wools—Elasticity of fibres—Tables of strength and elasticity.

Felting of wool—Nature of felting—Cause of felting—Cotting of wool—Use of yolk—Effects of moisture on wool.

Kemps in wool—Structure of kemps—Cause of kemps.

(b) In regard to its chemical composition.

Composition of fibres—Cotton—Silk—Wool—Molecular structure—Relation to albumenoids and gelatine—Horny tissue—Analysis of various wools—Products of decomposition—Water of hydration—Proportion of water in wools—Ultimate analysis—Suint or yolk—Its use—Its relation to wool—Its composition.

Mineral constituents of wool—Analysis of wool ashes—Relation of mineral constituents to dyeing.

Action of heat upon wool—Destructive distillation—Sulphur in wool.

Action of reagents upon wool—Alkalis—Acids—Strengthening and deterioration of wool by reagents—Experiments on strength—Relation of soaps and various waters to wool-washing—Washing and cleansing of wool—Action of gases upon wool—Bleaching of wool—Relation of wool fibres to mordants—Absorption of weak reagents by wool.

Chemical dissociation of wool from other fibres—Methods of separation and determination.

LECTURE IV.

Introduction—Recapitulation of nature of mechanical and chemical structure of wool.

2. WHAT VARIATIONS FROM THIS TYPE STRUCTURE ARE PRESENTED TO US?

(c) In fibres from the same animals and grown at the same time.

Variation in quality of wool—Distribution of quality—Classification of quality—Sorting of wool—Relation of quality of wool to counts spun—Microscopical character of various qualities—Variation of fibres in diameter—Industrial analysis of various classes of wool—Tables of qualities and weights derived from various kinds of wool.

(d) In fibres from the same animal grown in different years.

Effects of different seasons—Effects of feeding—Effects of pasturage on character of fibres.

(e) In fibres from the same animal grown under different climatic and other conditions.

Effects of environment—Change of climate—Geographical distribution—Merino, Australian, and other sheep—Angora goats—Deterioration of sheep.

(f) In fibres from different breeds of sheep grown in different countries.

Differences in wool fibres—Classification of fibres—Hairs and wool—Intermediate varieties—True wool fibres.

Structure of alpaca fibres—Characteristics of nomad and mountain wools—Mohair—Its structure and relations—English bright wools—Middle-class wools—Southdown wool—Merino wools—Australian Botany wool.

3. HOW FAR THESE VARIATIONS IN THE ULTIMATE STRUCTURE MAY AFFECT ITS USE IN THE MANUFACTURING PROCESS.

(g) Mechanically.

Relation of wool fibre to mechanical arrangement—Necessity of good machinery—Its adaptation to special work—Preliminary processes—Washing of wool—Drying of wool—Worsted and woollen yarn—Essential difference—Relation of wool structure to each—Mechanical operations—Imperfections in yarn—Degree of uniformity attainable.

Experiments with yarn—Weight and counts of yarn—Table of weights and counts—Series of examples of single and twofold yarns to test regularity in strength, twist, and counts—General results of these tests—Improvements in spinning.

LECTURE V.

Introduction—Mechanical and chemical structure of wool—Variation in effect in manufacturing process produced.

(h) Chemically.

Composition of wool—Relation to dyeing—Nature of colour—Nature of light—Relation of dyed fabrics to light—Spectral analysis of dyed fabrics—Structure of fibre in relation to dyeing—Cause of colour and lustre in fibre—Probable nature of union of fibre with colouring matter—Theories of dyeing—Classification of dyeing processes—Influence of time in dyeing—Nature of various colours in relation to fibre—Chemical nature of changes—Microscopical examination of dyed fibres—Effects observed by different processes—Importance of further knowledge—Improved methods of dyeing—Advance of technical education—Conclusion.

List of Figures in Text.

FIG.
1. Typical Wool Fibre 51
2. Fibre Testing Machine 142

List of Plates.

		PAGE.
	Merino Sheep (coloured)	Frontispiece.
I.	Cotton Fibres	16
II.	Flax Fibres	20
III.	Silk Fibres	22
IV.	Section of Skin	30
V.	Longitudinal Section of Hair	32
VI.	Transverse Section of Hair	34
VII.	Cells Constituting Hair	36
VIII.	Surface of Human Hair	38
IX.	Longitudinal Section of Hair Follicle	40
X.	Typical Wool Fibre	52
XI.	Various Hairs Magnified	58
XII.	Cheviot Sheep (coloured)	76
XIII.	Southdown Sheep (coloured)	84
XIV.	Lincoln Sheep (coloured)	88
XV.	Leicester Sheep (coloured)	92
XVI.	Fat-tailed Sheep (coloured)	112
XVII.	Alpaca Goat (coloured)	124
XVIII.	Angora Goat (coloured)	126
XIX.	Section of Wool Fibre	132
XX.	Kempy Wool Fibres	162
XXI.	Fleece of Leicester Hog	218
XXII.	Fibres of Fine Lincoln Wool	224
XXIII.	Fibres of Coarse Lincoln Wool	226
XXIV.	Fibres of Diseased Wool	238
XXV.	Fibres of Alpaca	240
XXVI.	Fibres of Pacpathian Wool	246
XXVII.	Fibres of Coarse Chinese Wool	248
XXVIII.	Fibres of Mohair	250
XXIX.	Fibres of Half-bred Mohair	252
XXX.	Fibres of Southdown Wool	254
XXXI.	Fibres of American Merino Wool	256
XXXII.	Fibres of Australian Wool	258

THE STRUCTURE OF THE WOOL FIBRE

AND ITS RELATION TO THE

Use of Wool for Textile Purposes.

LECTURE I.

SOME time ago, in the spring of 1880, I delivered a series of three lectures upon the Structure of the Cotton Fibre in its relation to the use of cotton for technical applications. These lectures have since been published, and have, I believe, been the means of calling increased attention to the necessity for a more extended knowledge of the structure of all our raw materials, so as to enable us to turn their various distinctive peculiarities to the best possible advantage in our manufacturing processes.

I was requested at the time these lectures were delivered to extend my investigations to the structure of wool as well as cotton, and thus make the complete course a *resumé* of the present state of our knowledge respecting the materials which enter into the fabrication of the mixed goods which have so long been known as the peculiar feature of the Bradford trade.

I have now great pleasure in complying with this request, and although I am quite aware that I can enter only a short way into the wide field which such an enquiry opens, I will, nevertheless, endeavour to the best of my ability to make the lectures as wide in their range and as practical as I can. I need not say at the outset that the subject is surrounded with very great difficulties, because most of you know that all experimental researches require great patience and perseverance, even when the subject matter of the enquiry is of limited range. It becomes increasingly so when, as in the case of this enquiry, the various ramifications of the question are so extensive, and such various sciences as anatomy, physiology, chemistry, and mechanics have to be called into requisition. In addition to this, I have been able to find even less literature upon wool than upon cotton; and, in consequence of this, I have, in many of the researches, been obliged to begin at the very foundation, and have not had the advantage of the previous experience of others in the same field.

As I remarked at the outset of my lectures on cotton, the day is gone by when we can expect in this country to hold our position as a manufacturing nation, unless we bring to bear upon all our processes the advantages which a thorough knowledge of the nature of the raw materials which we use alone can give. The rapid strides which are being made by our competitors on the continent of Europe and in the United States of America, and the readiness with which they are calling into requisition all the resources which modern scientific discovery and mechanical invention have placed within their reach, ought to stimulate us to renewed exertion. I am persuaded we are not one jot behind them, either in our intellectual attainments or our energy and determination; and I believe that if, instead of resting satisfied with our present position, we keep abreast of the times, and carry into our manufactories and workshops the knowledge which a sound technical education can impart, we shall be enabled to maintain our supremacy and take the lead, whether it be in articles of utility or taste. Fortunately for us, our rivals, at any rate so far as textile manufactures are concerned, have to work with the same materials as ourselves, and our insular position, and the fact that we are the great ocean carriers of the world, makes our country the great central emporium through which the raw materials for the world's use must pass, which gives us facilities for selection and comparison which are enjoyed by no other nation. We must take every advantage of this, and keep our eyes open to every new discovery in this direction, so that, like the late Sir Titus Salt with alpaca and Mr. S. C. Lister with silk waste, we may be enabled to use what others cannot use or reject, and thus lay the foundation of new industrial enterprises. In addition to this, we must also make ourselves thorough masters of the great principles and laws which underlie all the processes and reactions which the raw material undergoes while it is being transformed either mechanically or chemically into the finished condition.

Unless we do this we can never expect to obtain the best results, because we shall be sure to treat the raw material either too little or too much, or subject it to processes which are either unnecessary or unfit for obtaining the object which we have in view. To gain this end, it is quite essential that at the very outset of all our textile manufactures we should have a clear and distinct knowledge of the true nature of the raw material upon which we have to work. No comprehension of general principles can obviate the necessity for this, because this alone can enable us to select that raw material which will best subserve the purpose which we have in view, and then enable us to select our various transforming processes, so as to suit the raw material by bringing into play its peculiar properties without injury or detriment to its structure.

Attention to this will always enable us to use the least expensive raw material for the purpose, because, if the raw material is not treated exactly as it should be in our mechanical and chemical operations we shall be obliged to use a better material than we otherwise should, and thus give an advantage in price to our competitors.

The neglect of these precautions, which have in most instances arisen from a want of knowledge, has in the past been the cause of very great annoyance and pecuniary loss to the trade, because we must all be familiar with numerous cases where the lustre of the wool has been destroyed by the chemical means used to cleanse it, or the staple broken and destroyed by imperfect construction or setting of the machinery.

Nor is this all, for it frequently happens that the means employed in some of the earlier stages of manufacture are absolutely detrimental to those which are to follow afterwards, and which render it quite impossible to attain the results which were desired. You all know that the spinner and weaver, who are usually quite distinct from the dyer and finisher, very seldom either know or consider the processes to which the yarn or goods will be subjected during the dyeing and finishing, and hence it frequently happens that the latter has to remove defects which might be avoided by more care and forethought in the earlier stages of manufacture. On this point I need only instance such a case as the influence of temperature upon the wool fibre, which we shall afterwards see is a very important point in determining both the after strength and lustre of the wool, as well as the power which the fibre possesses to receive the dye. We all know how seldom the thermometer is called into requisition in the washing process to determine the heat of the water;—usually it is considered quite sufficient to guess the heat by the immersion of the hand, or the haphazard turning in of steam, a process which between two different conditions of the body or two different individuals, will not be the same within a very much wider range than we should imagine to be possible without trying the experiment. Take another case, viz., the use of oil along with the wool in the process of combing, or carding, or spinning, where the yarn is afterwards to be used in fabrics which are intended to be dyed into light and delicate shades, and requiring an even appearance over the whole surface, as well as where the wool is intended to retain its soft and supple condition. One of the secrets of the great success of the French dyers in certain classes of goods arises from the fact that the wool is worked dry, and thus the natural condition of the fibre is retained, and the constituent cells are better fitted to receive the dyestuff.

What we want is an intelligent understanding of every process, and the co-ordination of each to the after treatment of the fibre, so that every step will be a step in the right direction, and each process, while perfectly fulfilling its special function, not in any way interfering with any operation which succeeds it. It may seem at first sight as if this was a comparatively easy matter, and one which a very little practice would enable us to settle in such a way that very few mistakes would be made. Experience, however, teaches us otherwise; and it would not be difficult to instance very many cases where up to a recent period, and indeed, in some cases, even now, in our process of manufacture we have to undo, or at any rate put right in a subsequent process what we have put wrong in a former one. For example, how often do we find in the spinning of yarn that with the desire to produce solid bobbins in the preparing machinery, an excessive twist is put into the rovings, which in the spinning causes serious breakage of the raw material, and irregularity in the yarn which can never be removed? This excessive twist is often necessary because of an improper adaptation of the size and weight of the preparing bobbin to the quality and counts of the yarn to be wound on to it, as well as from the want in ordinary worsted machinery of a more automatic method of laying the yarn on to the bobbin. As another instance, in a different department, I had recently placed in my hands a sample of wool which had a very high lustre, and which lustre was almost entirely removed from the yarn before it was finished, in consequence of improper treatment in the washing of the wool, and several ingenious devices were being called into requisition to restore the lustre again to the fibre.

The same wool, in the hands of another firm, and only a short distance from each other, presented a wonderful contrast, and came up in the yarn bright and shining, although I have strong reason to believe that this firm might even still further improve, so as to retain a larger portion of the original lustre, if they used a different washing liquor. We must always remember, that we can only attain the greatest possible perfection when we have the best possible results obtained in every process through which the fibre passes, and when every stage in the onward course is arranged and carried out with the final consummation in view. This perfection we can only attain by a thorough technical knowledge of the special work which each process is intended to perform, and this, in turn, will always depend upon our knowledge of the structure and affinities of the raw materials which we use. It is necessary, therefore, that in order successfully to use each raw material for its best purpose, and in its best way, that we should make ourselves thoroughly acquainted with its typical and special structure, both mechanically and chemically, and when this is done we can then enter into the principles of the transforming processes with an accurate knowledge of what we wish to produce, and a reasonable expectation of being enabled to accomplish it.

In these lectures we do not propose to deal with the mechanical transformations, but only with the raw material as a basis for textile manufactures, because the former would open up a much wider field than we have time to explore, and introduce us into the discussion of various kinds of machinery which are continually undergoing a process of improvement, so that machinery which is abreast of the times this year becomes obsolete in the course of a decade. What we seek to enquire into is the essential nature of our fibres, which must always form the raw material upon which our machines will have to work, and which by suitable selection and culture is likewise capable of improvement, so as to render it better fitted for our various requirements.

In our textile manufactures the raw materials are very various, and derived from many sources, and our complicated civilisation demands from the vegetable, animal, and mineral kingdoms continually larger and larger supplies. In the clothing for our bodies, the furniture of our houses, and the various articles for decoration, as well as utility, which are now deemed almost indispensable in all civilised countries, we have an increasingly wide field of demand; while the quickening impulse of competition in trade necessitates the employment of new forms and combinations, as well as the discovery of new fibres which can enter into our manufactures.

As a rule, the fibres which are generally in use are the product either of plants or animals, and consist of such substances as cotton, flax, hemp, jute, china grass, silk, wool, goats' hair, camels' hair, and the hairy covering of many other animals. These various fibres differ very widely in their nature. They all possess a very different mechanical structure and chemical composition. This necessitates in every case a different method of treatment so as to enable them to be spun into yarn, and a different series of chemical reactions, so as to impart to them the various colours which they are required to receive, so as to fit them for the manufacturing process. We shall have to look at some of these differences further on, but meanwhile we may remark that between the fibres of vegetable and animal origin there is one great chemical difference. The basis of all vegetable cells is cellulose, a substance which, when perfectly pure, consists of carbon, hydrogen, and oxygen in the proportions indicated by the formula $C_6 H_{10} O_5$, and which possesses great chemical inertness, having very little affinity for other bodies, and which can scarcely be acted upon by any reagents except strong acids and alkalies. This substance, you will remember, I treated upon at considerable length in my lectures upon cotton. The basis of all animal fibres is gelatine, or some albumenoid body allied to it. We never find a trace of cellulose in the animal kingdom. While our albumenoid molecule contains the same substances in its composition as the molecule of cellulose, it also contains two others,—nitrogen and sulphur,—so that its structure is much more complicated, and we shall have to look more particularly at it when we come to consider the chemistry of the wool fibre. This substance, or its co-geners, forms the solid walls of the animal cells which build up the fibres, and whether the materials we have to work upon be the secretion from a worm, such as silk, or the hairs of a goat, or the wool of a sheep, it is the material basis which forms the largest portion of the solid structure. Gelatine has a higher specific gravity than cellulose, and hence animal substances sink in water while vegetable substances swim. As a general rule, the ultimate vegetable cells are larger than the animal cells, and hence there are a larger number of the latter in the same space, and the tenacity of gelatine is also greater than that of cellulose, so that animal substances and fibres are as a rule stronger than vegetable fibres. As I have already pointed out in the case of cotton, so also most of these animal fibres are too minute to be examined with the naked eye, except in their general aspect. Hence, we require the use of a powerful microscope when we wish to notice their structure more closely, and especially when we are examining the differences between the various fibres in detail. These differences, although they are so minute, and in some instances they vary only by quantities which are represented by thousand parts of a linear inch, are nevertheless quite essential to be known if we are to obtain the best results from the material. In the same way, small chemical differences are equally important, because of their reaction when the raw material is required to be treated chemically. In my lectures on the cotton fibre I gave a full account of the large microscope which I employed in these researches, and the various accessories which were attached to it, so as to enable me to determine with absolute exactness the very minute measurements involved in the differences between the diameter of the fibres. It is, therefore, unnecessary for me to enlarge upon it here, further than to say that I employed the same micrometer and similar powers, so far as the eye pieces and object glasses are concerned. In some cases I used powers as high as 8,000 diameters, a power which, if we could see a linear inch under the microscope at once, would make it appear as large as 666 feet, and a single fibre of Leicester wool would appear about 6 inches in diameter and 6,800 feet long, or very nearly the third of a mile. In working with the instrument I have also in these researches endeavoured, as far as possible, to make as many confirmatory observations as I could, so as to eliminate the errors which are so apt to arise when only one set of observations are taken.

One of the greatest difficulties with which I have had to contend in preparing these lectures, has arisen from the impossibility of so arranging my subject matter that it would present a consecutive series of observations, and not necessitate any recapitulation. This, however, I have found to be quite impossible, because the various parts of the subject do not shade into each other, but from lack of wider information present gaps which I shall be obliged to leave others to fill up, and have been linked together by ties which, in some cases, necessitate a restatement of facts already given.

The subject of the structure of wool fibre is more difficult than that of cotton, because the structural differences between the various classes of wool are more varied than those of different classes of cotton, and the effects of climate and species are more marked in the animal than the vegetable kingdom. Chemically, too, the difficulties have been greater because there is a greater vital action in the sheep than the cotton plant, and the composition of the wool is more affected by the state of health of the animal and the food upon which it is kept. It is not possible for us to enter upon the consideration of the structure of the wool fibre without first having some general knowledge of the various fibres, besides wool, which are used in textile manufactures, in order that we may be enabled to understand the differences which exist between them, especially so far as regards the mechanical arrangement of the ultimate parts of the fibre. This alone can enable us to see how far this difference affects the use to which it can be put in our manufacturing processes, and which fibres are suitable to be used together, as well as the part which each is best fitted to serve in the fabric.

It is calculated that more than one-tenth of our population is dependent upon the cotton, flax, wool, and silk manufactures which are carried on in this country, and these four fibres may be taken as typical in their character, so far as manufacturing is concerned, because they each possess special properties which fit them for use as raw material. These four substances, indeed, enter into the composition of nine-tenths of the clothing of the whole civilised world, and with the exception of food products, their cultivation occupies the largest share of the world's labour.

There is, of course, a very wide difference between the structure of vegetable and animal fibres, and they can each be very readily detected when placed under the microscope. In this manner it is possible often to detect adulterations, such as the mixture of cotton with wool in blankets or woollen goods; the mixture of cotton or flax with silk in sewing silk or goods; or of inferior with higher priced fibres of the same kind in various classes of silk, woollen, or worsted goods.

Let us look at a few of the more prominent characteristics of these various fibres.

COTTON.

Amongst the vegetable fibres the first place must be assigned to cotton, because it supplies by far the largest weight of material for the clothing of mankind, and can be manufactured into an almost unlimited variety of textures, suited for almost every possible purpose, whether for utility or ornament. Cotton may be defined as the woolly denticulated fibrous material which envelopes the seeds of various species and varieties of the genus *Gossypium*, belonging to the natural order *Malvaceæ*. The cotton fibres are firmly attached to the seeds, for which, indeed, in the economy of nature they were doubtless intended to serve the purpose of parachutes, so as to assist the dissemination of the seed by the action of the wind.

When the cotton is separated from the seed, after the boll is open and ripe, a process which is accomplished by the operation of ginning, the fibres or filaments when examined under the microscope present the appearance of continuous twisted and flattened or collapsed tubes, with a distinct cellular structure. The appearances of the various kinds of fibres which are present in a lock of cotton, differ only in regard to the nature of the internal cavity of the tube and the thickness of the tube walls. In half ripe or immature cotton the fibres are pellucid and ribbon-like, as though the tube had been squeezed quite flat, and with little or no twist visible. When the fibre is fully ripe and matured the tube walls are quite distinct and well defined, and the twist more regular and perfect. Upon this peculiar and characteristic twist in the fibre, and which is a peculiarity of cultivated cotton, depends to a large extent the power which cotton possesses of forming strong threads or yarn, because the necessary friction which prevents the fibres drawing out is obtained by the strands interlocking into the grooves of contiguous fibres. The various classes of cotton differ in the amount of twist which they possess, as well as in the length and fineness of the fibre; but the general features which we have indicated are common to them all, and render the fibre easy to detect when it is associated along with other substances in any textile fabric or yarn. Plate I. will give us a much better idea of the appearance of cotton than any description of cotton which can be given. Here we have B the unripe fibre, with its thin, pellucid, and ribbon-like structure. Then the half ripe fibre, C, with its slender cell walls and twisted form; and lastly, the fully matured and perfectly ripe cotton, D and E, with its distinct cellular structure, and solid thick cell walls with regular and uniform twist in the filaments. We have also sometimes a structureless fibre represented at A which does not spin well, and will not dye; and which, when occurring in large quantities, materially decreases the value of the cotton. This, as we shall afterwards see, corresponds to the "kemps" found in wool. A section of the cotton fibre presents the appearance of a collapsed tube with a general section not unlike that of a double-headed tee rail, such as is in common use on our principal railways. The walls of the tube vary in thickness with the degree of ripeness of the fibre, and appear to be formed by the deposit of concentric layers of fibrous matter upon the outer sheath or membrane of the fibre, which seems to be a continuous lamina of cellulose. There are many varieties of cotton, each of which has its distinctive peculiarities; but arranging them in the order of their length of staple, beginning with the longest, they may be classed—1, Sea Island; 2, Egyptian; 3, Peruvian; 4, American; and 5, Indian or Surat.

The American cotton grown in the United States may be taken as the typical fibre, and possesses an average length of staple of about 1 inch, and a diameter of $\frac{1}{1200}$ of an inch. For comparison, the following table may be useful:—

	Average length of fibre.	Average diameter of fibre.
Sea Island cotton	1¾ inches	$\frac{1}{1800}$ of an inch.
Egyptian ,,	1½ ,,	$\frac{1}{1620}$,,
Peruvian ,,	1¼ ,,	$\frac{1}{1260}$,,
American ,,	1 inch	$\frac{1}{1200}$,,
Surat or Indian ,,	¾ ,,	$\frac{1}{1180}$,,

Plate I

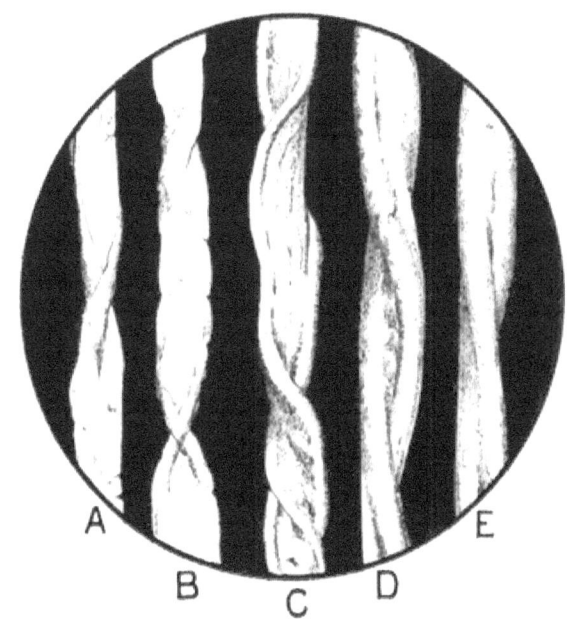

325 DIAMETERS.

COTTON FIBRES.

A. Glassy Structureless fibre.
B. Thin pellucid, unripe fibre.
C. Half ripe fibre, with thin Cell wall
D & E. Fully Mature and ripe fibre with full twist and thick well defined cell wall.

The chemical composition of the cotton fibre is véry simple. When fully ripe it is composed of pure cellulose, which we have already seen is a compound body, $C_6H_{10}O_5$. It is, however, never quite chemically pure, but always contains some unchanged juices and mineral substances along with oleagenous and waxy matter.

The cotton fibre holds a unique position in the order of vegetable textile fibres, because it is obtained from the plant by the simple process of picking when the boll or seed capsule is open and ripe. The cotton is ready for the process of manufacture without any other preliminary operation, except the separation of the fibre from the seed matrix upon which it grows. Most other vegetable tissues are procured, not from the fruit or seed, but from the stem and branches or leaves of the plant.

In very nearly all the more common plants, a casual observation, with a moderate magnifying power, of a section of the stem or branch, reveals the existence of a fibrous layer, of more or less tenacity, which is situated on the outside of the central part of the stem and next up to the bark. The fibres which compose this tissue descend vertically and rectilinearly, and form a series of concentric rings, and are composed of a large number of separate fibres, which are united together by a resinous and glutinous substance secreted from the outside of the primary layer of the fibre wall.

These fibres have received the general term of bast

fibres; and flax, hemp, jute, and china grass, as well as many other less known substances, are the isolated liber or cellular tissue of various plants which possess this characteristic. For textile fabrics the most typical may be taken to be represented by flax.

FLAX,

Which forms the raw material out of which linen is manufactured, is the fibre obtained from the stem of a plant called *Linum usitatissimum*, belonging to the natural order *Linaceæ*. The stem of this plant consists internally of woody shore or boon, and externally, immediately beneath the bark, of the cellular tissue from which the flax is prepared. When the plant is ripe it is cut down, dried, and the seed beaten out. The seed, when pressed, yields linseed oil, and the inspissated remains of the pressed seed is manufactured into oil cake, which is largely used as food for cattle. The thrashed stems of the plant are then steeped in water, a process which is termed "retting," and which produces a peculiar fermentation by means of which the glutinous and other matter in the stem is destroyed, and the woody fibre so disintegrated that it can be separated from the flax fibre, which forms the outer layer, by a simple mechanical process. When the separation is complete the fibrous flax is made up into bundles, and is ready, with suitable machinery, to undergo the usual textile process of combing or carding, and spinning and weaving.

When viewed under the microscope, the flax fibre

exhibits the appearance of a hollow cylindrical tube, which is open at both ends. The tube is, however, not continuous, as in the case of cotton, which we have already seen is a single cell, but is separated by distinct joints or knots, which appear at intervals irregularly distributed in the length of the fibre, at distances varying from two to six times the diameter of the tube. The diameter of the fibre varies in different qualities of commercial flax from about $\frac{1}{1100}$ of an inch to $\frac{1}{1800}$ of an inch. This description will be better understood by reference to Plate II., where we have a correct representation of a number of flax fibres when viewed with transmitted light and magnified about 400 diameters. Here the tubular structure of the fibre is distinctly seen, as well as the dividing septa or knots. These divisions mark the extremities of the cells, which during the growth of the plant formed the channel within which the juices and sap circulated, and the thickness of the cell wall was produced by secondary deposits upon the primary sheath. When the fibrillæ are treated with a solution of iodine and sulphuric acid, the spiral character of the secondary deposits can be very clearly seen, and the spiral form of the deposit detected; but there is no disposition, as in the case of cotton, to form a spiral tendency or twist in the fibres themselves, the spiral tendency being strictly confined to the secondary deposits within the cell walls. When spun into yarn the adhesive power which the fibres possess does not depend upon the arrangement of the fibres into contiguous grooves, as in the case of cotton, but upon the mechanical twist which is put into them by the operation of spinning, and also to the rough nature of the outer sheath of the fibre, which is more or less pitted in its character, arising from the incrusting deposit of resinous matter which can never be entirely removed. This resinous matter is of a yellowish grey colour, and formed, as we have already seen, the cement which in the plant stem united the separate fibrillæ into vascular bundles. The thickness and density of the tube walls render the fibre of flax stronger in proportion than that of cotton; but as the tenacity of the separate cells at their point of junction depends upon a chemical rather than a mechanical union, it is more readily injured by the action of reagents. Like cotton, the chemical basis of the ultimate structure of flax is cellulose; but it is never in the same pure condition as in cotton, because on the large scale we can never entirely remove the encrusting matter, and this always interferes with the impregnation of the fibre with dyeing solutions. It affords, however, a means of chemically distinguishing between cotton and flax, when they are mixed together in any fabric, by the difference in the reaction of caustic alkalies upon them. Equal parts, by weight, of caustic potash and water at a boiling temperature may be employed, and when the cotton and flax are immersed in the liquid for about a minute, and the excess of solution removed by pressing between blotting paper, the resinous matter always associated

Plate II

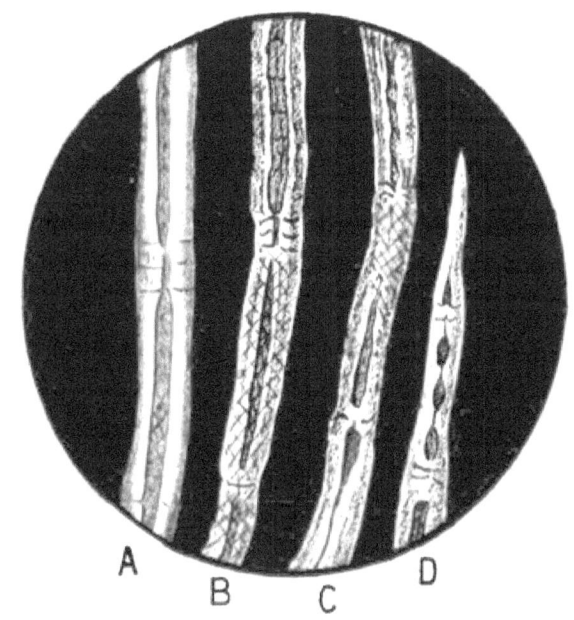

450 Diameters.

FLAX FIBRES.

A. Fibre treated with Nitric Acid.
B. Fibre treated with Nitric Acid, and then Sulphuric Acid and Iodine, to show spiral fibres.
C. Fibre with solid structure.
D. End of fibre with undeveloped cells.

with flax causes it to assume a dark yellow colour, while the purer cotton either remains white or turns a bright yellow.* M. Kuhlmann, in some of his researches, found that when very concentrated cold solutions of caustic potash were used cotton remains grey, while flax assumes an orange yellow colour, which he thinks is due to the presence of pectic substances associated with the flax fibre.†

The strength of the fibre walls in flax enables it to resist the solvent action of sulphuric acid longer than cotton, and the more distinctly tubular form of the flax fibre, the collapsing of which is prevented by the frequently recurring joints or knots, which act like the flanged rings in a boiler flue, enables it when immersed in oil to retain a quantity of it even when submitted to considerable pressure; so that when a mixed cotton and flax fabric is immersed in oil, and examined under the microscope with transmitted light, the flax fibre appears quite transparent while the cotton remains comparatively opaque.

SILK.

Amongst animal fibres the first place must be assigned to silk,—not only on account of the beauty of the fibre itself, but also because in every respect it is one of the most perfect substances for employment in the textile arts. Silk is in reality a rod of consolidated flexible gum which is secreted from two

---

* Dyeing and Calico Printing, W. Crookes, F.R.S., p. 15.
† Do. do. do. p. 65.

glands situated on each side of the body of the silkworm, which is the early stage of an insect belonging to the family of the *Bombycidæ*. These two glands terminate in two narrow excretory ducts, which are dilated so as to form a reservoir, and the common orifice of this reservoir opens outside the mouth of the worm in a short tubercule situated beneath the labium. This tubercule is called the spinnaret; and, on each side of the spinnaret, are two little glands which produce a sticky matter, very much like silk itself, by which the produce of the two larger glands is made to adhere together so as to produce one fibre. The silk fibre thus consists really of two fibres which are cemented together side by side, and under the microscope, while it shows no signs of structural markings, looking more like a polished metal rod, it usually exhibits an indication of the place at which the junction has been formed by a slight groove. Sometimes this depression becomes so deep as actually to divide the fibre into two, as though the two component fibres had either never been properly cemented together, or had been torn asunder by some after process either in unwinding or spinning. This is much more distinct in some qualities of silk than others.

Plate III. gives us a good representation of the usual appearance of silk fibres, where we see no central cavity as in cotton or flax, and no indications of any cellular structure or surface markings, but a comparatively smooth, glassy surface. The fibre itself

400 Diameters

SILK FIBRES

A A Fibres showing longitudinal groove.

B. Fibre in which the groove deepens into complete separation of the

is semi-transparent, but its high lustre depends upon the uniformity of the outer layer, which reflects the light without dispersion. In the economy of nature, the silk fibre is produced by the worm so as to form the cocoon or case, in which the creature is enshrined during its pupa state. When the cocoons are finished by the worm, they are taken and placed in vessels heated with hot water, or in an oven, which melts the cementing gum employed by the worm to cause the various layers of the cocoon to adhere together, and enables the fibres to be unwound, and at the same time destroys the chrysalis. Many cocoons contain as many as 1,500 feet of silk.

In section, the silk fibre consists of three parts,—a central silk cylinder composed of a substance called sericin, or fibroine by chemists, and which forms the principal part of the fibre, outside this is a layer of albumen, and on the surface of this a thin coat of gelatine. The fibrione is composed of carbon, hydrogen, nitrogen, and oxygen, and some chemists think it is a perfectly definite and stable compound which may be represented by the formula $C_{24}H_{38}N_8O_8$. Both the outer layers of the fibre are eminently fitted to receive the various colouring matters which are used in producing the brilliant tints which we usually see imparted to it when in the dyed state. The perfectly homogeneous structure of silk renders it stronger in proportion than any other fibre, and thus eminently fits it for those textile fabrics where strength and lightness, as well as beauty of colour and high lustre are desirable. In these respects it has no rival.

WOOL.

Amongst animal fibres, next after silk, comes wool and the various other hairy coverings of creatures allied to the sheep and goat. Here we enter upon the real work of our lectures. We cannot, however, enter upon it all at once,—we still need a few preliminary observations; but as we can best incorporate these into our general remarks under the various heads into which we shall divide our subject, we shall fix these divisions first, so that we may have a consistency and definiteness in our enquiry.

It seems to me that we cannot do better than treat the wool fibre in exactly the same way as we treated of cotton in our last lectures. This will have the additional advantage of enabling us to make a much better comparison between the two fibres than we could possibly do if we adopted any other method.

As in the case of cotton, so in our investigations on wool, we shall confine ourselves principally to the fibre before the process of manufacture; but our object will of course be to see how far the nature and structure of the fibre is capable of modification and improvement, and how far any changes in its composition and structure may either be introduced in the process of manufacture, or from their nature influence that process for good or evil.

Our divisions will therefore be as follows:—

I.—*What is the typical structure of a wool fibre?*
   A. In regard to the mechanical arrangement of its ultimate parts.
   B. In regard to its chemical composition.

II.—*What variations from the type structure are presented to us?*
   C. In fibres from the same animal and grown at the same time.
   D. In fibres from the same animal and grown in different years.
   E. In fibres from the same animal grown under different climatic and other conditions.
   F. In fibres produced by different breeds of sheep in different countries.

III.—*How far these variations in the ultimate fibre may affect its use in the manufacturing process.*
   G. Mechanically.
   H. Chemically.

In looking at these various questions, I am afraid that I shall be obliged sometimes to use terms and phrases which will not be quite intelligible to you all. I shall, however, as far as possible endeavour to use as few of these terms as I can consistent with a fair scientific exposition of the subject, and when I do use them I will try to explain their meaning as I go on, or at any rate to place them in such connection as to enable you to understand what I mean. To assist the reader a complete glossary will be found at the end of the volume. Where I cannot do this I hope the diagrams will enable you to see with the eye, and thus render verbal explanations unnecessary.

We must, however, remember that parts of our subject will necessarily require a certain amount of anatomical, physiological, and chemical as well as mechanical knowledge; and while I shall be as simple as I can, I hope that what I say may stimulate those of you who are students to a stronger desire for education, and lead you to the study of these subjects, which I am sure, even apart from any industrial applications, will yield you a rich reward for your labours. Silk, as we have already seen, is a stiffened gum, which is secreted from the body of a worm, but wool is an entirely different substance. It is in nature similar to hair, from which it differs in appearance only in possessing a certain wave-like structure of the fibre, about which we shall have to say more hereafter. It is an appendage of the skin, and, if we are to understand our subject thoroughly, we shall have to look at the way in which wool or hair grows upon the skin, and its relationship to it. Hair, wool, and even the feathers of birds are similar to each other in their essential nature, and are all produced in the same manner by an increased production of epidermic or skin cells at the bottom of a flask shaped follicle. This follicle is formed in the substance of the true skin, and is supplied with an abundance of blood by a special distribution of vessels in its walls. These vessels are continued as a fine network a short distance beyond the root, and thus feed the cells till they are fully developed; and in the case of some diseases of the hair, such as *pica polonica*, they become enlarged and allow the blood to penetrate up into the substance of the hair, so that if the hair is cut or broken it bleeds. If we pull a hair out by the root we find a bulbous enlargement at the bottom end, of which the exterior is tolerably firm, but the interior consists of a soft substance or pulp. The continual production of this pulp in the bottom of the follicle, and its conversion into the substance of the hair as it is pushed upwards to the surface of the skin, is the cause of the growth of the hair; but it gives no explanation of the differences which are manifested in the special forms which different hairs and wools assume on different animals, although the appearance of the bulbous parts are very similar. All the parts of the hair are only modifications of the various parts of the skin, which have had a vertical rather than a horizontal determination given to them. This is probably occasioned by the presence of nerve fibres, which penetrate the outer sheath of the hair within the follicle at its lower part, and thus the hair is put in direct connection with the nervous system. A sudden shock to the nerves will sometimes cause the erection to be so great as to warrant the expression that the hair stands on end.

At first sight it might appear that the skin is a very simple membrane which covers the whole exterior of the animal body, and that the hair or wool simply grows upon the surface in the same way that we saw the cotton fibre proceeding from the outer layer of the seed wall; and that it possesses some root-like attachment which enables the hair to remain fixed to it. The skin is, however, a much more complicated structure, and it is quite necessary for us to understand something of this structure before we can be able to investigate the formation, growth, and nature of the wool fibre.

The skin of all the higher vertebrated animals consists of four strata or layers. Two of these layers, called respectively the *cuticle* or scarfskin, and, beneath it, the *rete mucosum*, lie on the outside, and form what is called the *epidermis*. This epidermis serves as the protection for two deeper seated underlayers, which are called the *superficial* or *papillary* layer, and the deep seated *stratum* or *corium*. These two together are called the *dermis* or true skin. We may tabulate these various strata as follows, beginning at the outside:—

1. Cuticle or scarfskin } Forming the epidermis.
2. Rete mucosum
3. Papilliary Layer } Forming the dermis.
4. Corium

When we were looking at the structure of the cotton fibre, we found that the solid material of all plants was built up of small sack-like bodies called cells, which enclosed within their walls, during the growth of the plant, the protoplasm or juice by which the cell and plant was nourished.

In the same way all animal substances are in like

manner built up of cells, which differ only from those of plants in their size and chemical composition. The method of growth of these cells is identically the same, and in their earlier stages it is quite impossible with the microscope alone, if we neglect the position where they are found, to distinguish one from the other. The *protoplasm*, which forms the ultimate germinating material in each, is undistinguishable by any means at our command.

If we take a brush, or any rough substance, such as a piece of cloth, and rub it upon the surface of our skin, especially in a dry place, we shall find a quantity of dry dust to fly off and attach itself to the cloth. Upon examining this under the microscope we find that this dust really is composed of a series of flattened scales or cells. These are called epidermal cells, and the whole of the skin which lies upon the surface is entirely composed of these microscopical scales, which are really dried up and dead cells which were produced from a series of more rounded cells which lie immediately beneath these flattened ones. These scales form the cuticle or scarfskin. The rete mucosum is a series of much more rounded cells, which have a distinct nucleus or germinating point, and it lies conformably upon the papillary layer of the dermis. The density and hardness of the epidermis decreases as we pass inwards from the outer surface to the rete mucosum. This difference in density is dependent on the mode of growth of the epidermis, for as the external surface is constantly subjected to destruction from attrition and chemical action, so the membrane is continually reproduced on its internal surface, new layers being constantly and successively formed on the derma to take the place of the old ones. The papillary layer of the derma lies immediately below the rete mucosum, and the upper surface consists of a series of conical prominences or papillæ, which pass upwards into the epidermal layer which lies above it. On the general surface of the body the papillæ are short and minute, but they increase in size and differ in arrangement in various special situations, as in the human body on the surfaces of the hands and feet, and other parts where great sensibility is requisite. This layer is chiefly composed of areolo-fibrous tissue, elastic tissue, and smooth muscular fibre, together with blood vessels, limphatic vessels, and nerves, and is highly vascular and sensitive.

The corium or deep seated strata lies lowest of all. The upper surface, which is connected with the papillary layer, consists of areolo-fibrous tissue, which is collected into cellular bundles called fasciculi, which are small and closely interwoven in the superficial strata, and large and coarse in the deeper strata; in the latter, forming an areolar network with large openings. These openings are the channels through which the branches of vessels and nerves find a safe passage to the papillary layer above, in which and in the superficial strata of the corium they are chiefly distributed.

Plate IV

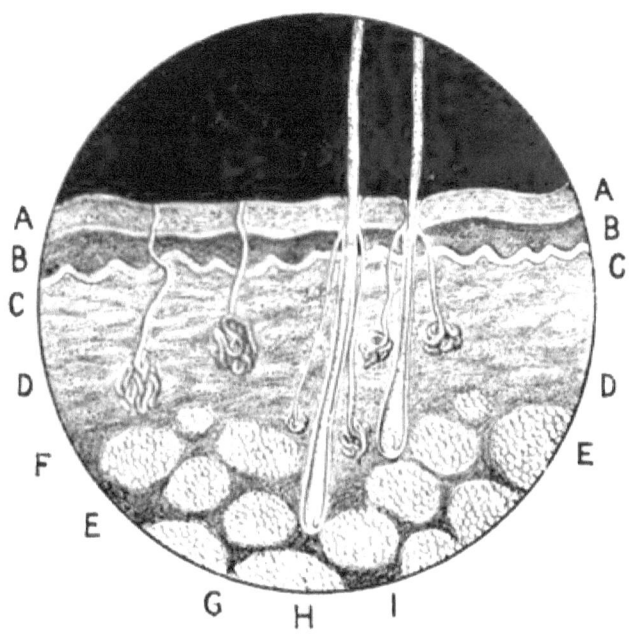

25 Diameters.

SECTION OF SKIN.

These dermal and epidermal layers are everywhere penetrated, from beneath to the surface, by a series of channels or openings called sudoriparous ducts, and through which the perspiration or moisture from the fatty or adipose layer, which lies beneath the derma, escapes into the air. The secreting glands which throw off this moisture are embedded in the substance of the derma and the subcutaceous tissue, and present every degree of complexity, from the simplest follicle to the compound lobulated gland.

In some situations their excretory ducts open, as we have seen, on the surface of the skin, while in others, they terminate in what is of most interest to us, viz., the follicles of the hairs or wool, which, like themselves, have their origin usually beneath the skin, and pass upward through it to the outer surface of the body.

Hairs or wool are therefore living appendages of the skin, produced by the involution and subsequent evolution of the epidermis; the involution constituting the follicle or sac in which the hair is enclosed, and the evolution the shaft of the hair. Before we look at the structure of this hair, and its relation to the skin, let me call your attention to Plate IV., which gives a representation of the section of the skin of an animal, from which we can obtain an idea of its structure much better than by any possible description.

A is the cuticle or scarfskin, with the dead flattened cells on the surface; B, the rete mucosum, with its more distinct cellular structure, and resting upon the conical prominence of C, the papillary layer. D is the deep seated strata or corium, with its areolar openings and vascular structure, and which lies upon E, the subcutaceous layer of adipose cells. F and G are two sudoriparous glands, with their winding spiral ducts, which terminate on the outer surface of the skin. H and I are two hair follicles, with their enclosing hairs, which have their origin at different depths in the subcutaceous tissue, and which are furnished on each side with two sebiparous glands, the excretory ducts of which, instead of rising to the surface of the skin, are connected by a short tube with the follicle of the hair. These glands secrete an oily substance, a kind of natural pomatum with which the surface of the hair is bathed, and thus the scales on the surface are greased and prevented from irritating the nervous lining of the follicle in their passage upwards. It also serves to support and feed the growing hair. The hairs or wool fibres themselves are formed within the follicle in identically the same manner as the formation of the epidermis by the papillary layer of the derma. Plastic lymph is, in the first instance, exuded by the capillary plexus of the follicle, and the lymph undergoes conversion, first into granules and then into cells, which, as the process of growth and extrusion proceeds are elongated into fibres, which form the central structure of the hair. The cells which are destined to form the surface of the hair go through a different process. They are converted into flat scales, and entirely lose

Plate V.

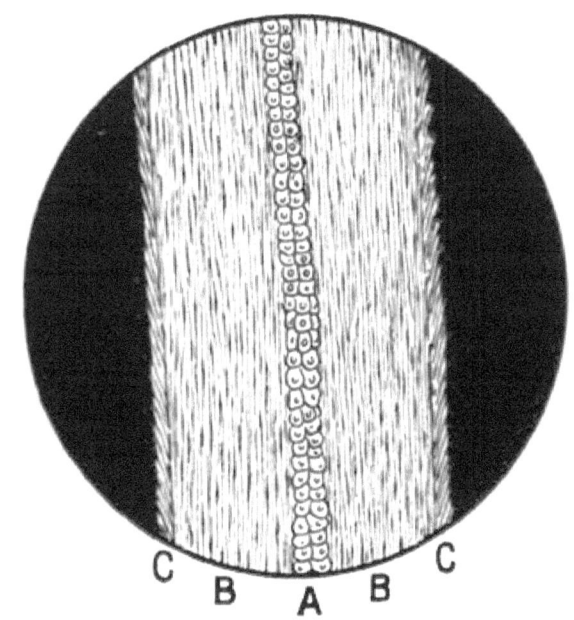

350 Diameters

LONGITUDINAL SECTION OF HAIR

A. Central Medulla with round nucleated cells.

B. Cortical substance with fibrillæ and linear nuclei.

C. Cuticle with laminated cells or plates, and serrated edge.

❖

their cellular form, and as they are successively formed each fresh one overlaps that immediately preceding it, and gives rise to the prominent and wavy lines which are always seen round the circumference of the outer sheath. Hairs are generally not quite round, but more or less flattened in form, and when the extremity of a transverse section is examined, it usually is found to possess an eliptical or reniform outline. This examination also demonstrates that the centre of the hair is porous and loose in texture, while its periphery is dense. Just as we find in a section of a plant stem that the central cells are usually large and distinct, while those which form the outer layers are more closely packed together, and at the extreme margin increase further in density, and change the character of the cells so as to form a bark or skin, so in the hair we have a similar phenomenon, which enables us to distinguish its cross section into a central or medullary part, a cortical or intermediate part, and a cuticle or skin forming the outer portion. If we examine a longitudinal section of the hair we find the same divisions distinctly marked,—the dense outer sheath of flattened scales, with an inner lining of closely packed fibrous cells, and frequently a well marked central vascular bundle of larger cells. These larger cells are, however, frequently wanting in many hairs. The extremity of the hair is usually pointed, but in some instances it is divided into several distinct filaments. The lower extremity of the hair is larger than the shaft, and forms a conical bulb, or bundle of

D

cells, which has a circular section, and constitutes the root or growing portion of the hair. Its larger bulk is due to the larger size of the newly formed cells, which have just been thrown off from the layers in which they are embedded. These cells shrink in volume as they are pushed upward from their various growing points, and as they become more consolidated, they form the shaft of the hair with its various parts. The hair makes its appearance on the skin of the animal before it possesses an independent existence.

In order that we may thoroughly understand the structure of the wool fibre, which as we have already seen is a peculiar modification of hair, it will be necessary for us to look more closely at the minute structure of the hair, and as we know more about the anatomy and method of growth of a human hair than any other, we shall take this as a typical example. Of course, as we all know, there are several kinds of hair growing upon different parts of the body. The long fine hair of the head, which in the case of the female, often reaches a very great length,—two and even three feet or more, with a diameter of about $\frac{1}{300}$ of an inch, which however differs very widely on different persons;—a short, stiff-pointed hair, from about $\frac{1}{4}$ to $\frac{1}{2}$ inch long, as on the eyelashes, and a fine downy hair about $\frac{1}{12}$ to $\frac{1}{8}$ inch in length, which grows more or less upon the whole surface of the body, and can be seen very distinctly if we look along the back of the hand with the light shining upon it. All these various hairs have a great similarity in

Plate VI.

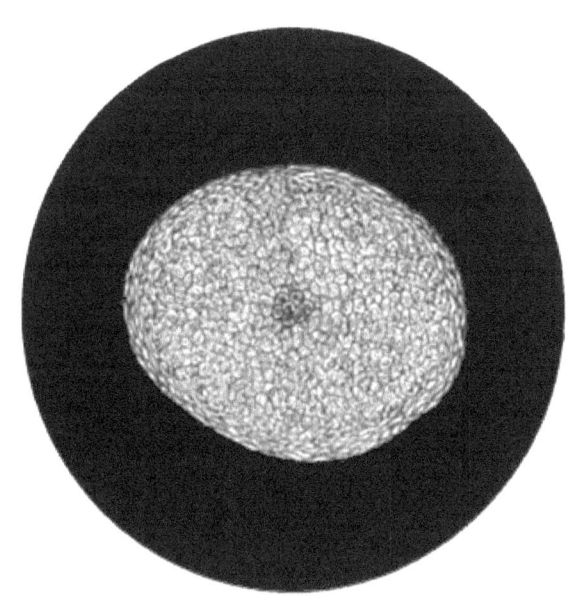

350 DIAMETERS

TRANSVERSE SECTION OF HAIR

Showing Central Medulla with round nucleated cells. Cortical Substance with angular cells, and Cuticle with elongated cells and laminated plates.

structure, differing indeed only in minute details, and possessing a common method of development. If we take a hair from the head, and cut it into section in the direction of its length, in the same way that a plank is cut out of the trunk of a tree, we have a very beautiful appearance presented, in which we can, if we magnify it, say about 350 diameters, see distinct evidence of three different structural parts. (1) A central medulla; (2) a cortical substance upon which the firmness, elasticity, and colour of the hair depends; and (3) on the outside a thin outer sheath or cuticle with serrated edge.

Plate V. gives a representation of such a longitudinal section after the hair has been treated with an alkali, so as to remove the natural fat and render the structure more distinct. A represents the central medulla, with its rounded and nucleated cells; B the cortical portion, with its elongated and striated cells, with fibrillation and linear nuclei; and C the outer sheath or cuticle, with its lammated cells and serrated edge.

Plate VI. gives a representation of a transverse section of the same hair, magnified 350 diameters, and where we can see the various parts mentioned above with even greater distinctness than in the longitudinal section. If we treat the hair with strong sulphuric or some other acid, at a gentle heat, we can break up the various parts of the hair into fibrous bundles, and then into the constituent cells, and then only do we come to understand how complicated a substance a hair really is. By counting a small portion of the cross section of a hair, in the cortical part alone, I found that the number of cells were not much less than 1,500 in number in that cross section; and, if we take them at an average length of $\frac{1}{400}$ of an inch, we arrive at the conclusion that there must be about 600,000 of them in every inch of the length of the hair. This hair was taken off the head; but I found in several coarser hairs a very similar average, the larger size of the hairs being made up by an increased diameter in the individual cells rather than in a greater number; but I also found that the number and size of the cells differ considerably in different individuals. Two other hair sections which I counted gave 900 and 1,100 cells respectively.

Plate VII. shows some of these constituent cells when they have been treated with various reagents, so as to separate them and bring out the various points in their structure.

A represent a number of cells, such as constitute the medulla or central portion of the hair. They are more or less angular, and also rounded, and vary in diameter from $\frac{1}{1000}$ to $\frac{1}{2000}$ of an inch, and are about the same length. They often exhibit a distinct nucleus, and sometimes one or more little rounded globules of fat or some other such substance; and, when they become consolidated, after being pushed forward from the bulb by the growth of cells behind them, they also contain air, which can easily be seen by macerating the hair in oil of turpentine, when the

Plate VII.

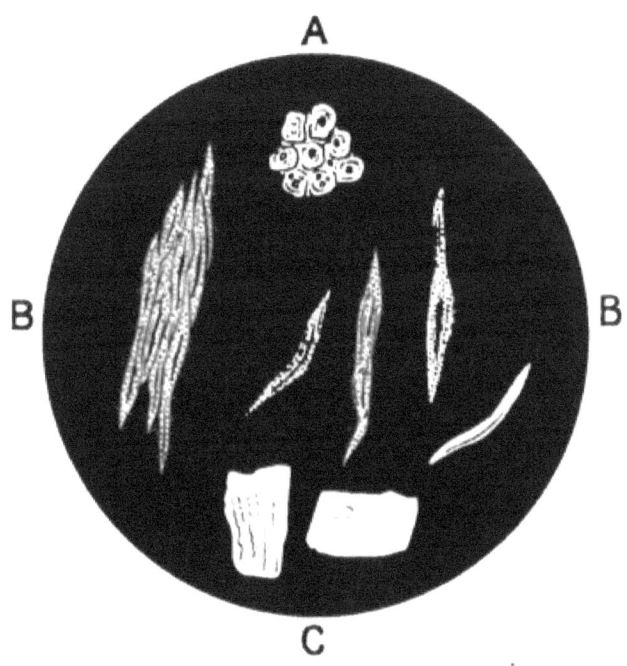

450 DIAMETERS

CELLS CONSTITUTING HAIR

A. Cells from medulla with nuclei and fat globules.

B. Cells from cortical substance with elongated nuclei and pigment cells.

C. Structureless horny scales from the cuticle.

STRUCTURE OF CORTICAL CELLS.

air is displaced by the liquid and escapes in minute bubbles. In many hairs I have found these larger medullular cells much diminished in size, and with a very faint nucleus, and in some entirely wanting. B represents a series of cells from the cortical part of the hair. Here we have them aggregated in fibrous bundles, and also separated from each other. These cells present uneven surfaces, and a more or less uneven outline, their true form being spindle-shaped; but they are mostly flattened and angular, or curved from mutual pressure, resulting from their aggregation into the shaft of the hair. These cells vary in length from about $\frac{1}{500}$ to $\frac{1}{300}$ of an inch, and in diameter from $\frac{1}{5000}$ to $\frac{1}{2000}$ of an inch. When separated from each other by the action of alkalies they swell up and become larger than when in the bundles in which they are associated in the substance of the hair, as if they were consolidated under pressure, and they also increase apparently in length as well as diameter, as if the whole enveloping membrane of the cell was distended in every direction by the swelling of its contents. They mostly contain elongated, dark-looking nuclei, and in coloured hairs, the small pigment granules to which the colour of the hair is due. These pigment granules are exceedingly minute,—not more than $\frac{1}{50000}$ of an inch in diameter, and are arranged in the hair in linear groups, their colour and number varying with that of the hair. At C we have a number of isolated scales from the surface of the hair, which are really flattened inspissated cells, similar in character to those which form the outer cuticle of the epidermis of the skin, and which have a common origin. To these scales we must call particular attention, because it is upon a variation in the character of them, and the method in which they are connected with the cortical substance beneath, that the great differences between wool and hair consists, as well as the peculiarity which enables wool to mat or felt together. To enable this to be understood more distinctly we must look at Plate VIII., which represents a hair viewed by reflected light, so that we can see the nature of the surface or cuticular coat. Here we see at once the cause of the serrated edge when the hair was viewed in longitudinal section. The whole surface of the hair, at any rate above the termination of the inner root sheath, is coated externally by a firmly adherent, thin membranous layer, consisting of flat, imbricated, epithelial scales. These scales have all their free margins directed towards the unattached end of the hair, and lie overlapping each other like the plates on the scaly back of a fish, or the tiles on a housetop. In the natural state of the hair, when it has not been treated by appropriate reagents, these scales lie so flat upon the shaft of the hair that it is almost impossible to see them, and their existence is only revealed by the presence of irregular transverse and anastomosing lines which cross the surface. If, however, the hair is treated with any reagent which disintegrates its component parts, the free margins of these scales are raised up,

175 DIAMETERS.

HUMAN HAIR

SURFACE OF HAIR treated with Caustic Soda, so as to show epidermal scales.

so that they at first stand off from the hair like the scales on a fir cone, and finally become detached from it altogether, so that they can be separately examined. I found that the number of them on the surface of the hair varied considerably in different individuals; but an average of ten different hairs from several persons gave 3,200 as the number of free margins in 1 inch. The length of the scales varied from $\frac{1}{600}$ to $\frac{1}{700}$ of an inch, and about $\frac{1}{1800}$ of an inch in diameter. The whole cuticle of the hair was formed of from three to five layers of these cells, and they are so closely cemented together, that when seen in section the cuticle presents the appearance of a transparent membrane with a serrated edge. When viewed in relation to wool these scales are of great importance, because, as we shall afterwards see, upon them depends the distinction to a large extent between many classes of wool. They also vary in their nature and arrangement on the hairs of different animals, so that it is often possible to distinguish by microscopical examination from what animal the hair has been derived. I need not point out how very important this is when it is necessary to determine whether yarns are composed of one fibre, or a mixture, and also what the character of the mixture is. The cause of these variations also is of the utmost importance, because a knowledge of the underlying causes enables us to modify them so as to produce a variation in effect, which is often of the greatest value. To know this, we must look at the method in which the hair grows, both upon the fœtal skin and when the creature has obtained a separate existence; because, in the first case, it is dependent upon the selection of sire and dam, and in the last upon the peculiar climatic and other conditions by which it is surrounded, as well as to a certain extent upon the food which is eaten.

We have already seen that the hairs are enclosed at the attached end within a follicle or pouch, which is really an involution of the epidermis itself. These hair follicles are about $\frac{1}{10}$ to $\frac{1}{4}$ of an inch deep in the human subject, and enclose the hair round like a bag or elongated sack, extending in the short hairs down into the upper layer of the cutis, but in the longer and stronger hairs into its deepest portion, and even in some cases, down into the subcutaneous cellular fibre. This will be readily seen by looking at Plate IX., where we have a transverse section of a hair, with its follicle, magnified about 100 diameters, in which we see the root sac penetrating down below the derma into the mass of adipose cells which lie beneath it. The walls of the follicle being a simple involution of the epidermis, we find, as we might naturally expect, that the walls exhibit a similar structure and correspond to the layers of the epidermis. We have, thus, three separate parts distinguishable in the follicle walls.

(1) An external transparent layer, which corresponds to the cutis of the skin, and is marked A.

(2) A much thicker, very fibrous, and vascular por-

Plate IX.

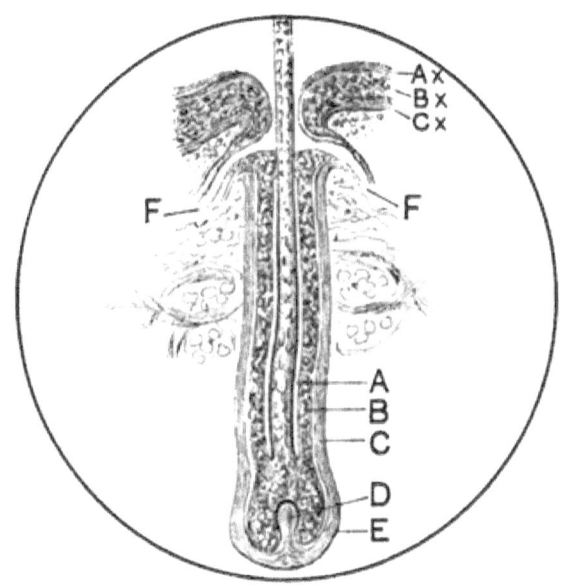

50 DIAMETERS.

SECTION OF HAIR FOLLICLE.

- A. External transparent layer.
- B. Fibrous layer corresponding to Rete mucosum.
- C. Transparent sheath or basement membrane.
- D. Papilla.
- E. Bulb of Follicle and Hair.
- F. Sebaceous glands.
- Ax. Cuticle of Skin.
- Bx. Rete Mucosum.
- Cx. Papilliary layer.

tion, which forms the bulk of the follicle proper and is marked B, and which corresponds to the rete-mucosum of the skin, and which in the lower part of the follicle, at the bulb E, comes in direct contact with the cells of the growing hair and the papilla D.

(3) A transparent sheath, called the basement membrane, which is marked C, of which the papilla D seems to be an involution, and which forms the internal covering of the follicle. It is a firm, elastic, yellowish membrane, and terminates near the point where the sebaceous ducts F open into the hair follicle. "Externally this membrane is connected with the outer root sheath, and internally with the outer layer of the cuticle of the hair, and hence no interval exists naturally between it and the hair. At first sight it appears as a perfectly homogeneous membrane; but, on closer examination, it is found to be distinctly cellular. It consists of two or three layers of polygonal, longish transparent cells, with their long axis parallel to that of the hair. The outermost layer, called Henle's layer, consists of long, flattened, non-nucleated cells, from $\frac{1}{700}$ to $\frac{1}{500}$ of an inch in length, with fissures between them, thus forming a fenestrated or perforated layer. The innermost layer, called Huxley's, consists of one or two layers of shorter or broader polygonal cells, from $\frac{1}{1200}$ to $\frac{1}{600}$ of an inch in length. Their nuclei, which exist only in the lower part of the coat, are often broader at the end than in the middle, and are sometimes curved and pointed. At the base of the hair follicle, the

inner root sheath consists of a single layer only of beautiful polygonal nucleated cells, which becoming soft, delicate, and rounded, gradually pass into the outer layers of the round cells of the bulk of the hair."*

The shaft of the hair comes in close contact with the enclosing walls of the follicle, just below the point where the sebaceous ducts enter at F, and is also less consolidated than higher up; the outer cuticular layer of the shaft being in close contact with the outer layer of the follicle itself, and the two cannot indeed be easily distinguished, except by the use of an alkali as a reagent, when the shaft of the hair shrinks in upon itself and assumes an undulated form by the involution of its outer coating. Within the root sheath, below the point of stricture, the cells of which the cortical part of the hair are built up, are more rounded and of larger diameter than when the hair passes out of the follicle. They are, however, less in length, and it seems as if, as the process of growth proceeds and the cells are carried outwards further and further from their point of origin, the consolidation which takes place elongates the cells at the expense of their diameter, and renders the hair shaft more dense and fibrous. The cuticle of the hair also undergoes a similar change. At the root of the hair, in the bulb, just where the epidermal cells are thrown off from the growing points, they are round and nucleated, but this rapidly disappears, and they assume the form of

---

* Micrographic Dictionary, p. 334.

the flattened imbricated scales which afterwards cover the surface of the hair. In the lower parts, however, they stand more outwards from the surface of the hair, and are thus more distinctly seen without the use of a reagent than when the hair has passed out beyond the surface of the skin. The shaft of the hair itself when it passes out beyond the follicle is, as a rule, straight, and to a certain extent stiff; but it possesses a very remarkable degree of tenacity when subjected to strain in the direction of its length, as well as power to undergo flexure without a rupture of the cells of which it is composed. Its cellular structure also enables it to retain its circular form under great pressure. It is also very elastic, and, when subjected to strain, draws out like an elastic band for a considerable length before it breaks. It should be observed that the follicles do not stand perpendicularly in the skin, otherwise the hair on leaving the surface would always stand erect. The natural position of the follicles is oblique, and hence the hairs lie smoothly, especially if they are allowed to take their natural sweep round the crown, which is their natural centre of radiation. Indeed, the hair on every part of the body, both in man and the lower animals, is arranged in various geometrical curves or currents, so as most suitably to conform to the contour of the body,— this is well seen in the arrangement of the hair on the body of a horse. At the sides of the hair follicles, and passing into the outer layers of which the follicles are composed, there are involuntary muscles, which are called the erector muscles, by means of which the hairs are drawn into an upright position when acted on by the nerves. Their contraction also assists the sebaceous glands to discharge their contents. To their action also is due the mottled condition of the skin, which we often call goose-skin, because it resembles the skin of that bird when the feathers are plucked out.

"The rudiments of the first hairs appear in the human fœtus about the end of the third month, and, just as in mammals, are at first solid knoblike outgrowths of the stratum Malpighii into the corium, especially of the deepest layer of columnar cells. In some instances the corium shows a slight elevation preceding the formation of the rudiment of the hair, but this is absent in many instances.

"The rudiment of the hair rapidly elongating becomes cylindrical, and we notice in it the following different elements: the majority of the cells are small and polyhedral, in the marginal layer they are hexagonal or slightly columnar; the former possess a spherical, the latter an oval nucleus; the cells and their nuclei in the axial portion of the hair rudiment are slightly flattened. There is a distinct limiting membrane between the marginal layer of cells and the surrounding tissue; this membrane represents the rudiment of the glassy basement membrane. Each of the hair rudiments is from the earliest time surrounded by a thick layer of a tissue altogether different from the rest of the corium, and representing the rudiment of the hair-sac; it is well marked off from the corium, is composed of a network of flattened, spindle-shaped or branched cells, and stains as a whole better than the rest of the corium; although relatively very bulky, it nevertheless can be traced directly to a thin layer similarly constituted and situated immediately underneath the epithelium of the surface, that is to say, a layer which gives origin to the papillary body of the corium.

"There is a definite distinction between the hair-sac and the surrounding corium in the full grown hair, and we see this is borne out by the development. The branched cells of the rudiment of the hair-sac soon make their way into the above solid cylindrical hair rudiment, and thus give origin to the branched nucleated cells that are present in the adult state between the cells of the outer root sheath.

"The tissue of the hair-sac grows much more rapidly than the hair rudiment, and having closed round the deep extremity of the latter, grows now against it as the papilla, and thus produces the inflection and enlargement of the bulb. Henceforth the multiplication of the cells at the bulb naturally leads to the new cells being pushed up in the axis of the hair rudiment towards the surface, and becoming elongated constitute the elements of the hair substance, and its cuticle and inner root sheath. The cells of the primary solid cylinder represent the rudiment of the cells of the outer root sheath only. The gradual conversion of the cells of the bulb into the spindle-shaped horny scales of the substance of the hair, the differentiation at the bulb of the cell layers, and their conversion into the cuticle of the hair and the inner root sheath are easily understood from the description given above of these parts of the adult hair.

"One of the latest parts to appear is the mouth of the hair follicle, as the hair exists for some time beneath the skin before its appearance outside. The hair itself and the inner root sheath, having reached the stratum corneum of the surface, for a short time continues to grow underneath it for a considerable distance in a horizontal or slightly oblique direction; ultimately, however, the stratum corneum is broken, and the mouth of the follicle having thus been established, the hair henceforth grows beyond the free surface, loosing the adhering parts of the inner root sheath from the neck outwards.

"As soon as the rudiment of the papilla makes its appearance, the hair follicle, then still a solid cylindrical mass of cells, pushes out, near its connection with the surface epithelium, a small knob composed of the same polyhedral cells as the hair follicle; this knob gradually elongates, divides at its extremity, and its branches are converted into the alveoli of the sebaceous gland. The duct is therefore an outgrowth of the neck of the hair follicle.

"'According to Lowe, the correctness of whose statements must be questioned, the marginal layer of the epithelial cells lining the limiting *membrana propria* of the alveoli of the sebaceous gland is alone derived from the deepest layer of columnar cells of the epidermis, while the rest of the gland cells are offsprings of the stratum corneum.'

"The fully developed fœtal hair is very thin, its follicle and papilla do not reach into the subcutaneous tissue. It becomes replaced in many localities soon after birth by a much coarser hair, whose follicle and papilla pass down into the depth of the subcutaneous tissue. This new hair is produced from the outer root sheath of the primary hair-follicle, as will be presently described.

"Every hair in the young child, as well as in the adult, sooner or later undergoes a peculiar change, which leads to the formation of Henle's hair knob, or the intercalated hair of Götte, or the bed hair of Unna, differing in several important respects from the normal or perfect hair, and called by Unna the papillary hair. The mode of change of the latter into the bed hair is the following: the cells of the bulb over the papilla cease to multiply, and consequently the hair and its inner root sheath stop growing; first the inner, then the outer root sheath atrophy; but the root of the hair remains connected with the papilla for some time by a thin streak of cells, ultimately also this disappears. This process of atrophy extends up to near the point where the erector pili is attached to the hair sac; here the external root sheath becomes conspicuously enlarged, and the hair root terminates in it with Henle's 'hair knob,' being an enlarged broomlike extremity, which with its fibrous horny elements branches out amongst the adjacent cells of the outer root sheath. The inner root sheath is wanting just at the extremity, but is met with at a short distance higher up. The hair continues to grow at its knob at the expense of the adjacent flattened cells of the outer root sheath, and in this condition, viz., as a bed hair, it may retain its position and existence for a considerable time. In many instances it is, however, eliminated spontaneously or by the growth of a new hair produced from the cells of its (viz. the bed hair's) outer root sheath.

"As mentioned previously, this part of the external root sheath, viz., about the region of attachment of the erector muscle, contains on its surface sometimes few, sometimes many, smaller or larger, knob-like or cylindrical solid projections of epithelial cells. Now, in some instances, one of these grows into the depth as a cylindrical solid cell-mass, either making for itself a new path, *i.e.*, becoming provided with a new hair-sac, or advancing in the path of the former hair; this is the rudiment of the outer root sheath of the new hair. Its extremity becomes inflected over a new papilla, just as was the case in the fœtal process. The cells of this inflected part rapidly increase in numbers, and thus form the bulbous extremity, in connection with which the hair itself and its inner root sheath are formed in exactly the same manner as in the embryo. Now, the new hair, as it grows upwards in the axis of the new outer root sheath, either passes altogether at the side of its bed hair and ultimately reaches the surface, its follicle becoming provided with a new neck and mouth; or it makes its way into the follicle of the bed hair. In this case, the hair knob being pressed by the pointed extremity of the new hair, is gradually pushed upwards towards the free surface, and finally is altogether ejected.

"Hair follicles with two hairs, one an old hair knob and the other a young, newly formed papillary hair and growing from the depth, are to be explained in this manner.

"Stieda exhaustively proved the degeneration of the old papilla and the formation of a new one; Feiertag, Schulin, and especially Unna by his elaborate and careful researches, fully established it.

"Biesiadecki, v. Ebner, and Renny, however, still adhere to the older doctrine (Langer), according to which the old papilla persists, and in connection with it the new hair is produced."*

As we have already remarked, the hair is capable of considerable modification under various conditions. This is indeed a peculiarity of all epidermal growths, as will be very readily recognised when we remember that the nails at the extremities of the toes and fingers, and in quadrupeds the hoofs of the feet, and even in some animals, such excrescences as the horns on the head, have a common origin.

In the hair, one of the commonest variations consists in a waved character being imparted to it, so

---

* Klein's Atlas of Histology, pp. 325-327.

that instead of standing out stiff and erect it possesses a curly nature. This can be imparted to all ordinary hair by the application of heat and pressure, but it speedily passes away when these artificial means are removed. This arises from unequal contraction of the different parts of the hair. Under variation in climatic condition the hair tends to assume this character, and it is very well seen in the hair of the negro, which has far more the appearance of wool than hair. This likeness does not, however, exist further than the mere curl is concerned, because a microscopical examination of the hair of the negro clearly demonstrates that it possesses the same structure as that of the European. Moreover, even this woolly character is not constant in the negro race, because different classes present every gradation, from a full woolly lock down to a curled or even flowing hair. The true distinction between wool and hair lies in the nature of the epidermal covering with which the cortical part of the shaft is covered, and in the method of attachment of the scaly plates or flattened cells to the inner layer upon which they rest, and not upon the curly nature of the whole fibre itself, although there can be no doubt but that this waved appearance is one of the recognised characters of wool. There are, however, to be found numerous hairs which possess no curl, and yet have the epidermal characteristic of a true wool, which consists in the power to felt or mat, arising from the greater looseness of the scaly covering of the hair, and which, when opposing hairs come into contact, enables these scales to interlock into each other, and holds them together quite independent of any friction or twist imparted to the fibre by mechanical means. This peculiar characteristic will be more readily understood by looking at Fig. 1, where we have an imaginary section of a typical wool fibre opposed to another similar fibre, so that when they are drawn

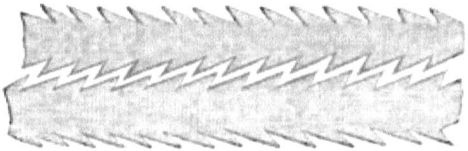

Fig. 1.

along over each other the scales interlock, serration into serration, and thus become perfectly united together by the wedged edges of the scales entering into the spaces between the scale and shaft of the opposing fibre. We have already seen that in the case of human hair the free edges of the scales are always pointed upwards towards the unattached end of the hair. This is also the case in wool, and when it is in its proper position on the back of the animal, quite independent of other causes which we shall afterwards have to name, the scales of the woolly hair are all pointing in the same direction, so that their tendency to mat or felt is reduced to a minimum, otherwise the fleece or pelt of the creature would become one matted tangled mass. The scales being in the same direction, the hairs have the tendency to slide over each other without interlocking, and thus prevent the disagreeable results which would otherwise occur. If we look at Plate X. we shall see there a representation of what we may consider a typical wool fibre, and by comparing it with Plate VIII. we shall see the great difference between the wool and the hair. In the wool, the cylindrical or cortical part of the fibre is entirely covered with very numerous lorications or scales, the free ends of which have a pointed rather than a rounded form. This enables them more readily when opposed to each other to find their way under the opposing scales, and to penetrate inwards and downwards proportionate to the pressure which is applied to bring them together. In the wool fibre also, the free margins of the scales are much longer and deeper than in the hair, where the overlapping scales are attached to the under layer up to the very margin of the scale, which can at its extremity even, only be detached by the use of a suitable reagent. In wool this is quite unnecessary, because the ends of the scales are free to about two-thirds of their length, and are to a certain extent indeed turned partially outwards, as can readily be seen by looking at the edges of the wool fibre, where the denticulated structure is quite distinct against the dark back-ground. This ideal diagram approaches nearer to the fibre obtained from the wool of the merino sheep than any other, and as we shall afterwards see this is one of the most valuable and beautiful wools which is grown, and one which either pure, or mixed with other breeds, yields a large proportion of

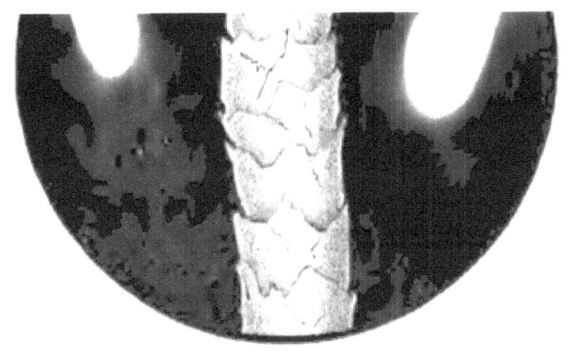

250 DIAMETERS.

TYPICAL WOOL FIBRE.

Shewing the pointed and serrated edges of the epidermal scales when treated with Caustic Soda

the wool which is used in our best manufactures. This, then, we may take as our typical wool fibre, and we shall find that just as the mechanical structure of any wool approaches this standard it becomes better and better fitted for our textile purposes, and just as it departs from it does it become less useful and less fitted for those peculiar uses to which wool can be put. We shall afterwards see, that in different classes of sheep, every variety of intermediate structure occurs between true hairs and the fullest development of the woolly nature of the fibre, and that under certain conditions, these wide differences may even exist in the fibres taken from the fleece of the same animal; we shall, however, also see that just in proportion as the conditions surrounding the sheep are favourable to the finest development of all its best qualities, and in proportion as the purity of the breed is maintained does the production of hairy fibres diminish and true wool replace them. We shall in our next lecture see that there are other fibres besides those which are grown upon the sheep which partake of this peculiar property, but that none possess it so universally and so uniformly. Even the wool of the sheep is subject to great differences in this respect, arising from a variety of causes, and hence the great necessity for studying these causes, so that by suitable selection and cultivation we may be enabled to produce the best and most uniform raw material. However correct our mechanical processes of spinning may be, we have already seen, when we were looking at the cotton fibre, that we can never get beyond the degree of uniformity which is manifested in the raw material itself, and this is equally true as regards the wool fibre also. Perfectly uniform material to work upon is the basis of perfect spinning, and although we can never expect to reach this standard, there is no limit assigned to the nearness with which we may approach to it. Every step we take towards this end is a step in the right direction, and a knowledge derived from observation and experience of what we require is the only basis upon which we can work. Hence, our typical fibre becomes invested with a deeply practical as well as theoretical interest, and forms the key to our future progress and success, and in our next lecture, therefore, we shall look shortly at the various classes of sheep which are found in the different quarters of the world, so that we may understand the nature of the conditions to which they are likely to be subjected, and prepare ourselves for the closer study of their different and characteristic fibres as they are affected by these conditions, and how far they fit or unfit them for use in textile manufactures.

LECTURE II.

IN our last lecture we looked shortly at the various classes of fibres which are used in textile manufactures, and saw that they were derived from various sources, both in the animal and vegetable kingdom. Cotton and flax were selected as types of the latter division of the organic world, and silk and wool as the types of the former.

We saw that the wool was only one of a numerous class of similar fibres, which, like wool, are modified growths of the epidermal covering of the higher animals, and we looked specially at the case of human hair, because we know more of its histology than that of any other fibre. In the human hair, we found that when treated with an alkaline ley, and examined under the microscope, the whole surface of the hair was covered with a series of fine, delicate epidermal scales, which, under ordinary circumstances, are attached close to the shaft of the hair, and correspond to the scales of the scarf skin on the surface of the body. In the case of wool, we found that the surface of the shaft of the fibre was also covered with scales, but that in proportion to the diameter of the fibre they were stronger and less numerous; they also bend outwards from the shaft of the fibre, at a higher angle, and hence possesses a serrated edge, which always presents the points of the scales in the direction of the growth of the fibre, that is to say from the base upwards to the point of the fibre. When, therefore, two fibres are reversed in position, and drawn over each other in the direction of their length, so that the point of one hair touches the base of the other, these scaly edges interlock into each other and a matting or felting is the result; the tenacity with which they can hold together being only limited by the strength of the fibres themselves. In the case of wool, this matting action is much increased by the tendency of the fibres to form a waved or curly structure, which enables them to wrap round each other, and thus form a firm tenaceous mass. Although the true cause of the curl in wool is not yet known, still there seems to be a close relation between the tendency to curl, the fineness of the fibre, and the number of scales per inch on the surface. This is very clearly shown in a series of experiments recorded by M. Lafoun in the Annales de l'Agriculture Française, 1832. The experiments were made with the wool of some German merino sheep, at Hohenheim, in Wurtemburg, and

Schleisheim, near Munich. Three times a year the whole of the flock was inspected,—before winter, when the selection of the lambs is made,—in the spring,— and at the shearing time. Each sheep was examined separately, and the examination included the length, elasticity, pliability, brilliancy, and fineness of the wool. The latter property, which is measured by the diameter of the fibre, was ascertained by actual determination with the micrometer. It was found that this fineness differed in different parts of the fleece, as we might reasonably expect; and when the wool in the fleece was sorted into its different qualities, in the manner usual in France, the results are given in the following table:—

No.	Quality.	Curls or curves per in.	Diameter of fibre.
1	Super Electa	27 to 29	$\frac{1}{815}$ of an inch.
2	Electa	24 „ 28	$\frac{1}{755}$ „
3	Prima	20 „ 23	$\frac{1}{660}$ „
4	Secunda Prima	19 „ 20	$\frac{1}{588}$ „
5	Secunda	16 „ 17	$\frac{1}{554}$ „
6	Tertia	14 „ 15	$\frac{1}{510}$ „
7	Quarta	12 „ 13	

It will be seen in this table that the finer the wool the greater the tendency to curl, for when the diameter of the fibre is $\frac{1}{840}$ of an inch, the number of the curves is more than double of that which pertains to the fibres whose diameter is $\frac{1}{510}$ of an inch.

The same variation can be seen if we compare the curves and diameter of the fibres in the wools of our own country, as will be seen from the following table:—

No.	Name.	Curves per inch.	Diameter of fibre.
1	English Merino	24 to 30	$\frac{1}{1562}$ of an inch.
2	Southdown	13 „ 18	$\frac{1}{1212}$ „
3	„	11 „ 16	$\frac{1}{1000}$ „
4	Irish	7 „ 11	$\frac{1}{830}$ „
5	Lincoln	3 „ 5	$\frac{1}{560}$ „
6	Northumberland	2 „ 4	$\frac{1}{380}$ „

As we have already stated, the growth of serrated fibres is not confined to the sheep alone, but is very widely diffused in the animal kingdom. Almost all the higher mammals have a hairy coating of some kind or other, and in by far the largest number, we find a tendency to produce an undergrowth of fine woolly fibre, especially during the colder seasons of the year. The difference which exists between the hair of man and that of the lower mammals, consists really only in a different proportion of size and arrangement in the cells composing the different parts of the fibre, as well as in a greater or less development of the scales or plates which form the epidermal covering. When viewed under the microscope, the hairs and wool of different animals present, therefore, a great variety of structure and appearance, especially when seen by transmitted light, which brings out the arrangement, structure, and grouping of the cells in the interior of the fibre. So far, however, as our present subject is concerned, we are more especially interested in the external covering, and here the differences are equally well marked. Fig. XI. gives a representation of various hairs from the kangaroo, camel, rabbit, and ornithorynchus paradoxus, a

Plate XI.

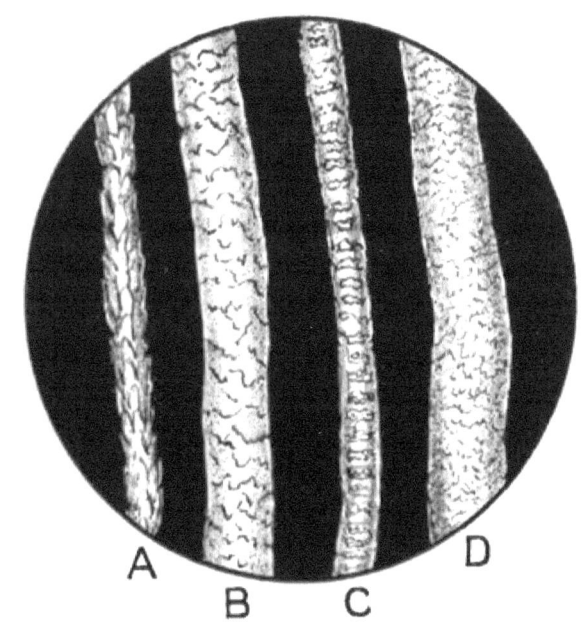

140 DIAMETERS.

VARIOUS HAIRS MAGNIFIED.

A. Hair of Kangaroo.
B. „   „ Camel.
C. „   „ Rabbit.
D. „   „ Ornithorhyncus Paradoxus.

singular animal found in Australia, which has a head terminated in a bill like a duck.

In looking at these hairs we see how diverse is the structure. In the kangaroo the scales are quite distinct and imbricated, and stand off from the surface of the hair with a wonderful regularity of arrangement. In the camel's hair we find an approximation to the appearance of true wool, where the scales take the form of irregular lorications of the surface of the hair, and the upper edges of which separate from the face of the shaft, when the hair is bent, as well as felt when they are met in the opposite direction by similar opposing scales. The hair of the ornithorynchus presents a very much finer imbricated surface, but with the same general structure; while in the hair of the rabbit we have a series of laminated plates, which rise from between the more solid parts of the cortical substance which exhibits large distinct semi-transparent cells. We might almost indefinitely extend the list of different hairs, but these will suffice to show some of the variations which are found.

The division of the animal kingdom, which, however, yields the true wool, and that which is most largely employed in textile manufactures, is the *Ruminantitia*, or animals which ruminate or chew the cud, and which includes the sheep, goat, camel, &c. The typical wool is produced by the sheep, and before we can proceed further with the characteristics of the various kinds of wool, and the peculiarities which they present, we must give some attention to the origin and varieties of the sheep, and its various characteristics, as modified by climate and culture. The ancestors of the sheep, like those of all our domestic animals, and indeed of all the present race of living animals, is lost in the obscurity of the past. Long before the dawn of history, and when man was in a primitive condition, living in caves and lake dwellings, we find the bones of the sheep, already domesticated, mingling with those of the fiercer animals which he captured by pitfalls or in the chase; and these primeval sheep doubtless supplied him with wool for clothing, flesh for meat, when unsuccessful in hunting, and probably milk also as an article of diet. As the habits of man became more settled, his principal wealth consisted of flocks and herds, and mankind might be roughly divided into shepherds and agriculturists, and hence we read in the earliest authentic record of man that "Abel was a keeper of sheep, while Cain was a tiller of the ground." Even at this early date, probably the care and attention bestowed on the sheep would improve its useful qualities in a marked degree, and render it increasingly serviceable to man in a variety of ways.

The existence of a race of wild animals, both in Asia, Europe, Africa, and America, which possess a similar affinity to the sheep that the wolf does to the dog, has led some naturalists to suppose that they may have been the original stock out of which the domestic sheep has been obtained by cultivation and breeding; but the probability seems to be much higher that these wild animals, along with the domestic sheep, may have had in the remote past a common ancestor, from which they have diverged during the course of ages.

The natural division in the zoological scale to which the sheep belong, constitutes the fifth family of the natural order *Ruminantia*. This family is called the *Bovidæ*, from the Latin *Bovis*, an ox, because it includes within it the various species of animals which we usually term cattle, and also the antelopes, besides goats and sheep. The goats and sheep form the second group of this family, and are easily distinguished from each other by their appearance as well as by their structural differences. Both the sheep and goats are furnished with horns, which are compressed, usually angulated, rugose, and turned more or less backwards, and sometimes twisted into a close spiral. Except in some of the domesticated varieties, both sexes are furnished with horns, but those of the female are much smaller than the male, whose horns sometimes reach very large dimensions. When in the wild state all these animals associate in flocks, and inhabit the mountainous districts of every quarter of the globe. The goats, as a rule, prefer the highest ground, and are more hardy than the sheep, while the latter prefer to remain in the richer pastures in the bottom of the valleys, or on the plains at the base of the mountain.

The goats *(Capridæ)*, are distinguished by having the horns simply recurved, and by the total absence of the lachrymal sinuses and glands between the hoofs. The males are always furnished with a beard beneath the chin. The habits of all the goats in all parts of the world are the same. The external covering of the goat consists of long hair, which differs in thickness and length on different parts of the body, and which varies in quality and fineness in different species, and during different periods of the year. The coat is thick and solid, and consists of two different classes of hair; the outer coat being much longer and thicker, while the undergrowth consists of a kind of woolly hair, which has a greater tendency to curl and mat together. Like the sheep, the quality of the hair can be greatly improved by breeding and cultivation, and can be made to grow long, fine, and silky, until it forms a beautiful material for textile fabrics. No cultivation, however, can prevent the growth of the outer hair, as in the case of the sheep, or change the undergrowth of fine hair into true wool.

Intermediate between the goat and the sheep is the Aoudad *(Ammotragus tragelaphus)*, a remarkable sheep-like creature, which is found in the mountain ranges of north Africa, ranging from Abyssinia to Barbary. It is of a reddish-brown colour, and has a strange looking appearance, occasioned by a large quantity of long hair which hangs down from the front of the neck and the base of the fore legs. Like the goat, it has no lachrymal sinuses, but it possesses a gland between the hoof in common with the sheep. The true sheep *(Ovidæ)*, are distinguished structurally from the goats by the possession of both lachrymal sinuses and of glands between the hoofs, which produce a fatty secretion. Their horns are also, unlike the goat, frequently twisted into a spiral. The forehead or outline of the face is convex. There is no lachrymal or respiratory opening under the eye, and the nostrils are lengthened and terminate without a muzzle. The beard, which is so conspicuous in the goat, is wanting in the sheep. The covering of the body is long and woolly, with an undergrowth of finer wool. In the wild state, the longer wool is mixed with hair like that of the goat; but, unlike the goat, by cultivation and domestication, this hair can be entirely done away with or bred out, and the whole covering of the skin made to consist of true wool only. Even in its most cultivated state, however, there are occasional hairs of a coarse and solid character appear amongst the wool, especially about the neck and base of the legs, which are often the source of annoyance in the manufacture and dyeing of wool.

Few creatures seem to be capable of greater variety than the sheep, and in consequence of this, and our ignorance of its origin, it is a matter of very great difficulty to classify the various different forms which it has assumed under different conditions. Some naturalists suppose that there are only three:—

   (1) The *Ovis ammon* or argali, which is the wild sheep of Asia and America.

   (2) The *Ovis musmon* or moufflon, which is found in southern Europe and the north of Africa.

(3) The *Ovis aries* or domestic sheep, which abounds in Europe, and notably in England.

The *Ovis Montana* or Big Horn, which is found in the Rocky Mountains of America, is considered by this division to be the same as the argali, and is frequently called the American argali.

Other naturalists make a wider division, and regard what under this classification are considered to be sub-varieties as distinct varieties. Prof. Archer regards the class ovis from an industrial point of view, and as having relation only to those sheep which are domesticated or useful to man as consisting of thirty-two varieties, of which four are inhabitants of Europe, fifteen of Asia, eleven of Africa, and two of America. This classification is as follows:—

I.—EUROPE.
1. The Spanish sheep or Merino sheep *(ovis Hispaniam).*
2. The common sheep *(ovis rusticus).*
3. The Cretan sheep *(ovis strepsiceros).*
4. The Crimean sheep *(ovis longicaudatus).*

II.—ASIA.
1. Hooniah, or black-faced sheep of Tibet.
2. Cago, or tame sheep of Cabul *(ovis cagia).*
3. Nepal sheep *(ovis selingia).*
4. Curumbar, or Mysore sheep.
5. Gărăr, or Indian sheep.
6. Dukhun, or Deccan sheep.
7. Morvant de la Chine, or Chinese sheep.
8. Shaymbliar, or Mysore sheep.

CLASSIFICATION OF SHEEP.

9. Broad-tailed sheep *(ovis laticaudatus)*.
10. Many-horned sheep *(ovis polyceratus)*.
11. The Pucha, or Hindostan Dumba sheep.
12. The Tartary sheep.
13. The Javanese sheep.
14. The Barwall sheep *(ovis Barual)*.
15. Short-tailed sheep of northern Russia.

III.—AFRICA.

1. Smooth-haired sheep *(ovis Ethiopia)*.
2. African sheep *(ovis Guinensis)*.
3. Guinea sheep *(ovis ammon Guinensis)*.
4. Zeylan sheep.
5. Fezzan sheep.
6. Congo sheep *(ovis aries Congensis)*.
7. Angola sheep *(ovis aries Angolensis)*.
8. Yenu, or goitered sheep *(ovis aries steatiniora)*.
9. Madagascar sheep.
10. Bearded sheep of West Africa.
11. Morocco sheep *(ovis aries Numedæ)*.

IV.—AMERICA.

1. West Indian sheep found in Jamaica.
2. Brazilian sheep.

Extensive as this classification appears, there is reason to suppose that many of the sub-varieties which are known to exist, as the result of the intermixture of these various kinds of sheep, possess characteristics which, if we did not know their origin, would almost entitle them to be considered as separate varieties. It is also probable that many of these may be the result of intermixture and subsequent variation on account of locality and pasture. This will appear all the more reasonable when we come to see, as we afterwards shall do, that there are no less than thirty-one sub-varieties known of the common sheep, some of which differ from each other quite as much as many which are regarded as distinct varieties. Some authorities are of opinion that there are only two varieties of sheep, the long and the short-woolled, and that all the others have been obtained by crossing and variation produced by climate and pasturage.

The very wide area over which the domestic sheep is found, the general characteristics which all the varieties possess, and the habits which are so similar, seem to indicate that it was one of the very earliest of all the domesticated animals; and although we can probably never settle the question as to what was the exact character of the original creature from which it was first derived, we can form probably a pretty close approximation by looking at the two wild varieties which are still found in the four quarters of the globe.

The *Argali* inhabits the mountains and elevated plains of central Asia which stretch from the Caucasus, northward and eastward, to Kamtschatka and the ocean. They are usually found in small flocks, pasturing in the higher valleys and mountains during the summer months, and descending into the lower valleys and plains during the winter, so as to avoid the inclemency of the weather and scarcity of food on the higher lands. They are agile and strong, but timid and shy, and in their habits very much resemble the domestic sheep. They are also easily tamed when taken young. Professor Low says: "The argali possesses all the genuine characteristics of the sheep, but is larger, being somewhat less than the size of a stag. It has enormous horns, measuring more than a foot in circumference at the base, and from 3 to 4 feet in length, triangularly rising from the summit of the head so as nearly to touch at the root, ascending, stretching out laterally, and bending forward at the point. It has a fur of short hair, covering a coat of soft white wool. The colour of the fur externally is brown, becoming brownish-grey in winter. There is a buff-coloured streak along the back, and a large spot of a lighter buff colour on the haunch, surrounding and including the tail. The female differs from the male in being smaller, in having the horns more slender and straight, and in the absence of the disc on the haunch. Both sexes have a shortish tail, whitish eyelashes, and the hair beneath the throat is longer than on the other parts of the body." When the argali is domesticated and removed from its wild habitat, the quantity of hair on the body diminishes and the quantity of wool increases.

The Rocky Mountain Sheep, or argali of the American continent closely resembles the Asiatic variety, but it is rather larger and stronger. It inhabits all the lofty mountain chains of North America, and moves in large flocks from the mountain fastnesses into the valleys and *vice versa*, with the changing seasons of the year. Its range extends within the temperate zone to the borders of the Arctic circle, and is described by some Spanish writers under the name of the Californian sheep.

The European and African variety is known as the *Musmon*. In Europe it still abounds in some of the islands of the Greek Archipelago, such as Crete and Cyprus; and its range extends through Corsica and Sardinia into the mountains of Murcia, in Spain, in which country it once abounded. The musmon is smaller than the argali, and although the male has a formidable pair of horns, nearly 2 feet in length, very thick, and differing from the horns of the argali by turning inward instead of outward at the points, in the female the horns are frequently wanting altogether. The body is covered with a hairy, brownish fur, beneath which is a short, fine grey-coloured wool, which covers all the body. When the musmon is captured and kept in a state of confinement it has all the habits of the domestic sheep, with which it is capable of breeding, and the offspring is also fruitful. Whether or not our domestic sheep is derived from any of these wild sheeplike creatures, there is no doubt but that its domestication first occurred in Asia, and from thence was introduced into Europe with advancing civilisation, and its introduction was always accompanied by a great increase in the comfort and wealth of the owners. In Europe, it appears first to have been brought into Greece, where, as is recorded by its early poets and historians, it was highly prized; and after the foundation of Rome, was probably brought into Italy by the Grecian colonists, and from thence it spread with the advance of Roman civilisation into Spain, Gaul, and Britain.

Although the wild sheep possess considerable interest, as exhibiting the probable original condition of the creature, undoubtedly our greatest interest lies in the domestic varieties, and in the sub-varieties which have been produced artificially by the mixture of races under cultivation. It is in these classes that we find the wool-bearing qualities of the sheep brought into the greatest perfection, and therefore rendered of the greatest use in the textile arts. Thus, while all the wild forms of sheep exhibit a great similarity in the structure of the hair, and in the mixture of true wool along with it, it is only when we come to the most thoroughly domesticated and cultured sheep, that we find the entire disappearance of the coarse hair, and its replacement by a pure and perfect wool,—a wool in which all the best and most desirable qualities as a textile raw material are found blended together. Nothing can show this difference more strikingly than a comparison between the coarse, hairy covering of the argali or the musmon, and one of the fine Saxony Merino; or one of the Australian Botany sheep, with its silk-like pure wool. As we have already stated, the sheep is found in every part of the globe; and in looking shortly at the principal varieties, especially of the domestic sheep, it will be better to adhere to the geographical divisions, beginning with the sheep of—

I.—EUROPE,

and taking as a starting point those which are found in our own islands.

SHEEP OF THE UNITED KINGDOM.

In reviewing the various classes of domestic sheep, it seems best that we should commence with those which exist in the United Kingdom; and all the more so because until a comparatively recent date, these English wools formed the staple article of consumption in the Bradford trade. As we might naturally expect, the great variety of mountain and plain, valley and marsh, as well as the detached islands of Scotland, exhibit a great variety in the characteristics of the sheep, and it is very difficult to make any exact classification of them all. The crossing of the various breeds has introduced many sub-varieties, and their character has also been much changed by the method of feeding adopted, by which it has been intended to improve the flesh as an article of diet as well as to improve the wool. The former of these considerations has always been a great point with English farmers, because the large manufacturing centres have formed one of the best markets in the world for butchers' meat, and hence, in many cases, there has been a willing sacrifice of those properties which might have tended to increase the quality of the wool in the endeavour to produce large and heavy sheep, and those which would fatten with the greatest rapidity,— the wool-bearing qualities being looked upon as almost subordinate. It will of course be quite impossible to give more than a very cursory account of the various breeds of sheep, because the length of time allowed for the lecture will not permit otherwise. The very great variety also which are found even within the limits of the United Kingdom presents another difficulty, and renders it quite impossible to do more than merely glance at the typical ones. The easy means of communication with different parts of the kingdom, and the desire for improvement, which has led to a large transference of stock from one part to another, have rendered classification either in regard to race or distribution extremely difficult. Several methods of classification have been suggested, but I have adopted that suggested by Prof. Low in his work on the Breeds of Sheep and Cattle, and extended by Mr. W. C. Spooner, in monograph of the History, Structure, &c., of the Sheep,[*] to which I must refer those who wish for further information than I can give here.

We may, therefore, consider a classification of the sheep of the United Kingdom to be generally made as follows:—

    I.—The wilder and most primitive breeds.
    II.—The forest and mountain breeds.

---

[*] "The Sheep." W. C. Spooner, M.R.V.C., Crosby. Lockwood & Co., 1878.

III.—The ancient upland breeds.

IV.—The long-woolled breeds.

I.—As we might naturally expect, the wilder and more primitive breeds of sheep are found in the most remote parts of the kingdom, where communication is difficult, and where improvements are likely to be most slowly adopted.

Highland Sheep.—In the extreme north of Scotland, in the Orkney, Shetland Islands, and the Hebrides, a race of sheep exists which seems to be allied to the Norwegian and Scandinavian race found on the opposite coast of Europe, whence it was probably derived. They are extremely hardy creatures, and more like a goat than a sheep in their appearance and habits. They have a short tail, and this distinguishing feature has earned their name,— "short-tailed sheep,"—by which they are known. In some of the islands they have been mixed in breed; but when pure, they are of various colours—black, brown, grey, white, and spotted. The fleece consists of a mixture of hair and wool. The wool does not increase in length from year to year, but falls off each year on the approach of summer, leaving the hair alone as a covering during the hot season. The fleece is not therefore shorn, but plucked off the sheep, and is fine and soft; but, as it contains only few serrations, is not well adapted for felting, but can be spun into yarn, from which coarse garments are made. Attempts have been made to improve this breed, but the probability is that it will be superseded by some of the hardier varieties of sheep already in existence, such as the Cheviot.

Welsh Sheep.—In the mountains of Wales there are, according to Prof. Low, two different varieties of sheep which are natural to the locality. One, which he terms the sheep of the higher mountains, and the other the soft-woolled sheep. The higher mountain sheep is various coloured, like the Highland sheep, and goat-like in appearance; but it has a long tail and a ridge of hair on the back, with the throat and dewlap white, and the face and legs always black. They are very wild and active, and always prefer the highest pasture ground. This mountain sheep is probably the original stock of the Radnor sheep, which is larger and heavier, with a better fleece, but still retaining the black face and legs. The soft-woolled sheep are the distinguishing breed of Wales. They are small and active, with a white face, and furnish the wool from which the famous Welsh flannel is made. The flesh is firm and sweet, and much in request as an article of diet. The fleece always contains a certain mixture of hair, although less than in most mountain sheep, and this is particularly noticeable on the throat.

Irish Sheep.—The sheep of Ireland, like those of Wales and England, are of two distinct varieties,— those which inhabit the mountains, and those which are found in the valleys. The mountain sheep are found principally in the counties of Wicklow and Kerry. The former are the most valuable, and closely resemble the Welsh mountain sheep. They are wild little animals, without horns, and with white faces and legs. On the higher pasturages the wool is coarse and much mixed with hair; but when removed to better grazing ground the wool becomes softer and longer, and the hair less, although it never entirely disappears, but is confined more particularly to the ridge of the back. When crossed with a better breed, such as the Southdown, considerable improvement has been effected, and, as the lambs feed quickly, and are therefore soon ready for market, they are much esteemed by the farmers. The Kerry sheep are larger than the Wicklow breed, but they lack many of the advantages which the latter possess, and neither as wool-bearers nor for food are they so suitable at the same early age. The mutton, however, is good.

The sheep which are found in the plains of Ireland are much larger than the mountain races. They are large, long-woolled animals, resembling the native sheep of the Midland Counties of England. Within late years very great improvements have been introduced into them by crossing with other and more cultivated races imported from England. This has been abundantly seen in the improved quality and character of the wool which has been received in the English market.

II.—In looking at the breeds of mountain sheep which inhabit England and Scotland, it becomes a matter of considerable difficulty to exactly distinguish between them, because they range over the whole of the kingdom from the south to the extreme north, along the mountain range and its offshoots which forms the backbone of England. In the south we have the *Exmoor and Dartmoor* sheep in Devonshire and Cornwall; the *black-faced heath* or moor sheep in the higher ranges of Derbyshire, Lancashire, Yorkshire, Cumberland, and Westmoreland, until they meet with the *Cheviot*, which inhabits the mountains in Northumberland and the south of Scotland. The *Herdwicks* are found in Cumberland and Westmoreland; and the *Penistone* sheep inhabits the hills of Yorkshire, Lancashire, and Derbyshire, in the immediate neighbourhood of the town of Penistone. There is also a cross breed with the black-faced sheep which is larger than the Herdwick sheep, and is called the Lonk, and is considered by some as the best adapted for the hilly districts.

The Exmoor and Dartmoor Sheep are small, with white faces and legs, and are well adapted by their hardy character for the poverty of pasture which is found in the higher lands of Cornwall and Devon. The Exmoor sheep are the smallest of the two, and the males have a slight beard under the chin not unlike a goat. They are wild and restless, and covered with soft wool. When crossed with the Leicester they are much improved in size, and when fattened the mutton finds a ready sale on account of its excellent quality.

The Black-faced Heath Sheep is larger and more robust than the Welsh mountain sheep, and in some of its characteristics resembles the sheep of Persia and

Wallachia. Both the male and female have horns, which are very large, and spirally twisted in the male, but sometimes entirely wanting in the female. The limbs are lengthy and muscular, and the form is robust. The face and legs are black, the fleece being coarse and shaggy, and while the colour is sometimes black or grey there is no tendency to brown or russet, and in this respect these sheep differ from all the other mountain breeds. The wool is of a medium length, and the fleece when washed weighs about 3 to 4 lbs., and is never heavy on the body. The character of the wool also is such that it can only be used for the coarser class of yarns, such as those employed in the manufacture of carpets. The most serious defect, however, is the frequent occurrence of "kemps" in the wool. These are wiry hairs without any serrations on them, and are entirely destitute of the felting properties necessary to give them a good spinning quality, and what is worse, they resist all reagents in dyeing, as they seem to possess no open cells into which the dye can penetrate. These sheep do not appear to amalgamate readily with other races; but, by cultivation and selection of suitable sire and dam, considerable improvements have been made in their properties. Crossed with Cheviot, Leicester, and Southdowns, several sub-varieties have been produced, which are a marked improvement on the old stock, both for food and wool-bearing qualities. The great hardiness of the race, and its fitness for enduring the hardships and exposure necessary to the

Plate XII

THE CHEVIOT SHEEP.

heath-covered hills in winter,—the scanty food upon which it can live, and the little attention which it requires, render it one of the most extensively cultivated of the English sheep.

The Cheviot Sheep is one of the most valuable breeds in the kingdom, and takes the place of the black-faced heath sheep in the mountains in the Lowlands of Scotland, from which it derives its name. It has extended from there, southward, into the hilly districts in the border counties of England, and northwards into the Highlands, where it has in many places supplanted the native mountain sheep. It is a very hardy creature and thrives well on very poor pasture, surviving with comparative ease the very severe weather to which it is subjected in the winters, which render the Cheviot hills quite unsuited for other breeds. They are thus described: "They have white faces and legs, open countenances, lively eyes, and are without horns. The ears are large and somewhat singular, and there is great space between the ears and eyes. The carcass is long; the back straight; the shoulders rather light; the ribs circular, and the quarters good. The legs are small in the bone and covered with wool, as well as all the body, with the exception of the face." Plate XII. gives a very good illustration of this valuable sheep, which may be taken as the type of the mountain breeds. Although the Cheviot is a mountain sheep, it is less active and more docile than many other mountain breeds, and has been much improved in certain districts by crossing with other long-woolled sheep, as well as with Down sheep. The wool is usually fine in quality, and grows thick upon the body, thus forming a good protection against the weather. The fleece usually weighs from 3 to 4 lbs. Although since the introduction of Botany wool it is not used so much as formerly in the production of cloth, it is extensively used in the manufacture of Tweeds and Cheviots, as its name implies. The crossing with other sheep, especially the Leicester, has materially improved the character of the wool, but it has tended to detract from the hardy character of the race, and hence throughout a large part of the districts where it is found it flourishes best in its purest state. These improved sheep are called Border Leicesters or Leicester Cheviots.

The Herdwick Sheep are found only in the mountains of Cumberland and Westmoreland, and are, like the Cheviots, able to live on coarse fare and endure great exposure without injury. They are without horns, and the wool is coarse and open, the fleece weighing about 3 to 4 lbs. They fatten slowly, but when matured the quality of the mutton is excellent. Unlike most mountain sheep, they remain attached to a particular spot, and seldom stray far away from it.

The Penistone Sheep is distinguished from all the mountain sheep of this country by its extreme coarseness of form, especially at the extremities, and the large, muscular and bony character of its long tail. The weight of the fleece is from 4 to 5 lbs., and the wool is of a silky appearance and medium length, but it is harsh and wiry, and only fitted for the coarser class of fabrics. The males have large horns, lying close to the head and projecting forward. The limbs are bony; the feet large; the shoulders heavy, and the sides fat. They feed well, and the mutton is of first-rate quality.

III.—*The Ancient Upland Breed* of sheep comprise, with the sub-varieties produced by crossing, the whole of the most valuable wool-bearing sheep of the United Kingdom, as regards the fineness and quality of the fleece. They are the inhabitants of the south, east, and west of England, and the Downs of the southern counties, and possess many of the most valuable qualities which are to be desired in a sheep. The distinctive classes are usually named from the districts in which they are found; but they are all more or less intermixed with other breeds, and into no class of sheep have greater improvements been introduced than into these by judicious crossing. The Southdown, which is included in this class, is, however, one of the purest and most unmixed breeds in the kingdom, and is the type of the short fine-woolled sheep, just as the Leicester is of the deep-grown woolled sheep.

The Old Norfolk Sheep were formerly found very extensively in the higher lands of Norfolk, Cambridgeshire, and Suffolk; but latterly they have been to a great extent replaced either by a cross with the Southdown or by the Southdown itself. They somewhat resemble the black-faced heath sheep, but have longer bodies and much finer wool. They have black faces, with horns in both sexes, long limbs, and are very active in their habits. The wool is mostly used for carding purposes, and made into livery-cloths, either alone or mixed with finer wools.

The Dorset Sheep is probably the best of all the old horned sheep of the country, and has been preserved pure from a very remote period. They are strong, hardy, active sheep; much wilder and less docile than Southdowns, which they exceed in size. They have longer legs than the Southdown, white faces and legs, and horns of moderate length in both sexes. The wool is moderately long,—longer than the Southdown,—scarcely so pure in quality, but brighter in appearance and almost entirely free from grey, and the weight of the fleece is from $3\frac{1}{2}$ to 4 lbs. The great value of this sheep, however, consists in its prolificness, since they rear a larger number of lambs than any other sheep, and at an earlier period. It is from this source that the supply of Christmas lamb in the London market is derived. This is a matter of considerable importance, because, since the great decline in the price of English wool, the farmer has to pay special attention to the rearing of sheep and lambs for the meat market.

The Somerset Sheep is a variety of the Dorset sheep, but more of the Leicester character, and differing from the Dorset in having a pink nose in place of black or white. The wool also is longer and heavier.

The Portland Sheep is also a variety of the Dorset, and is raised on the island of the same name. They have horns, and white faces and legs. The wool is coarser than on the Dorset sheep, and the fleece very light, but the flesh is delicate and excellent, and they are principally reared for the London market, where they command a good price.

The Old Wiltshire Sheep are nearly extinct, having been almost entirely replaced by other and more profitable breeds, or crossed with Leicesters, and so merged into half breed sheep. They are large in size, and horned in both sexes, with Roman noses, and white legs and faces. They carry very little wool, the fleece only weighing about $2\frac{1}{2}$ lbs., and they fatten slowly.

The Old Hampshire and the *Old Berkshire* sheep somewhat resembled the old Wiltshire, and both have now become practically extinct, having been replaced by Southdown and other more cultivated and useful sheep, though at one time they abounded in large numbers in the counties which are associated with their names.

The Hampshire Down Sheep is now found generally in the northern division of the county, and extending into Berkshire and Wiltshire. The precise origin of this variety is difficult to discover; but it probably originated in the native sheep which existed there before the time of the Romans, and its present characteristics have been obtained by judicious crossing with more improved sheep. This sheep is larger

G

than the Southdown, with longer legs and coarser bones, but the quality and weight of wool is somewhat similar.

The Improved Hampshire Sheep are examples of successful crossing, and a proof of what can be done by the male parent in the course of a few generations in changing the character of the original, and producing a breed which is more valuable in every way than either of the sources from whence it was derived. They unite the qualities of the original Hampshire with the Sussex and Cotswold sheep, and thus produce a first-class sheep, both in size, appearance, and wool-bearing properties.

The Southdown, or Sussex Breed is a typical sheep. It is unquestionably one of the purest and most valuable sheep in the kingdom, and its descent can be traced to a period antecedent to the Norman Conquest. It stands first amongst all the short-woolled English sheep, not only on account of the fineness and quality of the wool, but also of its fattening and meat giving character. These sheep have reached their present perfection by constant and unremitting attention to the purity of the original breed, and the careful weeding out of any sheep which showed any retrograde characteristics. The utmost attention has also been paid to the feeding and rearing of them, and this has not only tended to the increase of their numbers, but to the improvement both of the flesh and wool in every respect. Latterly they have been crossed to some extent with heavier woolled sheep, and this along with improved farming has tended to strengthen the character of the fibre. Nothing can show the sterling qualities of this breed better than the fact that, with the large influx of foreign fine wool into this country, the Southdowns have not only maintained their numbers, but actually increased, although the wool is now principally used for combing purposes, whereas at one time it was exclusively used for carding. They have also very much extended in the area which they cover, and have, in many instances, supplanted entirely the native sheep in those localities which are suited for their habits and constitution. This improved sheep has thus been described: "The head is small and hornless, and the face brown-grey in colour, and neither too short nor too long. The lips are thin, and the space between the eyes and nose narrow. The under jaw is fine and thin; while the ears are tolerably wide and well covered with wool. The forehead also, and the space between the ears is covered with wool. The eyes are full and bright, but not prominent, and the orbit of the eye not too projecting. The neck is of medium length; thin towards the head, but enlarging towards the shoulders, where it is broad and high, but straight in its whole course above and below. The breast is wide, deep, and projecting forwards between the fore legs, indicating a good constitution and a disposition to thrive. Corresponding with this, the shoulders should be on a level with the back, and not too wide above; they should bow outwards from the top to the breast, indicating a springing rib beneath, and leaving room for it. The ribs coming out horizontally from the spine and extending far backwards, and the last rib projecting more than the others. The back flat from the shoulders to the setting on of the tail. The loin broad and flat, and the rump long and broad. The tail set on high, and nearly on a level with the spine. The hips, wide, with the space between them and the last rib on either side as narrow as possible, while the ribs present a circular form like a barrel. The belly is straight as the back. The legs neither too long nor too short. The fore legs straight from the shoulder to the foot, not bending inwards at the knee, and standing far apart both before and behind. The hocks having a direction rather outwards, and the twist or the meeting of the thighs behind being particularly full. The bones fine, yet having no appearance of weakness, and the legs of a dark colour. The belly well protected with wool, and the wool coming down, both before and behind, to the knee and to the hock. The wool, short, close, curled, and fine, and free from spiry projecting fibres."*

Such is a description of this favourite sheep, which has extended itself into all parts of England, Scotland, and Ireland, and a representation of which is given in Plate XIII. It has almost supplanted the native breeds in Norfolk, Cambridgeshire, and many other counties; and in Hampshire, Wiltshire, and Dorset it has been extensively crossed with the native

---

* "The Sheep." W. C. Spooner, M.R.V.C., p. 41.

THE SOUTH DOWN SHEEP.

breeds. The breed is well adapted for hilly pastures wherever the chalk prevails; but as it has not the hardy character of many of the mountain races, it cannot replace the Black-faced heath sheep, or the Cheviots, or the mountain sheep of Wales and Ireland. The superior quality of the mutton, and the due proportion of lean and fat in the carcass, render it a greater favourite than even the Leicester sheep in the London market, and for this purpose, therefore, it has been crossed with Shropshire rams so as to produce a sheep partaking of the character of both parents, and having earlier maturity and superior feeding qualities to the pure Southdown.

The Shropshire Speckle-faced Sheep is a cross breed between the original horned sheep and the Southdown. The original sheep was probably the Morfe Common sheep, which is still found near Bridgenorth, and which produces a superior quality of wool; but as it has been crossed with other breeds, particularly the long-woolled Leicester and Cotswold sheep, as well as the Southdown, a corresponding variation from the original has been produced.

The Ryeland Sheep has been preserved from a remote time in the County of Hereford, and from thence has extended itself into Shropshire, Monmouthshire, Gloucester, and Warwickshire, where it has received various names. These sheep are small, without horns, and distinguished for the great fineness of the wool, which is superior for carding purposes to all others which are produced in England, the merino alone excepted. The introduction of fine foreign wool into the country has much interfered with the cultivation of this sheep, because any attempts to improve its character so as to compete with this have resulted either in the deterioration of the sheep for food purposes, or else its deterioration as a wool bearer if the former character was preserved. The cross with the Leicester has been most successful, but the quality of the fleece has been entirely changed and rendered fit for combing purposes.

IV.—*The Long-Woolled Breed of Sheep* are diametrically opposite to those of which we have last been speaking. They are distinguished for their great size and the great length and weight of the fleece, and in this respect the most improved breeds of England are without any rival in the world. They are properly the natives of the rich marshy pastures of the west and midland counties of England, from whence with the improvements in agriculture and the demand for long wool, they have spread into all parts of the country. Even in those counties where the short-woolled sheep abound there has been extensive crossing with the Leicester and allied breeds. Wherever suited to the district they have been found more profitable than the short-woolled sheep, not only on account of the greater weight of the wool which they produced, but also in one particular variety on account of their earlier maturity and greater aptitude for fattening. While many of the upland and mountain breeds of sheep have been preserved pure, the ancient long-woolled sheep have, in almost all cases, undergone modification by crossing so as to secure certain improvements. It is a matter of considerable difficulty to trace the original stock from whence the various breeds have been derived. Prof. Low thinks that there were originally two distinct varieties, one of which belonged to the marshes and fens and of which the Lincoln and Romney Marsh sheep are now the representatives; the other inhabiting the inland plains, and which are now represented by the Tees-water, Leicester, and other varieties. The wool from these sheep has a peculiar interest for those engaged in the Bradford trade, because it was from the use of these wools that the worsted trade, as distinguished from the woollen trade, originally took its rise, and they formed the staple articles of consumption before the demand for soft goods, and the introduction of such large quantities of Botany and other fine wools into the district, and they still hold their own in the manufacture of the warps for the all worsted goods.

The Lincoln Sheep stands at the head of the long-woolled sheep, not only on account of the length of the wool, but also of the weight of the fleece, which averages from 8 to 9 lbs. weight. The old pure Lincoln breed is now almost extinct, because it has been found that by crossing with the New Leicester a breed of sheep has been obtained which we may term the New Lincoln, and which possesses a greater aptitude to fatten, an earlier maturity, as well as an improved form. A larger number of sheep can also be kept on the same extent of land. In consequence of this, although the size of the sheep has been slightly reduced, it is the best wool producer as well as the largest sheep in Europe. It is of a large and coarse form. The fleece often weighs as much as 10 or even 12 lbs., and hangs down all round, almost touching the ground. When spread out on the sorting board some of the largest fleeces seem almost too large to have ever been upon a single sheep's back, having even reached the enormous weight of 24 lbs. We must remember, however, that some of the largest sheep reach from 350 to 360 lbs. weight when slaughtered. The length of the wool on the longest part of the fleece also sometimes reaches an incredible length. I myself retained for some time a lock from a fleece I sorted which measured over 36 inches in length. The wool, although bright and silky, is coarse in texture, but within recent years their introduction into Australia and New Zealand for crossing purposes has produced a class of sheep which have a beautifully pure and silky hair along with a great length. These sheep are principally found in the fen district of Lincolnshire, but from thence they have extended into Norfolk, Cambridgeshire, and the adjoining counties, and crossed with the Leicester into every district in the United Kingdom where suited for the growth of long-woolled sheep. Plate XIV. gives a good illustration of this celebrated sheep.

THE LINCOLN SHEEP.

The Romney Marsh Sheep is another breed of long-woolled sheep inhabiting from time immemorial the fen district on the southern coast of Kent from which it derives its name. The native breed of this district were large and coarse animals, rather smaller than the Lincoln, but since they have been crossed with the New Leicester they have much improved in every point, and now are represented by a large handsome sheep which yields moderately fine and deep-grown wool.

The Tees-Water Sheep originated in a large and ancient breed of sheep in the valley of the Tees, which separates the counties of York and Durham. It was a large, tall sheep, of very coarse form, with large head, rounded haunches and long limbs. The wool was very long, but rather scanty; and, since crossing with the Leicester, has much improved—so much so that the cross has entirely supplanted the original.

The Warwickshire Sheep was another variety of long-woolled sheep, rather smaller in size than the Tees-Water, with heavy bony frame, long thick legs, and great splay feet; but this animal has almost if not entirely become extinct, having been replaced by more improved animals such as the New Leicester.

The Bampton Nott is found in the fertile valleys of Devonshire and Somersetshire, round the village of Bampton, from which it derives its name. Crossed with the Leicester it has produced a valuable breed of sheep, in which the original defects of the native breed have disappeared. A smaller variety called

Southam Notts also exists, and these two classes of sheep, crossed with the Leicester, represent the long-woolled sheep of Devonshire, and the southern part of Hampshire.

The Devonshire Southam Sheep originated in the southern part of that county in the neighbourhood of the Vale of Honiton, and up to the borders of Dartmoor. From thence they have extended into Cornwall, where they are extensively bred, and have been much improved by crossing with Leicesters. They somewhat resemble the Romney Marsh sheep, but with brown faces and legs. Crossing with Leicesters has removed this colour as well as materially improved them in every other respect, so that they fatten earlier, and a finer and more silky fleece is obtained. The quality is moderately fine and the staple long. The fleece is about 9 lbs. weight.

The Cotswold Sheep derive their name from the hills of the same name in Gloucestershire, where they originated, or at any rate have existed for a period beyond authentic history. They are of large size, without horns, and with a long and abundant fleece. They are principally found in the valley of the Severn, and on the surrounding hills. The wool from these sheep has long been celebrated for its length, and in consequence of this property a few were exported to Spain in the reign of Edward IV., where they were much prized and increased in numbers. Some writers have supposed that they were the originators of the Spanish Merino sheep, but it is probable that they were crossed with already existing Merinos to the advantage of both. The introduction of Leicester sheep into the Cotswold district has greatly improved the old native breed, and the new Cotswolds have a decided advantage over the old on account of the greater hardihood as compared with the pure Leicester and the deeper grown nature of the wool than in the original stock. The wool, when washed, is of a good colour, and averages from 6 to 8 inches in length, and the fleece weighs from 7 to 8 lbs. The Cotswolds have also been crossed with the Hampshire Down sheep, and produced what is known as the New Oxford Sheep.

The New Oxford Sheep originated about the year 1830, when Mr. Twynham crossed a Hampshire Down ewe with a cross between the New Leicester and Old Cotswold. The resulting sheep approximated to the Cotswold in the wool, and the Leicester in the carcase, while it much exceeded the parent in size and hardihood. The fleece weighs from 8 to 9 lbs., with a firmer and finer staple than the Cotswold wool and yet retaining the full length.

The Leicester Sheep, or, as it is now called in its improved condition, the Dishley or New Leicester, is perhaps the most celebrated of all the long-woolled sheep, not even excepting the New Lincoln. In figure, hardihood, and quality, both for wool and mutton, it is almost without a rival, and has been used perhaps more extensively than any other to cross the native breeds of long-woolled sheep in other districts with a view to improve them. It originated with a Mr. Bakewell, who obtained it by a judicious crossing with various long-woolled sheep, which he had selected with the best specimens of the Old Leicester breed which it has now almost replaced. It is now preserved pure as a breed, and while there is no long-woolled sheep which has been crossed with it which has not improved, it has never itself received any further additional advantage by crossing with them. It occupies the same position in regard to the long-woolled sheep that the South Down does amongst the short-woolled.

The following is a description of this typical sheep, which may be compared with the illustration given in Plate XV.:—"The head should be hornless, long, small, and tapering towards the muzzle, and projecting horizontally forwards. The eyes prominent and with a quiet expression. The ears thin, rather long, and directed backwards. The neck full and broad at its base where it proceeds from the chest, but gradually tapering towards the head, and being particularly fine at the junction of the head and neck, the neck seeming to project straight from the chest, so that there is, with the slightest possible deviation, one continued horizontal line from the rump to the poll. The breast should be broad and full; the shoulders also broad and round, and no uneven or angular formation where the shoulders join either the neck or the back; particularly no rising of the withers, or hollow behind the situation of these bones. The

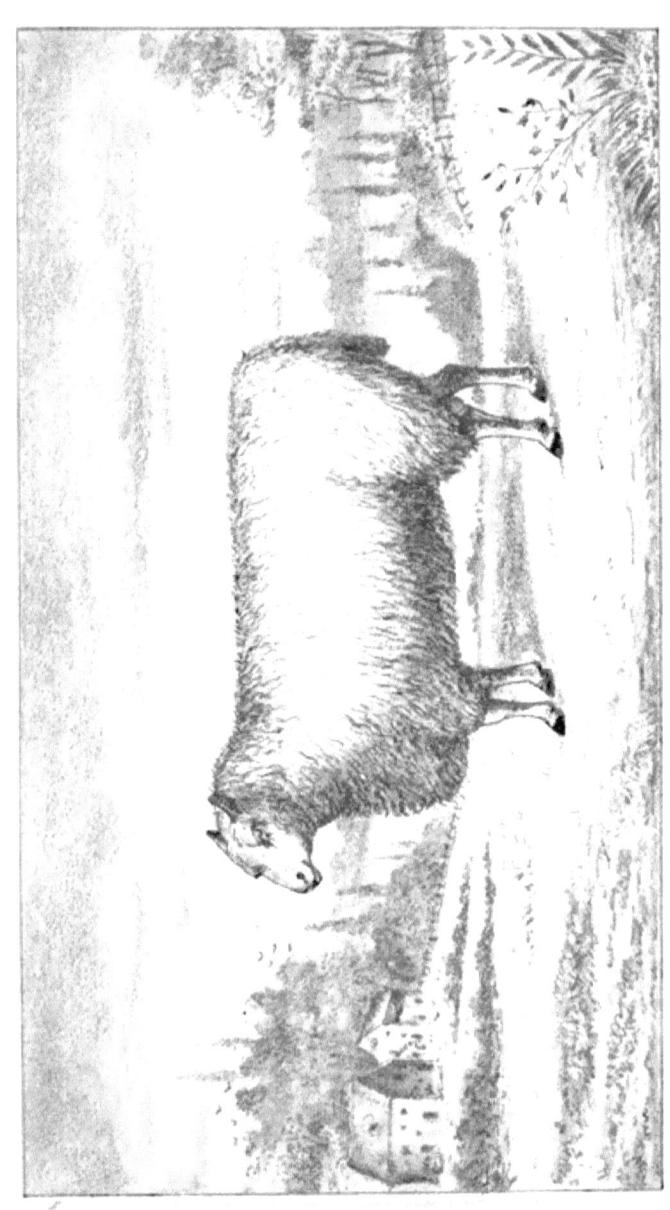

The New Leicester Sheep.

arm fleshy through its full extent, and even down to the knee; the bones of the leg small, standing wide apart, with no looseness of skin about them, and comparatively bare of wool. The chest and barrel at once deep and round, the ribs forming a considerable arch with the spine, so as in some cases, and specially when the animal is in good condition, to make the apparent width of the chest even greater than the depth. The barrel ribbed well home, with no irregularity of line on the back or belly, but on the sides the carcase diminishing gradually in width towards the rump. The quarters long and full, and as with the fore legs, the muscles extending down to the hock. The thighs also wide and full, the legs of moderate length. The skin is thin, but soft and elastic, and with a good quantity of white wool, not so long as in some breeds but considerably finer."

In addition to its unrivalled qualities as a wool producer, the New Leicester has a greater dead weight when slaughtered compared with the live weight than any other sheep, while the flesh and fat are accumulated more externally, and acquired in the greatest degree in the most profitable places and the least in the coarse points.

FOREIGN SHEEP.

Difficult as the task is to describe and arrange all the different breeds of sheep which are found within the United Kingdom, it becomes more difficult when we have to classify those which are found scattered over the four quarters of the globe. Many of the breeds have only a local celebrity, and only small quantities of the wool are received into the English market. The increase of international communications, however, has within the last few years greatly facilitated the transport of wool, and the great demand for new makes of textile fabrics has stimulated the introduction of new fibres, so that large quantities are now received from countries where but a few years ago the export of wool was unknown. Of many of these fibres it is extremely difficult to say which class of sheep has supplied them, as they are principally known as wools named after the port whence they are shipped, and are often mixtures from several varieties of sheep. There are, however, scattered through all the more civilised countries of the world various breeds of sheep which have distinctive characteristics, and these we shall briefly describe, commencing with those which are found on the Continent of Europe, and in the British Colonies, on account of their great importance in this and other markets.

EUROPEAN SHEEP.

The first amongst all the European sheep, both on account of its intrinsic merits, and also of the close relation which it bears to some of the English and Colonial sheep, stands the *Spanish Merino* breed.

The wool of Spain has always been celebrated from the very earliest times, and during the period of the Roman Empire was justly considered to excel, both in quality and staple, all other known wools. During the Middle Ages, and the Saracen occupation of Spain, the woollen manufactures of that country were renowned throughout all Europe, and the Italian artizans received their finest wool from that country. With the expulsion of the Moors from Spain the manufactures fell into a state of decay, from which they have not yet recovered, and the introduction of the Spanish Merino Sheep into Saxony and Australia and other of our Colonies has deprived her of the monopoly which she once held of this fine breed.

There has probably existed from the earliest times in Spain two different varieties of sheep which corresponded to our long and short-woolled sheep, and which were further distinguished by their habits, each of them having representatives amongst the stationary and migratory classes; the stationary confining themselves to one district all the year round, while the migratory seek a different pasture at different seasons. The stationary sheep consist of two different breeds and a third or intermediate one.

The Chunah is a larger, taller, and heavier sheep than the Merino, with a smaller head, which is devoid of wool. The staple is about 8 inches long, and much coarser than the Merino, and possessing hardly any curve. It was probably to improve this breed that the Cotswold sheep were imported into Spain from England in 1464, and the descendants of this mixed breed may still be traced.

The Stationary Merinos are chiefly found in the pastures scattered amongst the Guadarrama mountains, the Somo Sierra ranges, and the whole country of Segovia, and hence are sometimes called Segovia Merinos. They produce fine, beautiful wool, but have not the same reputation as the migratory Merinos, which are so justly celebrated.

The Migratory Merinos, or, as they are called in Spain, *Transhumantes,* are the most celebrated sheep in the world, and excel all others in the fineness of the quality of the wool. They are small in size, with flat sides, narrow chests, and long legs. The first impression made by their appearance is not often favourable; the wool lying closer and thicker over the body than in most other breeds of sheep, and being abundant in yolk, which is an oily, fatty, secretion mixed with the wool, is covered with a dirty crust, often full of cracks. The legs are long, yet small in bone; the breast and the back are narrow; the fore-shoulders and bosoms are heavy; and too much of their weight is carried on the coarser parts. The horns of the male are comparatively large, curved, and with more or less of a spiral form. The head is large, but the forehead rather low. A few of the females are horned, but as a rule are not. Both male and female have a peculiar coarse and unsightly growth of hair on the forehead and cheeks, which is cut away before the shearing time. The other part of the face has a pleasing and characteristic velvety appearance. Under the throat there is a singular looseness of skin, which gives a remarkable appearance of throatiness, or hollowness in the neck. The fleece when pressed upon is hard and unyielding. This arises from the thickness with which it grows upon the pelt, and the abundance of the yolk, which detains all the dirt and gravel which falls upon it. The wool, however, when examined, exceeds in fineness and in the number of curves and serrations which it presents, that of any other sheep in the world. The average weight of the fleece in Spain is 8 lbs. from the ram, and 5 lbs. from the ewe. The staple differs in length in different provinces. The wool is usually white, but darker on the legs, faces, and ears.

These migratory sheep are divided into two classes, the Leonese and the Sorians. The former are the more valuable. They pass the summer in the mountains of the north, and the winter in the plains of the south of Spain. They leave their winter quarters about the middle of April, and occupy about six weeks on their journey. During their journey they are shorn in large buildings built for the purpose. The sheep are packed close together the night before to cause them to sweat, which softens the yolk and renders the shearing operation easier. No less than 50,000 shepherds are employed in tending these sheep, which are divided into flocks of about 1,000 each. Formerly it was supposed that this change of pasture was absolutely necessary for the animal to retain its fineness of wool; but it is now found that this is not the case, as some of the German Merinos, which were

H

originally derived from Spain, and which are kept perfectly stationary, yield wool of equal quality.

For a long time the laws of Spain were very strict in regard to the exportation of these sheep, so as to prevent their introduction into foreign countries, and indeed, at one time, prohibitive,—the penalty being death in case of discovery. About 1723, however, they were introduced into Sweden, but have not flourished well in that country, probably on account of the coldness of the climate, which is not in favour of the growth of fine wool. Shortly afterwards they were introduced into France; but the breed was not kept pure, and deteriorated either through want of care or admixture with inferior races.

The Elector of Saxony introduced them into Germany in 1765, and in 1775 they were also taken into Austria, in both of which countries they have flourished in a remarkable manner, so much so that the German Merinos now more than rival the Spanish in the quality of the wool. The two classes of sheep which were introduced into Saxony and Austria are still perfectly distinct. *The Saxon breed* is called the Escurial. These sheep have longer legs than the Austrian, with a long spare neck and head with very little wool upon it, but the wool is shorter, finer, and softer in the fleece, which weighs from $1\frac{1}{2}$ to 2 lbs. on the ewes, and 2 to 3 lbs. on the wethers and rams.

The Austrian Merinos are called Infantado or Negretti, and have shorter legs than the Saxon, with a comparatively short head and neck and short turned-up nose. The wool grows upon the head as far as the eyes and down to the feet upon the legs. The wool is very thick in the fleece and often very matted and tangled, while the yolk upon the wool is so stiff as to render washing difficult. When cleaned, however, the wool is very fine and long. The weight of the fleece is from $2\frac{1}{4}$ to $3\frac{1}{4}$ lbs. in ewes, and 4 to 6 lbs. in wethers and rams. These sheep, especially the Saxon, are very tender and require very careful attention both in regard to the pasture upon which they feed and the nature of the pasture ground. They are always housed at night, even in the summer except during the very finest weather, and are never returned to the pasture till the dew is off the grass. During the winter they are entirely kept within doors and fed with hay, straw, and corn. Although various attempts have been made to cross the Saxon and Austrian Merinos no advantage has resulted from it, and the best results are in each case derived by keeping the breeds as pure as possible. Both these classes of sheep are stationary, and although originally derived from ancestors in the migratory Merinos of Spain have suffered no deterioration in consequence.

It seems, indeed, probable that the practice which is still maintained in Spain of moving the flocks is not a necessity of their existence in the best possible condition. The long, tiresome journeys, which occupy several months during the year, are always accompanied with many casualties and great mortality amongst the sheep, as well as causing great inconvenience in the country through which they pass, which necessitates much land remaining uncultivated and special legislation to regulate the migration.

The Merino Sheep was introduced into England by George III. in 1791—although a few sheep were obtained earlier—and the breed still remains, but has not been found so suitable in many respects as some of the native breeds, although crosses with it have much improved the quality of many of our native breeds. Although the quality of the wool on the English Merinos was quite equal to that obtained in their native country, it was found that they did not possess one of the necessary qualifications which in this country is essential, viz., the principle of early maturity and the general propensity to fatten. In all countries where the fleece is looked to as the great source of profit to the farmer, this is quite a secondary consideration, but in England the mutton is as valuable, or indeed more valuable than the wool, especially since the great reduction in the price of the latter; and hence many of our own breeds of sheep will always be cultivated in preference to the Merinos.

Notwithstanding this disadvantage so far as the meat bearing qualities of the Merino are concerned, it stands first in the quality of the wool, and no sheep has had a more important part to play in the history of the industries of the world. The fineness of the fibre, the lustre of the hair, the unrivalled felting properties, and the great strength of the fibre in proportion to its diameter, all combine to render the Merino a typical wool—and the fact that admixture with almost all other races of sheep introduces many of its characteristics into their wool as well as renders them capable of extension over a very wide geographical range has made the Merino sheep one of the most valuable of all domesticated animals, and one which has rendered the very greatest service to the cause of human civilization.

FRENCH SHEEP.

As we might naturally expect, a country so extensive and diversified as France contains a very large number of different breeds of sheep, and of late years especially considerable improvements have taken place in most of them arising from the introduction of foreign blood, which has been rendered easier by improvements in transit and the competition which the native wools have had to meet in the various markets. The original sheep were probably, as in England, of several varieties suited to the different physical conditions of the country. The mountain breed partook of the character of the usual mountain sheep which still linger in the districts of Navarre and Bearn, with long legs, thin body, and coarse fleece.

In Picardy the sheep closely resemble some of the English breeds, such as the Romney Marsh sheep, and indeed are a cross between them and the sheep of the neighbouring provinces of Flanders.

In Normandy there is a large breed of sheep which

weighs as much as 15 to 16 lbs. per quarter, and which produces a fine long wool, and is also esteemed for its mutton, which finds a ready sale in the Paris market.

Along the coast of Bretagne, Poitou, Guienne, and Gascony the breed of sheep is entirely different, being much less and short-woolled, but the wool is fine and valuable.

At the lower or Basses Pyrenees the sheep yield wool which is fine in quality and from 6 to 7 inches long, but in the central or High Pyrenees a different breed is found, which somewhat resembles the Norfolk sheep, with black faces and legs.

In the district of Rousillon the presence of the Merino Sheep may be distinctly traced, and many of the flocks are scarcely inferior to the Spanish Merino, from which, indeed, they were derived. The chief difference between them being that the wool does not grow so close in the fleece, but hangs in detached locks with a beautiful spiral waviness. The same class of sheep extend into Languedoc.

The whole district of Arles is famous for its sheep farming, and the sloping pastures in the district of Crau, from the mountains down to the sea coast, abound in large flocks which are hardy, healthy, and good wool bearers. Most of the sheep in this district are migratory, being driven in summer from the plains of Arles and the valley of the Rhone towards the Alps, which divide Provence and Dauphiné from Italy.

The fine-woolled sheep of the southern provinces

have had a considerable influence on the sheep of the inland districts northward, and most of the wool is in much repute. In Dauphiné it is finer than in most of the southern provinces. In Auvergne there is a mountain breed with black and white heads, but the wool is not much esteemed.

SWISS SHEEP.

The mountains and valleys of Switzerland have long been distinguished for some of the breeds of sheep, the origin of which has no doubt been a breed which probably originally came from Italy when the sheep was first introduced there from the East, or perhaps an older breed still, which may, like some of the Spanish sheep, have been indigenous to the soil, but now lost by crossing with more improved breeds. In many of the valleys the sheep are not unlike some of the English breeds, and have been imported, or sheep to improve them have been obtained, from Germany, Flanders, and Great Britain. As might be supposed from the general character of the country, a mountain breed flourishes best, and has been much improved since the introduction of the Merino sheep. In some parts of the country there are also flocks of pure Merino, whose wool is much sought after and wrought into the finer goods produced in the various cantons.

ITALY.

No country produces pastures which are better fitted for the feeding of sheep than Italy, and during the time of the Roman Empire the country possessed the finest breed of sheep which were then known, and they were watched and tended with a care which was unknown elsewhere, and the wool used for the manufacture of the very finest fabrics. With the extension of the Roman Empire, however, and the increase of Roman colonies, the growing of wool was more extensively practised abroad, and the wools of Spain and Gaul were very largely used, and to a great extent supplanted those of native growth; the Italian sheep being more cultivated like the present sheep in England for the sake of the carcase for food. During the middle ages the foreign commerce of the Republics was such that they bought their wool from all the countries on the shores of the Mediterranean Sea, and even from Britain, but with their decay the breeding of sheep was much neglected, and a deterioration in nearly every class of sheep in the country followed. Within comparatively recent years,—since the unity of Italy has been attained,—there has been a revival of both commerce and agriculture, and many flocks of sheep and rams for improving the breed of native sheep have been introduced from England and Spain. Piedmont, and the districts at the foot of the Italian Alps, have long been celebrated for a breed of sheep which are excelled only by the Merinos, from which they may have been originally derived, and various kinds of sheep both for long and short wool are found in the plains of northern Italy.

GERMANY.

As we have already mentioned, the Merino sheep has been introduced into this country and into Austria, and has flourished so well under the care and attention bestowed upon it, that the Saxon and Austrian Merino has produced even better and finer wool than can be obtained from Spain. There are several breeds of sheep found in the various provinces of Prussia, most of which, however, were of an inferior character, but since the introduction of the Merino, and most of all since the establishment of government schools of agriculture, a great improvement has been introduced into nearly all of them, and in addition to this, many of the long-woolled sheep, including the New Leicester from England, have been imported, which have materially tended to improve the native races. The same remarks apply to the Austrian as well as the German Empire, and in every part of these two large continental states there is an increasing number of sheep bred either from pure Merinos or crosses with the native races. In the Duchy of Holstein, in the North of Germany, a peculiar and valuable variety of sheep exists which is the descendant of a primitive breed. It is of a moderate size and yields fine wool, but not a large quantity. In this district also the introduction of foreign sheep has been attended with great success, and many large flocks are found both pure or mixed with the native breed.

HOLLAND AND BELGIUM.

As might be expected, the sheep of these two countries more or less resemble the sheep of our own Island, with which, especially the Romney Marsh sheep, they have been intermixed. Early in the last century a large sheep from Guinea was introduced, which has still left its traces, and, crossed with the English long-woolled breed, has produced a valuable sheep known as the Texel sheep. In Friesland there is a similar breed, but with more English blood, and resembles somewhat the Irish long-woolled sheep. In 1789 the Merino was introduced into these countries, but has never acquired the same hold as in Germany, although it has been used in several districts to improve the quality of the wool.

RUSSIA.

This vast empire has always been celebrated for its wools, and although many of them are coarse, yet from the extent of the country and the vast difference in climate which is found in a country stretching from the Arctic Circle to the Black Sea and the Danube, we may naturally expect to find a great variety of qualities. The fact that very large numbers of the people are more or less of wandering habits, and their principal wealth flocks and herds, contributes to make it one of the largest of wool growing countries. In the northern parts of the empire the sheep are small and short-tailed, and bear a coarse wool much mixed with hair and frequently of a very brown or mixed grey colour. On the banks of the Rivers Don and Dneiper and in the districts of the Ukraine, the sheep are larger and yield a better class of wool, some of it indeed of a fair quality when care is exercised in the management, and it can be used for the manufacture of cloth. The shores of the Baltic, and the islands in the Gulf of Finland, have long been celebrated for their wool, and in these districts the native sheep have been considerably improved by the admixture with superior foreign breeds.

The finest wool growing district, however, in Russia, is the Crimea and the neighbouring provinces, where the climate and pasturage is of a character which is eminently adapted to sheep farming, and the wool is usually shipped from Odessa. In the Crimea and neighbourhood there are three classes of sheep. The common breed has a long tail covered with fat, and is white, or black, or grey, with long coarse wool. These sheep are kept in very large flocks, and are removed from the mountains to the plains along the sea coast according to the season of the year. There is a breed of mountain sheep which occupies the higher lands, and which yields a thick and rather fine fleece, and in addition to these two classes there is a breed which is a cross between these sheep and the Merinos, and which are receiving increased attention, and upon the cultivation of which the increase in the export of better class and finer wool from Odessa depends.

DANUBIAN PRINCIPALITIES.

Along both shores of the Danube the sheep is extensively cultivated. The native sheep of this region—the Wallachian sheep—is a large, noble looking animal, with spiral horns of large size and long silky wool, but the fleece is much deteriorated by a long growth of coarse hair. Until comparatively recent times, and especially on the Turkish side of the river, the state both of agriculture and sheep farming was in a most primitive condition, but of late years the introduction of better class sheep for breeding purposes, and specially the Merino, has tended to improve the native breed in every way. Indeed, in many districts the native is now either entirely displaced by the Spanish sheep, or a cross between it and the native, with the most beneficial effect on the wool; and this sheep, from its size and other useful characteristics, has spread into the neighbouring states and through Hungary and Bohemia. The Moldavian sheep differs from the Wallachian chiefly in the length of the tail and the form of the horn, which is not so spiral, and also in the quality of the wool, which is not so fine. Like the Wallachian there is a great mixture of hair and wool. The hair being coarse and about 11 inches long, and the wool about 5 to 7 inches. A similar sheep also exists in Bulgaria and Servia, and a smaller mountain breed in the Balkan ranges.

TURKEY IN EUROPE.

On the Roumelian side of the Balkan Mountains, and in the central plains of Turkey in Europe, the sheep, as may have been expected from the general condition of the Turkish Empire, have been much neglected, and are in some places probably worse than they were centuries ago, but with the partial acquisition of independence, improvements will be introduced and sheep farming extended. The native sheep of the plains are of two kinds: one somewhat similar to the Roumanian, and another which is smaller and probably a cross between this and the Balkan sheep. In some of the islands of the Greek Archipelago, the Musmon is still found as in Crete and Cyprus, and in the latter also a peculiar breed which is distinguished by the possession of four horns, two of which stand erect forwards, and two curved downwards behind the ears.

MONTENEGRO, ALBANIA, AND GREECE.

In the mountains of Montenegro and Albania there is a breed of mountain sheep which seems to be allied to the sheep found in the mountains of Greece, but the native sheep have in many instances in both these countries been superseded by better classes which have either been imported or obtained by crossing the native breed with imported sheep.

ICELAND SHEEP.

In the island of Iceland a peculiar breed of sheep

exists—indeed there are two different breeds,—one evidently the result of importation, probably from Norway or Sweden, and larger in size than the native breed, with a finer and whiter wool,—and the other a small active sheep in colour varying from dun to black. One great peculiarity of this sheep is that it seldom has less than four and often as many as eight horns. When the horns are not more than five they are placed in one row, and all spring from the frontal bone as in the case of the native sheep of Cyprus, but when there are more than five they are placed in two rows, one behind the other. They almost look more like goats than sheep, as the outer covering is long coarse hair with a close fine layer of wool underneath, which neither wet nor cold can penetrate. The ewes also, in districts where cattle cannot be kept, yield a valuable supply of milk, varying from two to six quarts per day.

SWEDEN, NORWAY, AND DENMARK.

The native sheep of these countries are not a very valuable breed, but they are very hardy and easily withstand the severe winters, besides yielding a sweet and nourishing mutton. They are usually of medium size with slender bodies, which are not readily fattened, and long bare legs. They have a small head and short horns, and the fleece is only sparse and open and frequently mixed with much hair, especially in the hilly districts and upon poor pastures. In the islands on the coast of Norway, there is a breed of wild sheep which are sometimes caught and shorn by the natives, but the wool is wild and coarse.

Sweden was the first country to see the advantage of improving the native breed or else supplanting it with the Merinos, and as early as 1723 these Spanish sheep were introduced, and the result was a great improvement in the native breed and a great increase in the manufacture of woollen goods in consequence of the improvement in the wool. These sheep were also introduced into Norway at a later period, and in both countries great attention has been paid to their cultivation so that they now exist in great numbers.

The Danish sheep originally were not unlike those of Norway and Sweden, and have been much improved by the introduction of Merinos, so that now considerable quantities of fine wool is exported from Copenhagen to Great Britain and Germany.

II.—Asia.

We have already pointed out that there is strong reason to believe that many of the Asiatic varieties of the sheep have taken their origin from the Argali or wild sheep of the Asiatic Mountains, which extends its range from the Caucasian Mountains to the shores of Kamtchatka along the whole chain of mountains which run along central Asia. We have already given a description of this animal (page 66) and of its habits, and it is not necessary, therefore, to refer to it further.

The general character of the Asiatic domestic sheep is somewhat similar to those which are found in

Palestine and Syria. In those changeless countries they have probably altered little in character since the days of Abraham. A few of the fat-rumped, but more of the fat broad-tailed variety are seen. In the latter the carcase is more or less neglected, and the hairy-woolly fleece is coarse and comparatively valueless, while the fatty portion of the tail is increased to one-fourth and even sometimes one-third of the total weight of the sheep.

The fat-rumped sheep have an accumulation of fat commencing at the posterior part of the loins, swelling gradually into a considerable mass towards the rump, which presents two considerable enlargements of a more or less globular form. This sheep extends through the northern part of Asia and into Russian Europe, and is the prevailing sheep of which the flocks of the Kalmucks and Turcomans and almost all the wandering tribes are composed. It is influenced to a certain extent by the climate and pasturage, but no attempts have been made to improve the breed by admixture with other races, and the fact that it can travel long distances, endure great hardships, and yields a plentiful supply of milk and coarse wool for the coarse fabrics used by the wandering tribes, renders it one of the most useful of the domestic varieties. In some districts of Russia, however, with care and cultivation, this sheep has been caused to yield fine wool with only a small admixture of hair.

The broad or fat-tailed sheep is probably a variety of the last named, and is found in Palestine, Syria,

THE FAT-TAILED SHEEP.

and Persia. These creatures have a monstrous round of fat like a cushion in place of a tail which sometimes weighs 30 or 40 lbs. The wool of these sheep is coarse, much tangled, and felted and mixed with coarse dark coloured hair. Large quantities of the wool of this sheep are exported from Bagdad, and the breed is found in all parts of Asia as far as China. Plate XVI. gives a fair illustration of this remarkable sheep.

As the majority of the Persians lead a pastoral life, much attention is paid to the breeding of sheep, and the best are found in the district of Kerman. Here the wool is fine in quality and is manufactured into goods which rival the beautiful goods of Cashmere.

The sheep in this district bear a fine spirally curled wool of a grey, or mixed black and white colour. They are below the ordinary size and their fleeces supply most of the wool from which the fine felt carpets of Persia are made.

TIBET SHEEP.

The sheep in this region are very numerous and are chiefly a small variety of the fat-rumped Persian sheep, and this class extends through Afghanistan and into the north of China. In some of these sheep there is a small portion of wool growing at the roots of short hair, but in others the wool is both long and fine, and out of the long wool, after careful separation from the hair, some of the fine shawls of India are manufactured.

I

INDIA.

The same variety of sheep above-mentioned are found in northern India, and the class of wool is the same, but in some districts such as Nepaul, there exists a small class of sheep which are well cultivated and yield a very fine class of wool which is used in making a variety of fine fabrics. These sheep, however, cannot endure the great heat of the plains.

In the Deccan there is another variety of sheep which is extensively reared. It has short legs, short thickish body, and short horns, with short black wool. Attempts have been made to introduce English sheep into India, but in the tropical regions there is always difficulty in regard to pasturage, and I have not heard what success has attended the endeavour. It is impossible to leave India without mentioning the Cashmere goat, which is found in the district of that name. It is allied to the native Tibet goat, but rather smaller. It is a fine looking creature with very large horns, which curve backwards and often extend half the length of the animal. The hair is longer than that of the Angora goat which yields the mohair of commerce, and is destitute of the undulating curves which are the true distinction between hair and wool. This hair varies from 6 to 18 inches long. The finest only grows upon certain parts of the goat, and it is said that a single goat only yields about 3 to 4 ounces. The strictest watch is kept to prevent these cultivated goats from being exported, and it is from their hair that the fine Cashmere shawls are made, which are unrivalled for texture, colour, and design.

CHINESE SHEEP.

The vast empire of China possesses several distinct varieties of sheep. In the north and along the borders of Tartary the fat-rumped and fat-tailed breed is found. The same is also found in the south, where, in different situations it produces almost every variety of wool. In some districts in the south there is also found a small variety of sheep which almost resembles some of the English breeds, and from the wool of which the natives make a fine class of serges. The larger varieties yield wool from which strong felted carpets are made. There is also in China a long-legged sheep which seems to resemble the African Adimain sheep. The tail is long and the wool short and coarse. Some of the sheep in the northern districts have four and even six horns the same as the Iceland sheep.

III.—AFRICA.

The general character of the sheep in the northern districts of Africa, around the basin and in the valley of the Nile greatly resembles that of Palestine and Persia modified to a certain extent by the difference in climate.

EGYPT, THE SOUDAN, AND ABYSSINIA.

Along the borders of the Red Sea and the eastern coast of Africa the general condition of the sheep is not satisfactory, as it is much neglected. In Egypt the condition is rather better, although the rearing of sheep is not largely carried on. The fat-tailed sheep prevail in Egypt, but those with long tails nearly reaching the ground are more numerous than the broad-tailed. In Upper Egypt the sheep are more numerous and of a large size, with tails which weigh from 18 to 25 lbs. Also the fat-rumped sheep which are rather smaller than the Persian. Beyond the confines of Egypt and stretching onward to the mountains of Abyssinia, there are many tribes who possess large flocks of sheep, some of which are well looked after and produce good wool. The Abyssinian sheep are somewhat similar to the native Persian, with an external covering of hair, which has, however, frequently a fine lustre and softness. In the mountains, also, are found the many-horned sheep, similar to those which are found in the rocky portion of the deserts of northern Africa.

MOROCCO, ALGIERS, AND TUNIS.

The native sheep of this district are only of a very poor character. They are of the middle size, with an arched forehead, pendulous ears, and shaggy hair, with long uncovered legs. They are found in large numbers in the oases which abound round the wells in the desert which stretches from the coast of the Mediterranean Sea inward towards the south. Since the colonization of Algiers by the French, attempts have been made, with success, to introduce better breeds of sheep, and the Merinos and other cultivated races have been imported, so that in some districts really good wool is now grown. Whether any attempts have been made to improve the native breeds I cannot say, but immediately we pass from the places in contact with European civilization to those where native rule pertains, we find all traces of improvement lost. In Morocco and Fez there is a considerable manufacture of coarse woollen goods, and also of felted materials made from the finer parts of the fleece, of which we have the best example in the felted skull caps which are so universally used by the Turks and Egyptians. Some of the native sheep of Tunis have been imported into Spain and America, and, crossed with Merino sheep, have been made to produce a good class of wool.

WEST COAST OF AFRICA.

Along the west coast of Africa several distinct breeds of sheep are found. In Guinea and the slave coast there are two which are quite different. One is of small size, and somewhat resembles the European sheep, and the other, which is most numerous, is larger and of a different character. The male is horned and the female generally hornless. The colour is usually grey, with black distributed about the head and neck, and a mane of long, silky, white hair. There is also a sheep which has a large quantity of hair flowing down towards the brisket, and which gives it a singular and curious appearance, and, one traveller says, they have so little resemblance to those in Europe that unless they were heard to bleat it would be difficult to tell what kind of animals they are. In Angola a very singular sheep is found, called the Zunu, which is found in no other part of the world. Its legs are long and slender, but muscular and strong. There is a slight elevation of the withers, the chest is narrow and flat, and the false ribs project and give the animal a strong resemblance to the Zebu. The fat is singularly distributed over the body and about the neck, which has given it the name of the goitred sheep. The body is covered with soft, short, pale brown hair, mixed with a fine undergrowth of wool. Somewhat similar sheep, but differing in colour and general form, are found along the basin of the Congo.

CAPE COLONY AND NATAL.

The most important sheep rearing district in Africa, however, is the Cape Colony and Natal, with the adjacent districts. The native sheep is of the broad-tailed variety, with long legs and a small body, with the fat collected mostly on the rump and tail. They are of every variety of colour, and covered with a strong frizzled hair, with the undergrowth of wool mixed with it.

When the colony was in the possession of the Dutch, they introduced improved sheep from Holland and Spain, and sheep farming became a very large industry. When the colony passed into the hands of the English, this industry increased in importance, and now wool of the very best quality, and in very large quantities, is exported to Europe.

When the Merino was first introduced there was considerable prejudice against it, but its success in one district gradually led to its introduction, along with Southdowns and Leicesters, into all the others. Attempts have also been made to introduce the Angora goat into this colony, and I understand that this has now succeeded, and that large quantities of goat's hair, which is as fine in quality as the native Mohair from Asia Minor, are now imported from Cape Colony into the United Kingdom.

Some idea of the great importance of this industry in the colony may be gathered from the fact, that 196,000 bales of wool were exported from this district in 1883.

IV.—AUSTRALIA AND NEW ZEALAND.

Nowhere in the world has sheep farming been carried on with greater success or on a larger scale than in our Australasian Colonies, and nowhere has the effect of climate and breeding been more marked in the improvement of the wool.

The settlement in New South Wales, which was originally intended as a convict station, and which is now the flourishing colony with Sydney for its capital, was the first place where sheep were introduced into the island. There were no sheep native to the soil, and the first were introduced from India. Those introduced were of poor quality. They had large heads, Roman noses, and slouch ears. They were narrow in the chest and shoulders, with long legs, high curved backs, and a coarse hairy fleece, more resembling goats than sheep. Even these sheep, under the influence of the splendid climate and rich pastures, became essentially changed in character, and in the course of a few years lost all their hair and increased the growth of wool, which was likewise much improved in quality. Southdowns and Leicesters were then introduced, and the crosses with these produced a fleece equal in fineness and value to that of the pure breed of these sheep in England. The success of the Merino sheep in every part of the world, led to the introduction of these into Australia, and the third or fourth cross with the prevailing sheep of the colony, produced an animal with the fleece equal in quality to the pure Merino in Europe, and the wool of the pure breed seemed to improve as much in quality as the native wool had done. Henceforth, the production of wool became the great staple trade of the colony, and the millions of sheep which cover the pastures of New South Wales, Victoria, Queensland, New Zealand, and Tasmania, are second to none in the world; some even rivalling the finest Saxony. The history of one colony is the history of all, and the immense increase of manufactures in Europe has sustained an ever increasing demand for the splendid wools which are now exported.

The rapid decrease of time required for the voyage to and from Europe by the introduction of steam, and the opening up of an entirely new outlet for the carcase of the sheep in the tinned and frozen mutton now so largely used, have afforded a new stimulus to the increased cultivation of sheep, which is rapidly telling in every part of the world.

Last year the following were the exports from the various Australasian Colonies:—

SHIPMENTS TO EUROPE FROM AUSTRALIA DURING THE SEASON, 1884.

Victoria	325,000	Bales.
New South Wales	307,000	,,
Queensland	66,000	,,
South Australia	118,000	,,
Total	816,000	,,

Including the wool sent to North America, the total quantity sent from these colonies, was one million and twenty-six thousand bales.

V.—AMERICA.

We have already pointed out (page 67), that the Big Horn or Rocky Mountain sheep is a native of America. But few of these creatures have ever been tamed, and, as wool bearing animals, they have really no interest.

UNITED STATES.

During the time that these States were colonies of England, various classes of sheep were introduced, and in many of the States sheep farming is an important industry, although it has hitherto been more or less subordinate to the growth of cotton and corn. During recent years, however, great efforts have been made to improve the character of the sheep. This has been stimulated by the increase in manufactures which has arisen since the war between the North and South, and the imposition of protective tariffs on all imported manufactured goods. At the present time there are many large flocks of first-class sheep of various kinds found scattered over the country, and extending into some of the better parts of Canada.

No country in the world surpasses some parts of the States as a field for sheep farming. The country is undulating or hilly, with the finest herbage and abundance of water. Recent experiments which have been made in the South with a view to rotation farming in the cotton fields, and which have demonstrated that sheep and cattle can be fed on the green parts of the cotton plant and the cotton seed cake after the oil is expressed, open up a wide field for an extension of sheep rearing, and there can be no doubt but that in the future America will take an increasingly important place as a wool producing country in every quality which can possibly be required.

I saw the statement in a Boston paper *(Boston Journal of Commerce)*, that this year the production of American clothing wool would exceed that of every country in the world except Australia, and would probably amount to 350,000,000 lbs. Whereas, in

1876, only eight years ago, it was only 115,000,000 lbs., which shows the very rapid advance of wool farming in the States. In addition to the large increase in the yield of wool, the Angora goat has been introduced into suitable localities in Texas, Georgia, and elsewhere, and very large quantities of mohair are now produced, which will probably render the country in a few years quite independent of foreign supplies.

SOUTH AMERICA.

Many of the States of South America possess large flocks of sheep which serve for the purposes of native manufacture and for export. Most of the sheep are the offspring of those which were originally introduced from Europe when the Republics were Spanish colonies, and they therefore partake of the character of the European wools. The immense plains which abound on the Atlantic coast form one of the best rearing grounds for sheep in the world, and some of the finest wool is now exported from the district watered by the River Plate and other regions. Indeed, in 1883, no less than three hundred and forty-five thousand bales were exported from this district, and thirty-three thousand bales from the west coast of South America. This quantity included alpaca.

ALPACA.

Before concluding our notice of the wool-bearing animals in America, it is impossible not to notice one which has played such an important part in the manufacture of Bradford goods. I refer to the Alpaca goat.

This goat belongs to the order *Auchenia* (from the Greek word *Auchen*, the neck), a genus of ruminating quadrupeds, of which the Llama is the best known. It is exclusively South American, and is found in the lofty ranges of the Andes. They are allied in character to the camel, and may be regarded as the American representatives of that family. They possess a stomach somewhat similar to the camel, and resemble it in general form, except that they are smaller. They have a long neck, small head, prolonged and moveable upper lip, and small apertures of the nostrils. They differ from the camel in the dentation, and partly in the more cloven feet and moveable toes. The nails are stronger and curved, and each toe is supported behind by a pad or cushion of its own. Considerable doubt exists as to the number of species in this order. The Llama and Vicugna are certainly distinct, but it is doubtful whether the Alpaca is not a mere variety of the Llama.

The Alpaca is smaller than the Llama, and the legs and breast are destitute of callosities. In form it somewhat resembles the sheep, but it has a longer neck and more elegant head. The head is carried erect, and the eyes are very large and beautiful. The general form of this creature is illustrated in Plate XVII. It is remarkable for the length and fineness of the wool, which is of a silky texture, with a very bright and

Plate XVII.

THE ALPACA GOAT.

silvery—almost metallic lustre. As we shall afterwards see, when examined under the microscope, the alpaca fibre seems to occupy a position intermediate between wool and hair, indeed, having many of the essential features of the latter rather than the former, as the epidermal scales are closer in their attachment to the stem of the fibre. If the creature is shorn each year, the length of the fibre reaches eight inches, but if allowed to grow it will attain a length of from twenty to thirty inches. The wool is not so curly as the wool of the sheep, but fine and very strong in proportion to the diameter. The colour varies very much. Some of the goats are yellowish brown, and some grey, and even white, while many are found which are quite black. I need not mention, in Bradford, that the late Sir Titus Salt was the first to introduce this important fibre into use as a material for textile fabrics.

MOHAIR.

Simultaneously with the great increase in the demand for lustre goods which led to the rapid rise of the alpaca trade, there has been a very large use of another and allied fibre—mohair.

This fibre is the wool of the Angora goat, a creature whose native home is the mountainous districts in the interior of Asia Minor, and of which Plate XVIII. gives the general features. The centre of the district is the town of Angora, about 220 miles from Constantinople, and from which the goat derives its name. The climate and soil seems to be peculiarly favourable to the growth of long silky hair, as many of the cats, dogs, and even the rabbits and rats of this region are famous for it. The Angora goat is a fine, noble looking animal, with large horns which are curved back over the neck, and its fleece is composed of long, beautiful, silky hair, varying in length from 6 to 8 inches or more. This hair, however, is a true wool, since it possesses a curly structure, with a fine development of the epidermal scales and a bright metallic lustre. From the earliest times this district has been famous for the production of a superior fine yarn and fine wool goods. Endeavours have been made to acclimatise this goat elsewhere, but for a long time without success, as, when removed from its native mountains, the wool deteriorated and lost its distinctive features.

They have, however, been introduced into Cape Colony, where in its pure state, and mixed with the native African goat, it produces a fleece which even exceeds in quality the native mohair, and large quantities of this wool are now exported to England. As we have already noticed, they have also been introduced into the United States, and large flocks, which are continually increasing, are now to be found there in suitable positions.

Plate XVIII.

The Angora Goat.

LECTURE III.

IN our last two lectures we have looked at the general conditions which regulate the growth of wool and the varieties of sheep which produce it, both in regard to their specific differences and their distribution on the face of the earth. We have seen that the difference between wool and hair is rather one of *degree* than *kind*, and that all the wool-bearing animals have the tendency, when their cultivation is neglected, to produce hair rather than wool. This tendency also always manifests itself whenever the conditions of soil and climate are unfavourable to the fullest development of the animal.

There is indeed great difficulty in giving any real definition which will exactly cover the difference between wool and hair. They have almost identically the same chemical composition, and to the unpractised eye they are almost equally difficult to distinguish by their mechanical structure, because the fine hair in some animals is very like wool, and the coarse wool on others closely resembles hair. The softness and pliability which is so remarkable in some wools is absent in others, and some true hairs are quite as soft and silky. The very fineness of the fibre cannot in the same way be relied on, as we have true wools which range from the very finest fibres of the Saxon Merino up to the longest locks off the flanks of the Lincoln Ram, which are as coarse and thick in diameter as any of the hair-bearing goats. In the same way even the curl in the lock, which is perhaps the best general and rough distinction between wool and hair, is found to pertain in some true hairs if we are to take the method of attachment of the epidermal scales of the fibre as any fixed guide. Colour and degree of transparency also cannot be relied upon, as we have as great variety in hair as in wool, and even the lustre is apt to deceive, because we have an almost metallic lustre in both. The Mohair is a true wool, if we are to take the arrangement of the scales as a guide, and the Alpaca wool is much nearer allied to true hair, and indeed many of the fibres are such, and yet both are distinguished by their high lustre.

Some writers have endeavoured to distinguish between wool and hair by the periodical decidence or falling off of the latter, which appears to be much more regular and periodical than the former. We see this in the case of the horse and cow, and this periodical shedding is much more marked in the case of the animals in their wild state than when they are domesticated. When under domestication many of these changes are modified, and in the case of man at any rate there is no periodical falling off of the hair. When in a wild state, or in the more neglected breeds of sheep, there is no doubt a periodical moulting or separation of the old pelt or fleece from the growth of new wool beneath, and at the commencement of summer this would gradually be thrown off if the sheep was not shorn, but in the more cultivated breeds this tendency is much less marked, and in some cases so entirely disappears that the wool will continue to grow from season to season. The reason is probably this: when under natural conditions the sheep is much more exposed to the effects of the different seasons of the year, both in regard to the inclemency of the weather, and more than all the scarcity of food, and this produces a marked effect on the strength and thickness of the wool fibre. When the winter season is over, and abundance of food becomes again possible, the wool increases in strength and shedding occurs, the fibre separating at the weak places. Indeed, amongst some savage races, this knowledge that starvation produced a deterioration of the fibre was turned to account, before the introduction of shearing, as a means of obtaining the fleece from the sheep. The animals were confined without food for some days until a short growth of weak and debilitated hair had been produced, and thus the fleece could readily be torn from the surface of the skin.

This definition of wool and hair, however, cannot be accepted as really distinctive, as there are numerous exceptions amongst animals which bear both fibres. Although no definition of the difference between them is quite possible, those who are accustomed to work amongst wool have no difficulty practically in telling the difference.

The true distinction between wool and hair, indeed, seems to be principally in the way in which the scales on the surface of the fibre are attached to the body of the fibre, or rather to the cellular mass of the fibre which lies immediately beneath them, and we can best understand this by dealing with the first division of our subject, viz.:—

I.—*What is the typical structure of a wool fibre?*

To answer this question it is necessary to look at it in a twofold aspect.

    A. In regard to the mechanical arrangement of its ultimate parts.

    B. In regard to its chemical composition.

A. Wool and hair are simply modifications of the same epidermal excrescence, and we have already almost anticipated what can be said definitely in regard to the typical structure of the wool fibre in our remarks at the close of the first lecture. There we saw that the fibre of true wool is always covered with numerous lorications or scales, the upper extremity of which are pointed rather than rounded in form, and which may be seen distinctly in the fibre delineated in Plate X. The scales also have a much larger free margin than in the case of hair, being only attached for about one-third of their length, and in many cases the free ends are more or less turned outwards so that they present a much more serrated or denticulated edge. The interior portion of the fibre, however, differs in no respect from hair, and cannot be distinguished from it, as there are many wools which differ in regard to the central part in the form of the nucleated cells just in the same way that different hairs do. We shall afterwards see, when we come to another part of our subject, that there is a very wide difference in the structure of different wools in regard to the nature of the scales and their distribution on the surface of the fibre, and also in regard to their number and strength. We shall also find that the structure of the fibres taken from different parts of even the same animal exhibits different modifications both in regard to the thickness and length of the fibre as well as its surface covering. The wool fibre is a long cylindrical structure, which varies in length and diameter in different breeds of sheep. In some it is only an inch or thereabouts in length, and in others extends to a yard or more, while the variation in diameter is from $\frac{1}{3500}$ of an inch in the finest Saxony to $\frac{1}{50}$ of an inch in the coarsest part of some of the deep grown English and foreign wools. We shall look at this variation more particularly further on. In the first growths of the wool, as is the case before shearing, the fibre has a more or less tapered form, and terminates with a pointed or rounded end. After shearing, as in wether fleeces, however, the thickness is more or less uniform from end to end, but still irregular as the health of the animal and the conditions under which it is placed have a considerable effect in this direction.

In looking at one of the best types of wool fibre we are struck with the beauty of the whole arrangement, by means of which lightness and strength, as well as pliability and brilliancy of surface are secured. This beauty of structure is wonderfully revealed when we carefully examine the cross section of a hair as exhibited in Plate VI.

In the central portion of the structure we have a strong cellular axis, which is usually composed of rather larger cells that those which immediately surround it. All round this cellular axis the mass of elongated cells, which form the bulk of the fibre, are arranged in compact regularly distributed masses, usually appearing to increase rather in size and diminish somewhat in density till we reach the scaly part or outer margin of the fibre. The closer arrangement of the fibres surrounding the central cells, and which forms the cortical substance of the hair or wool, enables the fibre to stand the crushing action which is always present when a cylindrical structure of any appreciable diameter is subject to flexure, and the larger cells and less dense arrangement on the outer surface render those parts more elastic, and therefore better able to withstand the flexure which they must undergo when extended or

Plate XIX.

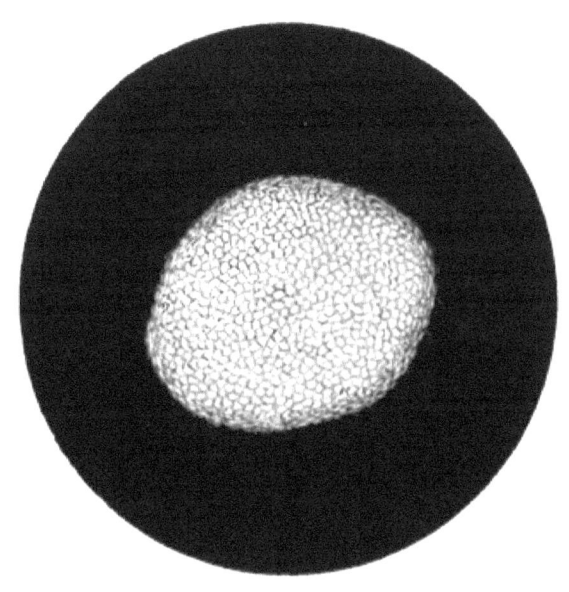

450 DIAMETERS

TRANSVERSE SECTION OF WOOL FIBRE.

(LINCOLN HOG)

compressed by the same action. The section of a wool fibre differs from that of a hair in having much less frequently a development of the central cells, so that in well grown and true bred white wool, the cells forming the cortical structure consist of cells with transparent laminated walls and hardly any trace of a nucleus,—indeed, even when acted upon by alkalis so as to disintegrate the cells from each other, they have the appearance of transparent jelly-like elliptical bodies, which vary in length from $\frac{1}{400}$ to $\frac{1}{700}$ of an inch, and in diameter from $\frac{1}{1500}$ to $\frac{1}{2000}$ of an inch. It is probable that when thus treated and separated from each other these cells are enlarged or swollen more than when arranged within the fibre. The appearance of a cross section of a wool fibre is something like what is represented in Plate XIX., where it will be seen that the cells are smaller and less marked than in the hair section. The arrangement of scales upon the surface, the free margins of which can slide over each other, secure the greatest amount of liberty to the surface of the fibre, without any rupture of the covering which would undoubtedly be caused by any more rigid arrangement of the epidermal part. The greater softness and pliability of the wool fibre, as compared with the hair where the free margins are less, is a striking proof of the value of this arrangement.

This peculiarity of the structure of the wool fibre has been known for a considerable length of time, although its importance and the exact nature of all the peculiarities which it exhibits have only been the subject of careful examination within comparatively recent years. As early as 1664 Dr. Hooke read a paper before the Royal Society upon the structure of various hairs, but the microscopic power at his command was only limited, and the observations consequently very incorrect. He considered the substance of hairs to be solid. About the year 1690 Leeuwenhœk turned his attention to hairs and wool; but although he figures in his works several specimens they are not correct, probably because of defective instruments for examination, as he was a most careful observer. About the year 1742 Henry Baker, F.R.S., read a paper on the subject before the Royal Society, but little advance was made until the invention of the compound microscope and its improvement at the beginning of this century. Mr. Youatt, whose work on sheep we have already mentioned, claims to have been the first person who really discovered the true nature of the surface of the wool fibre. We give it in his own words: "On the evening of the 7th February, 1835, Mr. Thomas Plint, woollen manufacturer, Leeds; Mr. Symonds, cloth agent, of London; Mr. T. Millington, surgeon, of London, an esteemed friend; Mr. Edward Braby, veterinary surgeon, at that time assisting the author in his practice; Mr. W. H. Coates, of Leeds, veterinary pupil; Mr. Powell, the maker of the microscope; and the author himself, were assembled in his parlour. The instrument was, in Mr. Powell's opinion, the best he had ever made. A fibre was taken from a Merino fleece of three years' growth. The animal was bred by and belonging to Lord Western. It was taken without selection, and placed on the frame to be examined as a transparent object. The power 300 diameters was used, and the lamp was of the common flat-wicked kind. The focus was readily found, as there was no trouble in the adjustment of the microscope, and, after Mr. Powell, Mr. Plint had the most perfect ocular demonstration of the irregularities in the surface of wool—the palpable proof of the cause of one of its most valuable properties—the disposition to felt. The fibre assumed a flattened, ribbon-like form. It was of a pearly grey colour, darker towards the centre, and with faint lines across it. · The edges were evidently hooked, or more properly serrated; they resembled the teeth of a fine saw." When examined as an opaque object with a view to determine the cause of this serration, "we were presented with a beautiful glittering column, with lines of division across it, in number and distance corresponding with the serrations that we had observed in the fibre that had been observed as a transparent object. These were not so marked as the inverted cones which the bat's wool presented, but they were distinct enough; and the apex of the superior one, yet comparatively diminished in bulk, was received into the excavated base of the one immediately beneath, while the edge of this base, formed into a cup-like shape, projected, and had a serrated or indented edge, bearing no indistinct resemblance to the ancient crown. All these projecting indented edges pointed in a direction from root to point."

The illustrations which are given in Mr. Youatt's work of the microscopical characters of various wools are most certainly the best which had been given up to that time, although in some respects they evidently exhibit a wider difference in allied wools than is found in the average fibres. Since then, however, much better illustrations have been given in various works on wool, such as Dr. Lankester's lectures at South Kensington Museum, various treatises on the microscope by Dr. Carpenter, Dr. Hogg, and others, and especially in the Micrographic Dictionary. Most of these illustrations, however, are only drawn with low powers, and mostly apply to "wool in general" rather than "wools in particular."

When we examine a fibre of fine lustre wool as an opaque object under the microscope, it forms a most beautiful picture. If the surface has been thoroughly cleaned, so as to remove all the natural grease from the surface, it appears, when the light is properly thrown upon it, like a laminated surface of silver. The scales have an almost transparent look, and a smooth, lustrous brightness, which well accounts for their excellent reflecting properties. Before preparation, and in the natural condition as the wool grows upon the back of the sheep, the scales, covered as they are by the natural oil, adhere more or less to the shaft of the fibre, and their transparency and thin edges, especially in the finer classes of wool, render them almost invisible except as fine anastomosing lines across the diameter of the fibre. When the wool is, however, treated to remove the grease by boiling in weak caustic alkali, the scales become more or less loosened from the surface, and we can then see their arrangement more distinctly, and the method in which their attachment differs from that of hair. When powerful microscopical power is used the surface of the scales is found to present a more or less reticulated or pitted appearance, which is much increased by the continued application of the hot alkali. This is the cause why too much washing injures the lustre of the wool. The action of the soap and hot water upon the surface of these fine scales destroys the continuity of the reflecting surface and causes it, like any rough surface, to disperse the light instead of reflecting it in solid sheets. The property of lustre in all wools is indeed one of degree, and is much more dependent upon the character of the surface of the individual scales upon which light falls than upon either their number or arrangement. As a rule, however, in the case of wool a fewer number of scales is accompanied by an increase in lustre because the reflecting surfaces become larger; but, in some cases, as we shall afterwards see, and especially in the coarser variety of wools, the larger surfaces of the scales are accompanied by an increased roughness in the texture of the scales, and thus the dispersion is increased in this way to a greater degree than is compensated for by the larger surface.

When the scales themselves are carefully studied under a variety of different illuminations, it is found that they present considerable differences in regard to their thickness and transparency. In the case of some wools, the scales have almost the density and texture of ivory, which, indeed, they closely resemble; while in others they have the appearance of opal glass, and we can easily detect the reflection of the light both from the upper and under surface. When the scales are very thin and transparent we have also frequently the production of iridescence or coloured fringes to the margins of the scales which give them almost the appearance of mother-of-pearl. These fringes are, however, too small to affect the general character of the light which is reflected from the surface. The transparency of the hair and its colour is largely dependent upon the mechanical arrangement of the cells within the cortical part, and when this is disturbed both are altered. It is well known that if a white transparent horse hair is stretched beyond a certain point it will obtain a permanent set, become suddenly opaque, and of a bluish green colour, and very brittle. This probably arises from the rupture of the surfaces of the cells from each other which breaks the optical continuity of the cortical substance. While the effect produced upon the light by the mechanical arrangement and structure of the surface of the wool is to a large extent the cause of the lustre, there is no doubt but that the chemical composition and nature of the individual scales, as well as of the immediate surface is also important, because a very small change occasioned by the action of various reagents upon them has a very great effect upon this property of reflecting light. Nor is the immediate surface of the wool all that is concerned in the production of a lustrous appearance, because in the case of many wools which have perfectly transparent and lustrous surfaces, this is modified by the structure of the cortical part of the wool, and more especially by the existence of pigment cells, which form more or less dispersive points and so tend to modify the general appearance of the reflection from the surface. In some cases these pigment cells only tend to increase the lustre, especially when the light is falling at certain angles, because they return the rays which would otherwise have passed through the more transparent fibre. The colour of these pigment cells also has something to do with the brilliancy, because some colours naturally reflect more light than others. This is not, however, of much importance to us as technologists, because there are very few coloured wools which are used in their natural condition, as they are seldom employed except into fabrics which have to be artificially dyed, and it is therefore of more importance to know how these naturally coloured fibres deport themselves in regard to dyeing materials than in regard to light before dyeing.

Just as there is a considerable difference in the number and size of the scales or flattened cells with which the surface of the wool fibre is covered in different breeds of sheep, there is also a difference in the mechanical structure of the cortical part of the fibre. In some wools these cells are considerably larger than in others, and the cells themselves when subjected to the action of reagents present different appearances so far as the relation between diameter and length are concerned, as well as the thickness of the cell walls. These walls themselves appear to consist of more or less concentric rings of transparent matter, which vary in thickness from $\frac{1}{5000}$ of an inch to a degree of tenuity which exceeds the power of measurement. As in the case of the cotton fibre, however, I have been quite unable by any microscopical power at my command to distinguish the texture of the ultimate layers of which these cells are composed, and which, so far as I can judge, seems to be a continuous membrane, which is, however, capable of permitting the passage of liquids through it and thus acts as a dialyser. Although the cells are closely packed together and do not seem to have any perfectly regular or systematic arrangement, they are attached at their outer surfaces in such a way as to withstand an immense strain, as we shall afterwards see when considering the power to resist tension in the different classes of wool. When subjected to tension, however, the surfaces seem to be able to slide over each other, the cell walls become more attenuated, and the nuclei more elongated, so that the whole cell is drawn out and the diameter of the fibre becomes less. If the tension is continued till fracture occurs, it seems generally to take place at the point of junction of the various cells and not by the rupture of the cells themselves. In all cases after the fracture of a fibre where I subjected it to the action of reagents which showed the individual cells, I could not detect in any case that the cells themselves were fractured. They seemed to have pulled out from amongst each other, and the spindle-shaped ends of the cells, where they had interlocked, were still visible, protruding from the fractured surface. When examined under the microscope the method of fracture of a wool fibre differs entirely from that of cotton. In the latter, the fibre being a hollow tube, collapses, and then usually fractures at one edge first, but the more solid and complicated wool fibre resists the strain more equally and fractures along the weakest part of the fibre at the junction of the scales, which appear as if torn out of the sockets. All fibres when closely examined are found to vary considerably in the diameter of the different parts, and, although the fibre usually breaks at the thinnest part, it is by no means universal, as some parts of the fibre which are large in diameter are sometimes apparently softer in texture, or at any rate less rigid to resist longitudinal strains.

In order to determine the strength of the fibres of various kinds of wool, I got a machine constructed on the principle of the steel yard, so that I could measure the limit of the elasticity of the fibres as well as the breaking weight. Fig. 2 gives a good illustration of this machine.

A is a base board of mahogany upon which is fixed a pillar, B. The top end is forked into a jaw, carrying on each side a screwed centrepiece, into

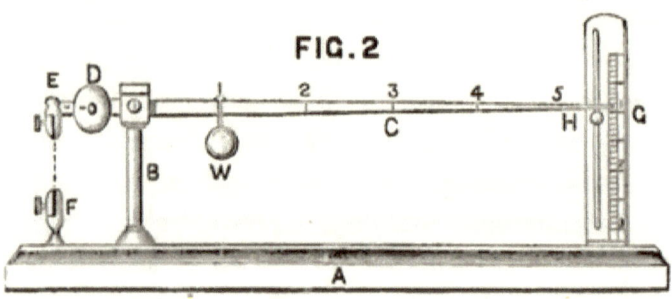

FIG. 2

which is fixed the fulcrum of the lever E, C, H. These two centrepieces can be screwed closer together, or further apart, as required, and the pivot which forms the fulcrum of the lever is pointed at each end, and fits into a hollow in the two ends of the centrepieces, so that it works perfectly free, and yet can have no lateral motion as would be the case if knife edges were used. The lever, C, is divided into five equal parts, each of which are equal to the distance of the centre of the jaw, E, from the centre of the fulcrum. D is a balance weight to counterpoise the longer arm of the lever, C. Each of the five divisions of the lever, C, are divided into ten parts. The range of the instrument depends upon the weight of the sliding weight, W, and this can be varied at pleasure. I used three different weights, viz., 50 grains, 100 grains,

MEASUREMENT OF STRENGTH. 143

and 1,000 grains, and the range of the instrument with these different weights was therefore as follows:—

Weight.	First Division.	Second Division.	Third Division.	Fourth Division.	Fifth Division.
Grs.	Grs.	Grs.	Grs.	Grs.	Grs.
50	50	100	150	200	250
100	100	200	300	400	500
1,000	1,000	2,000	3,000	4,000	5,000

By using the intermediate decimal divisions of spaces on the lever, we obtain, in the case of the 50 grains weight, an increase of 5 grains for each division; with the 100 grains weight, 10 grains for each division; and with the 1,000 grains weight, 100 grains for each division; and a little practice with the instrument enabled half of these divisions to be easily used, so that the range was from 50 grains up to 5,000 grains, with difference of not less than 2·5 grains when the 50 grain weight was used, 5 grains when the 100 grain weight was used, and 50 grains when the 1,000 grain weight was used.

At the end of the lever, C, a graduated scale, G, was placed, divided into spaces which enabled the elasticity of the fibre to be measured in terms of the distance of the two jaws, E and F, from each other. This distance was fixed at two inches. A separation of the jaws to the extent of one-tenth of an inch marked half an inch on the scale, and thus enabled very small ranges of elasticity to be readily seen. A small stop, which could be adjusted by a thumbscrew at the back of the plate, was inserted in a long slot in the divided plate, so as to prevent the fall of the lever when the point of fracture was reached. When the machine was used, the fibres to be tested were fastened into the two jaws, E and F, by relaxing the small setscrews at the side and opening the space between the two planes of which each jaw is composed. The length of the fibre between the two jaws was roughly adjusted until the pointer at the end of the lever arm pointed to 1 on the scale, G. A trial was then made of a number of the fibres under examination, so as to judge roughly of the elasticity and breaking weight. When this was ascertained a series of fibres were selected, and the adjustment between the jaws made as accurate as possible. The weight necessary to fracture the fibre, which had previously been roughly ascertained, was then accurately determined, as the rough adjustment had enabled the necessary weight and part of the lever on which it was necessary to place it to be ascertained, and thus much time was saved. When moving the weight along the arm in the final experiments, I used a fine silk thread to raise it with, attached to the ring which slid along the lever, and thus any pressure from the fingers either horizontal or vertical was avoided. In making the experiments, I found that very few fibres were equally sound throughout,—that is to say, that if, when the fibres were long enough, I took two inches at one end, then two inches or multiple of this number from the middle of the fibre, and then the same quantity from the other end, that there was considerable variation in the breaking weight as well as the elasticity in each of these separate two-inch lengths. Both these qualities depend on the weakest part of the fibre, and I found that some fibres fractured almost at once and exhibited little elasticity. In the tables which follow, however, I took the soundest and most uniform fibres which occurred in the lock, and when this was done there was found to be a considerable degree of uniformity both in the breaking strain and in the elasticity. I found also that both these qualities were considerably affected by the hygroscopic state of the fibre, and so as to ensure a uniform comparison I kept all the locks of wool to be experimented upon in a uniform temperature of 60° to 65° F., and all were taken from locks of wool out of the fleece unscoured, and therefore containing the natural fats within the fibre. In measuring the diameters of the fibre before and after breaking, I made a series of experiments on the diminution in diameter when the fibre was subjected to strain without breaking, so as to find out at what proportion of the breaking strain the fibre obtained a permanent set. Up to a certain point the fibre when released from strain regains its diameter by the shrinking in of the cells, but after a certain point it ceases to do this. Few fibres of any of the wools stretched equally along the whole extent of the fibre, but when subjected to strain disclosed thin and thick places, that is, lengths of greater and less elasticity, and the measurements of these were taken and averaged, after the fibre was broken, in the same way that I averaged the diameter when measuring previous to breaking, and before putting into the jaws of the machine.

The following tables give the result of these experiments :—

KIND OF WOOL.	Breaking strain in grains.	Elasticity in percentage of length.	Diameter of fibre before breaking in decimals of an inch.	Diameter of fibre after breaking in decimals of an inch.	Difference in decimals of an inch.
Human Hair.	1680	·374	·00342	·00283	·00059
	1750	·356	·00353	·00275	·00078
	1436	·389	·00301	·00241	·00060
	1620	·343	·00325	·00270	·00055
	1720	·371	·00342	·00283	·00059
Average.........	1641	·366	·00332	·00270	·00062
Lincoln Wool.	580	·240	·00185	·00161	·00024
	420	·288	·00173	·00152	·00021
	510	·313	·00196	·00167	·00029
	533	·310	·00188	·00166	·00022
	465	·270	·00165	·00150	·00015
Average.........	502	·284	·00181	·00159	·00022
Leicester Wool.	480	·240	·00175	·00131	·00044
	455	·275	·00143	·00122	·00021
	500	·300	·00182	·00158	·00024
	422	·280	·00163	·00141	·00022
	510	·270	·00158	·00138	·00020
Average.........	473	·273	·00164	·00138	·00026
Northumberland Wool.	420	·224	·00143	·00120	·00023
	330	·310	·00161	·00124	·00038
	540	·265	·00148	·00132	·00016
	418	·250	·00136	·00118	·00018
	440	·300	·00155	·00132	·00023
Average.........	429	·270	·00149	·00125	·00024

TABLES OF STRENGTH AND ELASTICITY. 147

KIND OF WOOL.	Breaking strain in grains.	Elasticity in percentage of length.	Diameter of fibre before breaking in decimals of inches.	Diameter of fibre after breaking in decimals of an inch.	Difference in decimals of an inch.
Southdown Wool.	82	·230	·00101	·00090	·00011
	75	·320	·00094	·00081	·00013
	93	·200	·00083	·00071	·00012
	102	·380	·00121	·00080	·00041
	80	·210	·00097	·00082	·00015
Average.........	86	·268	·00099	·00081	·00018
Australian Merino.	48	·387	·000540	·000354	·000186
	63	·421	·000583	·000332	·000251
	43	·334	·000471	·000320	·000151
	50	·283	·000521	·000391	·000130
	46	·251	·000472	·000361	·000111
Average.........	50	·335	·000517	·000351	·000166
Saxony Merino.	43	·321	·000317	·000210	·000107
	38	·284	·000321	·000220	·000101
	36	·253	·000340	·000230	·000110
	40	·241	·000381	·000246	·000135
	37	·263	·000331	·000213	·000118
Average.........	39	·272	·000338	·000224	·000114
Mohair.	600	·285	·00174	·00132	·00042
	540	·310	·00158	·00141	·00017
	580	·300	·00163	·00136	·00027
	620	·294	·00178	·00141	·00037
	590	·306	·00180	·00142	·00038
Average.........	586	·299	·00170	·00138	·00032
Alpaca.	150	·231	·000521	·000387	·000134
	162	·243	·000562	·000441	·000121
	144	·265	·000493	·000366	·000127
	153	·250	·000546	·000412	·000134
	138	·220	·000511	·000402	·000109
Average.........	149	·242	·000526	·000401	·000125

In looking at the figures given in this table, it will be seen that the strength of the fibres generally follows the diameter,—that is to say, that the fibres having the largest diameter, and, therefore, largest cross section, carry the greatest weight, and if these diameters are compared with those given in my work on the "Structure of the Cotton Fibre,"* and then with the breaking strain of the fibres of the various classes of cotton given in the same work,† it will be seen how much stronger the animal fibres are, in comparison to their diameters, than the vegetable fibres. For example, the fibres of Egyptian cotton average ·000655 of an inch in diameter, which is about $\frac{1}{1526}$ of an inch, and these carry a breaking weight of about 127·2 grains. This is just about double the diameter of the Saxony merino fibre, which has an average diameter of ·000338, or $\frac{1}{2958}$ of an inch. Indeed, one of the fibres given in the table, viz., the second of the fibres, is almost exactly half, being ·000321 of an inch, as against ·000327 of an inch in the cotton fibre, and this particular fibre had a breaking strain of 38 grains, as against 127·2 in the cotton fibre. Assuming the breaking strain of the two fibres to be directly as the areas of the two fibres, it should vary directly as the squares of the diameters, and hence the wool fibre, if as large in section as the cotton fibre, would carry 158 grains, since the area of the cross section of the cotton fibre is 4·16 times the area of the wool fibre. If the

---

* "Structure of the Cotton Fibre," p. 20. † p. 81.

areas of the two fibres were equal, the wool fibre would be fully 25 per cent. stronger. The cause of this is, probably, the fact that while in the case of the cotton fibre, which is a hollow tube, and when subjected to strain is apt to collapse, and then rupture at the edges of the ribbon which is formed by the collapsed tube, the interior of the wool fibre is much more filled up with regularly disposed cells, which tend to give the epidermal sheath of the wool fibre considerable support by preserving its circular form, and thus distributing the strain more regularly over the whole area. To set against this, however, there is the fact that the layers of which the cotton fibre is built up, while concentric, are continuous throughout the length of the fibre, while the cells composing the cortical and epidermal part of the wool fibre are not continuous, which introduces a great source of weakness, as we have already seen, as it is always at the junctions of cells in the transverse direction that fracture occurs. I have found such variation in the strength of fibres from different wools off the same class of sheep, that, like the variation in diameter, we can only consider these tables to give approximate results, but they will serve to give a general idea of the strengths and elasticities of the different varieties, and were the result of great labour and care.

I have already noticed that one of the great peculiarities which distinguishes wool from hair consists in the wavy or curled nature of the fibre, and I have in vain sought for any explanation of the cause of this peculiarity. It does not occur within the hair follicle, but soon makes itself manifest after the fibre has passed out of the surface of the skin. I can assign no mechanical cause for it, although it seems in some way to be occasioned by the unequal contraction of the cells on the two sides of the fibre, first in one direction and then in another. I cannot, however, detect any feature in the arrangement of the constituent cells which seems to me to account in any way for this peculiarity, and it appears to be, as in the case of the twist in the cotton fibre, inherent in the very nature of the wool.

In a paper which was read in 1867, before the Queckett Microscopical Club, by Mr. N. Burgess, the writer gives the following as the explanation. "I am of opinion with respect to the growth of wool, that as soon as the point of the fibre has protruded through the skin of the animal, a series of growths takes place, a small part of the epidermis is converted into wool, and then a rest ensues. One side grows faster than another, and hence probably the curly form of the fibre. When another growth takes place another ring is added, the new growth pushing up the hair from below and so adding to its length. This process is continually repeated, varying as to the length, straightness, and girth of the joints, and possibly with a variation in the thickness of the cylindrical portion of the fibre."* I do not, however,

---

* Jour. Queckett Micro. Club, vol i., p. 30.

think this is the true explanation, as the epidermis is not converted into wool, the fibre being formed within the hair follicle before its protrusion out of the skin, although the unequal contraction of the various constituent parts of the hair as the cells become more consolidated after leaving the skin, may account for the phenomena. We must remember that the cells which are to constitute the fibre are large and plastic within the lower part of the follicle, and become more consolidated as the fibre is pushed upwards. The cells which constitute the cortical part becoming elongated by the pressure to which they are subjected by the shrinking in of the outer cells. These outer cells shrink till they completely collapse, and thus form the epidermal plates, although they probably retain the laminated structure, and are capable of expanding again when subjected to variations in pressure, moisture, and temperature; and, as they shrink in, their gelatinous nature enables them to adhere together till they form a solid epidermal layer, which tightly binds the constituent cells of the cortical part. Unequal shrinking of this ring would give a tendency to curl. This curl in wool is not so important a feature as the twist in the cotton fibre, because there we have no other means of interlocking action upon which to rely in enabling the fibres to twist into each other, and thus afford the necessary friction to secure strength to resist the pulling out of the fibres when subjected to longitudinal tension; whereas, in the case of wool, we have the scales on the surface, which form interlocking surfaces quite independent of any twist in the fibres themselves. We may also notice that cultivation increases the curl of the wool fibre in just the same way as the twist in the cultivated cotton fibre, which shows very little of this peculiarity when in the wild state. And both wool and cotton, the one an animal and the other a vegetable product, both tend to revert to the non-twisted or straight condition when their culture and tending is neglected. There is no doubt, however, but that the curl in wool is a most valuable property, and from whatever cause it arises, it seems to increase or diminish just as the finer and more beautiful character of the wool does. The coarser wools exhibit the curl least and the finest the most.

Mr. Burgess, in the article quoted above, is of opinion that the sole cause of felting in wool arises from the curved nature of the hair, and has nothing whatever to do with the number of serrations on the surface. He says, "If a fibre be taken from the Merino, and another from the Lincoln sheep, and be laid side by side, the relative proportion of their curves will be as fifteen to one. If a number of these fibres were taken, each sort separate, it would be seen that the amount of the entanglement between the fibres would be fifteen times greater in the one case than the other. Suppose that instead of their natural form they are laid parallel to each other in a straight line by machinery, each fibre has a natural tendency to regain its original position. Suppose the now parallel fibres are twisted into a yarn, and then woven, and the warp is strained tight in the loom, many of the loose threads having been stuck down in the sizing process, it is evident that in this condition all the fibres are in a state of unnatural tension until they come out of the loom in the form of cloth. All external tension is now removed in order for the next or felting process; the loose fibres being released, the cloth being saturated with moisture, the whole has to undergo a process of heavy thumping, during which each fibre has a pressure applied first in one place and then in another. I believe that each fibre at every stroke is doing its utmost to regain its curved condition, and as it does so the cloth contracts and becomes thicker. This thickening is in proportion as the fibres of the wool have resumed their curved form from the temporary parallel condition. This, and this alone, is in my opinion the true cause of the felting process. . . . . It is well known to our cloth manufacturers that 'skin' wool, or wool cut after death, felts better than if cut from a living animal. Some may ask how is that to be accounted for? I answer that in death some parts of the animal are distended and others contracted, and this alteration being communicated to the fibrous covering, there would be more room for the contraction of the fibres in the process of manufacture than in those taken off while in the living state. Skin wool is sometimes taken off with lime, or sometimes by causing an incipient state of decomposition, when the wool separates from the skin, but other causes are at work which are not here discussed."

We think that this view is erroneous, because in that case very curly hair ought to felt quite as well as wool, but it will not, and also because the number of serrations are in some way related to the number of curves, and so the two causes probably go together. The very fact that skin wool felts better than natural wool is an argument in favour of the felting being largely dependent on the nature of the serrations, because, when skin wool is examined under the microscope, the action of the lime, or whatever reagent has been used in detaching it from the skin, causes the scales to be less firmly attached to the shaft of the fibre, and the free margins to stand out more prominently and thus increase the felting property. There are many wools which have a considerable number of serrations but do not felt well; but this arises, not from deficiency in curl, but from the fact that the scales have an attachment to the shaft of the fibre more allied to hair than that of wool, and this applies to the case of the Russian wool, which he mentions as follows: "If imbrications go for anything, Russian Douskoi should eclipse every other in felting, but here again facts are dead against that theory."

We have already noticed that in the case of all wools the direction of the free margins of the scales or lorications on the surface of the fibre is always towards the point of the fibre or in the direction of the growth, and pointed out that this is very important in the economy of the animal, because it always enables the hairs to slide over each other without felting, which they would certainly do if the free margins of the scales were opposed in direction in contiguous fibres. This freedom from felting when on the body of the animal is further increased by the fact that all fleeces and the surfaces of the individual hairs are always covered when in the natural state by a quantity of unctuous or fatty matter, which is secreted from the skin, and serves as a natural pomatum to lubricate the surface of the fibres, and thus enable them to slide over each other with greater freedom. This secretion, which is called yolk or suint, differs in quantity and quality in different breeds of sheep, and appears to have an important influence on the character of the wool, by promoting its softness and pliability, as well as preserving the surfaces of the wool fibres from injury, and thus enabling them to retain the felting property unimpaired until required for manufacturing purposes.

Under certain conditions the wool does felt on the back of the sheep, and forms what are known as *cots*, which are nothing more than a tangled mass of fibres, but are a source of annoyance to the manufacturer and loss to the farmer, as they deteriorate the value of the wool, and have to be removed in the process of sorting. The cause of this cotting is somewhat obscure, and varies much, both in different sheep and different seasons. I have frequently found that there is an absence of suint amongst the cotty mass as compared with the free fibres, but whether this is a cause or effect I cannot say, since either the tangling may arise from want of lubrication of the fibres, or the thickness of the felt may hinder the free discharge of suint from the skin. This tendency also varies much in individual sheep, and may arise from individual action, such as restlessness or rubbing when lying down, which causes the fibres to be thrown across each other in all directions, and thus they become entangled and matted. Of the chemical nature, and the purpose which this grease or yolk subserves in the nourishment of the wool, we shall have to speak more fully afterwards.

When intended for manufacturing purposes, the wool has to be freed from this yolk so as to prepare the fibres for a felting action, and by the processes of preparing the wool the fibres are transposed in position, so as to enable the opposing edges of the scales to come in contact with each other and interlock. This they do with great ease and tenacity, and this increases with the quality of the wool and the fineness and sharpness or pointedness of the scales.

When a piece of felted cloth is examined under the microscope, all the fibres are found to be lying in different directions, and the points of the scales driven into the openings beneath the scales of other fibres, and in many instances the fibres are twisted round each other in such a way as to render the attachments of the scales possible on all sides of the interlocking hairs. When subjected to beating and motion the interlockings are rendered more and more numerous, and the scales driven down into each other with such force that it is quite impossible to tear them asunder without the complete disintegration of the fibres themselves.

A single sight of such a piece of cloth enables us at once to understand the action of many of our machines and processes, such as "milling," where the texture of the cloth is rendered more dense and tenacious. It also enables us to understand why we can make strong threads of woollen and worsted yarn with a far less number of fibres in the cross section than would be required in the case of cotton. There is no doubt also that the felting action is further increased by the curl of the wool, which, when the pressure of weaving or spinning in the direction of the length of the fibre, and which had tended to straighten out the fibres is removed, causes them to shrink up again so as to regain a fuller curve, and thus brings the scales on the surface into closer contact. It is also a noticeable fact that if we wet a lock of wool the curl is considerably increased, but if the lock is subjected to tension while wet, and allowed to dry, the curl is completely removed, because the fibre cells take a permanent set under the strain. The same may be noticed in the human hair, especially when it is long. This arises from the fact that the cells in the interior of the hair are more or less pervious to water, which, when it enters, swells them out in the direction of the diameter and diminishes the length. Upon this principle the hair hygrometer is constructed. When the air is filled with moisture the hair shortens in length, and when dry expands, and thus moves an indicator over a graduated arc which roughly corresponds with the degree of moisture in the atmosphere. The cause of the increase in the curl arises from the fact that the cells are not all uniform either in their diameter or symmetrical in their arrangement, and there is, therefore, unequal expansion in various parts of the hair, and on different sides, which tend to distort the shape and twist the hair into curly or waved forms.

The action of water, especially hot water, in assisting the felting action is very curious, and is partly probably chemical, especially when acid is added, and there then seems to be no limit to the felting and shrinking action which accompanies it. The constituent cells of the fibre become softened by the action of the water and acid, and seem to be capable of uniting with each other when subjected to rubbing and pressure, until it is difficult, even under the microscope, to detect one fibre from the other, the whole seeming to form one solid mass, of which the parts unite closer and closer together the further the process is carried. It is not necessary for the fibres to be woven into cloth, or arranged in any regular manner so as to felt, indeed, the reverse is the case; for the less regularity there is in the arrangement of the fibres, the better and more perfect is the felting action. Hence the woollen thread, where the arrangement of the fibres is much more irregular than in the worsted thread, is best adapted for fabrics which are to be shrunk or felted afterwards.

It is quite impossible to pass from the mechanical structure of the wool fibre without noticing some of the variations which the fibre sometimes assumes from the normal type. While there is a general conformity to this type, there is almost a distinct individuality in every separate hair, and all more or less exhibit some peculiarity which serves to show how little there is in any organic structure which can be looked upon fixed and invariable. This tendency to variation does not astonish us when we remember that, as we have already noticed, such diverse appendages as the nails and hoofs as well as the horns of animals, and the scales of reptiles, or the feathers of birds, are all modifications of the same epidermal layers as the wool and hair. We may therefore look for considerable modifications in the structure of the individual fibres, and we are not disappointed. These variations may occur in all the separate parts of which the wool fibre is composed. Sometimes it occurs in the outer or epithelial layer of the fibre, and we have a great variation in the size and arrangement of the horny plates which cover it, two or three of the plates, or even more, being fixed as it were into one, until we have a considerable length of the fibre entirely destitute of the imbricated scales which are such a distinctive feature.

This part of the fibre then appears almost like an ivory ring on the otherwise scaly stem. In many cases this continuity of the outer plates or scales does not appear to be dependent upon the inner structure of the fibre, because that, when examined by transmitted light, remains the same, and the inner cells and even the distinctive medulla are quite visible. These form what are known as "flat kemps," and can be dyed when treated with care, because the central part of the hair is pervious to dyestuffs.

Sometimes, however, the change is more radical, and the whole substance of the fibre assumes a much more dense appearance, until even the cellular character of the cortical part is entirely obliterated, and the fibre assumes the appearance of an ivory rod without any internal structure being visible. This peculiarity is much less in the more cultivated than in the wilder and more neglected classes of wool, and is well known under the name of "kemps" or "kempy wool," and is a constant source of annoyance to the spinner and manufacturer, because such fibres not only have no felting or matting power, and thus weaken the tenacity of the yarn, but they always resist the action of the reagents which are used in dyeing, and are apt to remain uncoloured and thus spoil the surface of the fabric. So far as I can judge, they do not seem to differ in chemical composition from the other fibres; but they present such a different mechanical arrangement, and possess no absorbent power, and thus resist the entrance of the dyestuffs or only receive a topical tincture, which is almost always of a different shade from the other fibres which possess the usual structure and are dyed at the same time.

It is rather singular that these kemps are found in cultivated sheep, principally in certain localities of the body, and they are almost always the result of want of trueness in the breed of the sheep. In the finest wools they very frequently occur in the region of the neck, and are almost confined to a ruff round it just where the fibre of the body proper shades into the shorter and coarser hair of the head. They are also frequently found just where the fibre grows shorter on the legs. In the coarser kinds of wool they are found anywhere in the fleece, and are usually of rather larger diameter than the surrounding wool, and shorter in length. These kemps vary in length and coarseness according to the breed of sheep; as, for example, in the wild Highland sheep they are about 2 inches long and very thick, while in the cross-bred Australian sheep they are very short. In the finer wools I have often found them associated together in tufts, as if a small region of the skin was predisposed to their production, and in many cases this only occurs in small portions of the fleece, but in others it is widely distributed. Plate XX. gives a good representation of these kempy fibres in various degrees. The first two, A and B, are seen by reflected light. A is a fibre where the kempy structure is continuous throughout the entire fibre, which looks like a glass rod, but still has short and faint transverse lines which indicate the margins of the scales. When the change is a complete one, even the application of caustic alkalis fails to bring out the lamination of the scales with any degree of distinctness, and they seem to be completely attached to the body of the fibre up to the top of the scale. In some cases even the margins of the scales are quite obliterated, and the whole surface of the fibre has a silvery white appearance not unlike frosted silver. B represents a fibre where the change is only partial. The top portion of the fibre, as well as the bottom portions exhibiting the usual structure of wool, but the intermediate part having the scales closely attached to the surface, and the usual ivory-like appearance within the fibre. Whatever caused this change of character was evidently temporary, and the same follicle produced both wool and kemp. C is a kempy fibre seen with transmitted light, where we have the gradual passage of the kemp into wool clearly seen. In this case, with transmitted light, the kempy part retains almost the same transparency as the wool, but exhibits none of the interior arrangement of cells, and I may mention here that I have frequently noticed that fibres which have a tendency to kemp are also frequently distinguished by possessing an unusual distinctness in the medulliary cells. Indeed, it frequently happens that the kempy structure tails off in the same fibre, not as we should have supposed so much on the outer surface, but down the interior of the fibre, as though the change commenced in the central cells and was gradually extended to the outer

Plate XX.

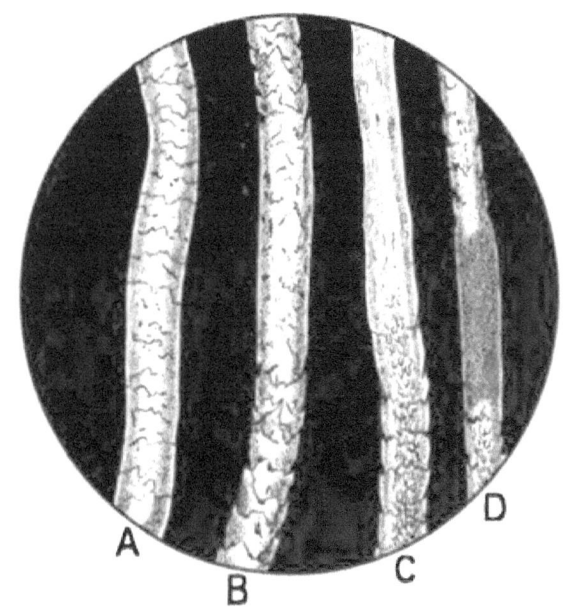

150 DIAMETERS.

KEMPY WOOL FIBRES.

A. Kempy Fibre, seen by reflected light.
B. Fibre, part Wool and part Kemp, seen by reflected light.
C. Fibre, part Wool and part Kemp, seen by transmitted light.
D. Fibre, part Wool and part Kemp, with Kempy part opaque when seen by transmitted light.

surface as the fibre grew. At the extremity, where the kempy structure first appears, the central cells are often not contiguous, as though the change commenced in a few cells first and then they became more numerous, both in a longitudinal as well as a diametrical direction. These kempy fibres often have a considerable degree of transparency when viewed with transmitted light, and in this respect they vary very much, but they are very seldom as transparent as the adjacent wool fibres. Sometimes, however, they are very opaque, as will be seen in the fibre marked D, where the light seems hardly to penetrate the centre of the fibre although it is refracted at the thinner edges, while the true wool, both above and below, is quite transparent to the same light. In this case, the same fibre, when viewed with reflected instead of transmitted light, exhibited no more signs of a dark colour in the kempy than the unkempy part, so that the want of transparency was not due to colouring matter.

Kempy fibres are not always white, as I have frequently found them in large quantities in coarse dark coloured foreign wools, and even in the coloured fibres of more cultivated sheep, both English and foreign.

Important as the mechanical structure and arrangement of the parts of the wool fibre are to us as technologists, they are not more important than the chemical structure and composition, because upon these latter considerations depend the deportment of the fibre in regard to its treatment in many parts of the process of manufacture, and more especially in regard to its relation to the dyeing of the yarn and goods.

Having therefore looked at the mechanical structure, we are now in a position to consider what is the typical structure of a wool fibre—

B. In regard to its chemical composition.

We have already seen in our first lecture that cotton and silk are probably definite chemical substances which have a definite and fixed composition, so that we can say that if perfectly pure they would always be composed of the same materials and in the same proportions. This, however, is seldom the case, as they are always more or less associated with other substances, in a state either of weak chemical combination or mechanically entangled.

Thus, cotton, if perfectly pure, would be identical with pure cellulose, which is composed of $C_6H_{10}O_5$; and silk would be represented by the formula $C_{24}H_{38}N_8O_8$. It will be seen from this that silk, besides containing an additional element, nitrogen, is far more complicated in its structure than cotton. This remark holds good of all animal fibres as compared with vegetable, and is specially the case in regard to wool, where we have two additional elements introduced beyond those contained in cotton, viz., nitrogen and sulphur.

We have already pointed out that considerable importance must be attached to the source from which fibres are derived, because this determines their relation chemically. All the fibres of vegetable origin are related to each other in having neutral carbo-hydrates as their basis, whether they be cotton, flax, hemp, or any of the bast fibres; while all the fibres which owe their origin to animals, such as hair, wool, or silk, have as their basis a series of substances which are called generally nitrogenous albumenoids, of which albumen, casein, gluten, fibrine, and gelatine may be taken as the leading examples. They are sometimes also called Protein compounds, because Mulder considered that all these bodies contain the same organic group—$C_{18}H_{27}N_4O_6$—to which he gave the name of Protein, combined with different quantities of sulphur and phosphorus. He also thought that the conversion of one of these bodies into the other depends upon the assumption or elimination of small quantities of one or both of these elements. Recent researches, however, have shown that this view is not correct, as few of the albumenoids contain phosphorus as an essential element, and the proportion of sulphur seems to be the same in all. Mulder thought that when treated with caustic alkali the sulphur and phosphorus could be extracted and the Protein remain, but the sulphur cannot be extracted entirely by the action of alkali, so that the Protein, if it exists at all, cannot be separated.

All the albumenoids exhibit the same or very nearly the same composition, and within the living animal albumen, casein, and fibrine, are constantly being changed from one into the other. When analysed by different chemists, they do not differ from each other more than analyses of the same substance would probably do in different hands, or if derived from a different source. We may look upon their ultimate composition as represented by the following analysis:—

COMPOSITION OF ALBUMENOID.

Carbon	53·5 per cent.
Hydrogen	7·1 ,,
Nitrogen	17·8 ,,
Oxygen	19·8 ,,
Sulphur	1·8 ,,
	100·0

The three albumenoids mentioned above differ most from each other in the method in which they pass from the liquid to the solid condition. Fibrine separates spontaneously in the solid form from the blood soon after its removal from the living body; while albumen, which is contained in the more liquid portion of the blood, does not become solid without the application of heat; and casein, which is contained in milk, cannot be separated as a solid by heat or spontaneously, but by the addition of an acid. These properties of the albumenoids are important to us, because, when we come to consider the case of the allied substance wool, we can readily see how it may be affected by slight changes in the temperature of the water used in washing it, which may alter the molecular condition of its constituent parts, and thus render it more or less fit, as the case be, for use in manufacturing processes. Albumen commences to coagulate or solidify at 140° F., and is completely solidified at 170° F.

All the albumenoids, as we should expect from their similarity of composition, have many properties in common. They all dissolve in caustic potash or soda, and also in very strong hydrochloric acid. When boiled with caustic alkalis, they yield solutions from which acids precipitate them in a more or less altered state, while sulphuretted hydrogen is given off. The solution in hydrochloric acid has a deep yellow colour, which, however, when brought into contact with oxygen, assumes a fine blue or violet colour. Mercuric nitrate imparts to the solutions of these bodies a very deep red colour, and this reaction serves as a very delicate test for their presence, and enables us to detect the solvent action of various reagents upon them.

All the albumenoids, as they exist in living plants and animals, are in combination with water of colloidation to a greater or less extent, and they can almost all exist in two states, soluble and insoluble in water, but when once dried they are insoluble both in alcohol and ether. When soluble in water the aqueous solutions are coagulated by alcohol and precipitated by salts of copper, lead, and mercury, and also by tannic acid, which has a strong affinity for them, and, indeed, this is the basis of the manufacture of leather.

All the albumenoids, when treated with oxidising agents, such as mixtures of peroxide of manganese, or bichromate of potash and sulphuric acid, yield the same products, viz., acids and aldehydes of the acetic and benzoic series. When subjected to dry distillation they are decomposed and a series of compound ammonias evolved. I may also state that all the albumenoids possess extremely low diffusive powers, and when examined with polarised light they turn the plane of polarisation to the left hand.

Gelatine is closely allied to the albumenoids, and seems to differ from them, indeed, only in not having any sulphur directly combined with it, and this body enters very largely into the composition of all the animal tissues and cells, since they all yield it when suitably treated. It swells up in water and dissolves on boiling to a viscid liquid, which becomes a jelly when cold, even if the solution only contains 1 per cent. of gelatine. Solutions of gelatine are precipitated by tannic acid, salts of mercury, and alcohol, but not by alum, or by neutral, or basic acetate of lead, ferrocyanide of potassium, or dilute mineral acids.

In the present state of our chemical knowledge we cannot determine what is the real difference between many of these allied bodies, and if we attempt to investigate them by separation and analysis, we probably destroy some of their characteristics as they exist in the organism, and can find no definite clue to the relations which they occupied to each other as integral parts of the membranes and cells.

Although the albumenoids are closely allied to wool and the epidermic structures generally, and

probably form the base of them, still they differ in
their ultimate composition in a slight degree from
these horny tissues, as they are sometimes called.
The epidermis of all animals, and the growths which
are connected with it, such as hair, wool, feathers,
nails, claws, horns, hoofs, and scales, are almost
identical in composition. They usually contain less
carbon and more nitrogen and sulphur than the
albumenoids, and also, as we shall afterwards see,
probably a larger quantity of water, but whether
this water is accidental and dependent upon their
mechanical structure, or associated with them in some
feeble form of combination as water of hydration,
it is at present impossible to say. The general
composition of these tissues will be seen from the
following analysis of hair, wool, horn, and allied
substances, which may be compared with the
composition of the albumenoids already given.

AVERAGE COMPOSITION OF HORNY TISSUE,
ACCORDING TO MULDER.

Carbon	50·54	per cent.
Hydrogen	6·91	,,
Nitrogen	16·83	,,
Oxygen	22·07	,,
Sulphur	3·65	,,
	100·00	

These substances have also been analysed by several
other chemists, and, although they differ from each
other in the exact amounts of the constituents, they
are sufficiently near to indicate that these bodies

have in all probability a fixed composition so far as the base is concerned, although they may be associated with varying quantities of other matter arising from local and other causes.

Wool has a very similar composition, as will be seen from two analyses by Scherer and Mulder.

Composition of Wool.

	Scherer.	Mulder.
Carbon	50·65	50·5
Hydrogen	7·03	6·8
Nitrogen	17·71	16·8
Oxygen	24·61	20·5
Sulphur	24·61	5·4
	100·00	100·0

Some years ago I made a series of analyses to determine, if possible, if there was any difference in the composition of various classes of English wool, and the following were the results :—

Composition of Wool Fibre.

	Lincoln Wool.	Irish Wool.	Northumberland Wool.	Southdown Wool.
Carbon	52·0	49·8	50·8	51·3
Hydrogen	6·9	7·2	7·2	6·9
Nitrogen	18·1	19·1	18·5	17·8
Oxygen	20·3	19·9	21·2	20·2
Sulphur	2·5	3·0	2·3	3·8
Loss	0·2	1·0	—	—
	100·0	100·0	100·0	100·0

These analyses were made after I had purified the staple, as far as it was possible, by maceration with water, alcohol, and ether, so as to remove all fatty matter, and the fibres were then dried at a steam heat so as to remove all traces of moisture. The loss in the first two analyses probably arose from the endeavour to estimate the earthy matter always associated with the fibre separately, and which consists of various salts, such as phosphates of lime and magnesia, sulphate and carbonate of lime, and peroxide of iron. In the last two analyses the amount of earthy or mineral ash is estimated along with the carbon. This mineral matter, according to M. Chevreul, amounts in different wools to from 1 to 2 per cent., and some other chemists have placed it higher, but there is reason to doubt whether some of the higher estimates have not arisen from the presence of mechanically attached impurities which the structure of the wool fibre greatly favours.

When dry sheep's wool is treated with hydrochloric acid, containing 0·13 per cent. of acid, anhydrous ether, cold water, and alcohol, in succession, and then again exhausted with alcohol and ether, the wool fibre is left free from all soluble constituents, and retains only such impurities as can be removed mechanically. When the wool is thus treated the ether takes up the fat, the water takes up the sweat which is associated with the fibre, and the other liquids take up the yolk or suint, which is a kind of natural soap secreted from the surface of the skin and always found attached to the surface of the wool. In some cases the amount of these foreign substances, after the wool has been thus treated, amounts to from 20 to 50 per cent. of the air dried wool.

From a summary of the analyses of wool which is given in Gmelin's "Handbook of Chemistry," Dr. E. J. Mills, F.R.S., has arrived at the conclusion that wool is a definite chemical compound, which is known as *Keratine*, and may be represented by the formula $C_{42}H_{157}N_5SO_{15}$, which indicates a very complicated molecule.* The great complexity of wool will be seen best if we contrast it with cotton and silk, thus :—

	Formula.
Cotton	$C_6H_{10}O_5$.
Silk	$C_{24}H_{38}N_8O_8$.
Wool	$C_{42}H_{157}N_5SO_{15}$.

Here, while we have in the cotton molecule only 21 elementary atoms, we have 78 in the silk, and no less than 234 in the wool. In our lectures on the cotton fibre we endeavoured to realise what might be the possible grouping of the atoms within the molecule, but when we come to such complicated structures as the fibre of wool we cannot possibly attempt to do so, and it will probably be long before the science of chemistry enables us to enter upon this field of investigation.

How complicated this structure really is, and what a number of different substances may be obtained by its decomposition, will appear from the following results obtained recently by Schützenberger by decomposing purified wool with an aqueous solution of barium hydrate at 170° :—

---

* Journal Chem. Soc., March, 1883, p. 142.

PRODUCTS OF DECOMPOSITION OF WOOL.

Nitrogen (evolved as ammonia)	5·25
Carbonic acid (separated as $BaCO_3$)	4·27
Oxalic acid (separated as BaC_2O_4)	5·72
Acetic acid (by distillation and titration)	3·20
Pyrroline and volatile products	1 to 1·50
Elementary composition of fixed residue, containing leucine ($C_6H_{13}NO_2$), tyrosine, and other volatile products... C	47·85
H	7·69
N	12·63
O	31·83
	100·00

When wool is destructively distilled at a high temperature, like most organic bodies it yields a considerable variety of different substances. Williams, by distilling flannel with strong boiling potash ley, obtained a distillate containing a large quantity of ammonia together with butylamine and amylamine.

Flannel distilled by itself yielded an insufferably stinking oil (probably due to sulphur compounds), accompanied by large quantities of pyrrol, streams of sulphuretted hydrogen gas, and a small quantity of carbonic di-sulphide, with mere traces of oily bases.*

I am not sure myself whether we are quite right in supposing that we can exactly represent the structure of the wool fibre chemically by referring that structure only to the organic part of the fibre, and neglecting as a factor either the water of hydration or the mineral constituents. When we have exhaustively analysed the fibre, and broken up the structure into its ultimate atoms, we must remember that in some way or other

---

* Ann. Chem. Pharm., cix., 127.

they were associated with these inorganic factors in the living wool, and that they were associated with it in some such way that we cannot possibly remove them without destroying the structure of the fibre itself.

With regard to the water of hydration, this is an important matter commercially as well as chemically, because no one can afford to pay for water in place of wool, and it is well known that water is not unfrequently added in order to increase the weight. As the wool is obtained from the farmer it differs very widely in different classes and seasons as might naturally be expected, both in regard to the quantity of moisture and grease associated with the fibre.

I made a series of experiments with well washed wool to endeavour to decide how much water was really associated with the fibre as water of hydration,—that is to say, water which really belongs to the fibre in its natural condition,—moisture which it will take up out of the air when it is left exposed at ordinary temperatures. I found that after drying a number of samples of wool on a Petrie's air-drying machine at about 100° F., and then exposing them to the air in an ordinary warehouse unheated in any way, but with a temperature of about 50° to 60° F., that the following was the result :—

Lincoln hogs	7	per cent. gain.
,, wethers	9	,, ,,
Leicester hogs	6	,, ,,
,, wethers	10	,, ,,
Irish hogs	7	,, ,,
Southdown	9	,, ,,
Skin wool	10	,, ,,

I find, however, from my note book, that these trials were not made at the same time but extended over several weeks, and as there was no doubt a difference in the quantity of moisture in the atmosphere on the different days, this would influence the quantity of moisture gained by the wool. We may, however, take the average gain, which is 8·28 per cent., as a fair representation.

From these same wools which had gained what they would under the ordinary atmospheric conditions, I took samples of each and subjected them to half-an-hour's heating in a laboratory oven where the temperature was maintained at the heat of boiling water, which we may take at 212° F. Continued heating, even at this temperature, colours the wool yellow, and, indeed, this change occurs at a considerably lower temperature if continued long. When the various wools were withdrawn and weighed the following was the observed loss:—

Lincoln hogs	13	per cent. loss.
,, wethers	13½	,, ,,
Leicester hogs	14	,, ,,
,, wethers	13	,, ,,
Irish hogs	14½	,, ,,
Southdown	14	,, ,,
Skin wool	16	,, ,,

This gives an average loss of about 14 per cent., which appears to indicate a further loss of 5·72 per cent. as compared with drying at 100° F.

When this wool was again exposed to the ordinary atmospheric conditions it regained a considerable portion of the loss which had been sustained, but not all. On the average it only regained about 9 to 10 per cent., showing that subjection to a temperature approaching boiling point, even for a comparatively short period of time, destroyed a portion of its hygroscopic qualities, or else drove off more than the water of hydration, and had already commenced to disintegrate certain of the organic compounds which either form part of, or are present within the fibre cells.

Little attention has hitherto been given in England to the quantity of water which is necessarily associated with wool, but on the Continent there are official and public testing establishments in many of the large manufacturing centres both in France and Germany, where reports can be obtained in regard to the condition both of wool, tops, and yarn. It has been found by a number of experiments conducted in these places that if wool is subjected to the highest temperature which it can sustain without scorching that it will regain from 18 to $18\frac{1}{2}$ per cent. of moisture, and we may, therefore, regard this as its normal condition under the usual atmospheric conditions.

Of course, this loss in washed wool would probably indicate a considerably larger one in the wool as it comes from the farmer's hands, but there is always difficulty in measuring it because of the large quantity of grease, earthy matter, and other substances which are associated with the wool mechanically.

M. Chevreul gives the following as the composition

of samples of raw Merino wool, which were analysed by him after drying at a temperature of 212°:—

COMPOSITION OF RAW MERINO WOOL. (CHEVREUL.)
Earthy matter deposited by washing the wool in water	26·06	per cent.
Suint, a peculiar saponified grease, soluble in cold water	32·74	,,
Neutral fats	8·57	,,
Earthy matter obtained after the fatty substances were eliminated.	1·40	,,
Textile fibre	31·23	,,
	100·00	

In this case the water had all previously been eliminated by the drying at 212° F., and yet less than one-third of the total weight remained as pure fibre.

Faist gives the analysis of several wools in a similar manner, but made before the fibre was dried, and he has tabulated them thus :—

ANALYSIS OF RAW WOOL. (FAIST.)

	Hohenheim Wool (raw).	Hohenheim (washed and dried).	Hungarian (washed and dried).
Mineral matter	6·3 ... 16·8	... 0·94	... 1·0
Suint and fatty matter	44·3 ... 44·7	... 21·00	... 27·0
Pure wool	38·0 ... 28·5	... 72·00	... 64·8
Moisture	11·4 ... 10·0	... 6·06	... 7·2
	100·0 ... 100·0	.. 100·00	... 100·0

In this analysis, in the case of dried wool, the results agree fairly well with the results of my own experiments on washed and dried wool, where the drying temperature was 100° F., which gave 8·28 per cent. as the loss.

We have already seen that there is always associated with wool a considerable quantity of fatty matter. Part of this fatty matter, is only mechanically adhering to the surface of the fibre, and is the result of a secretion from the skin of the sheep which is known as the yolk, and bears an important part in the growth and preservation of the fibre. The remainder is chemically united with the fibre, or exists as cell contents in the interior.

With regard to the yolk, Mr. Youatt, in his treatise on sheep, makes the following remarks : " The filament of the wool has scarcely pushed itself through the pore of the skin, than it has to penetrate through another and singular substance, which, from its adhesiveness and colour, is called the yolk. It is found in greatest quantity about the breast and shoulders, the very parts that produced the best, and healthiest, and most abundant wool; and in proportion as it extends in any considerable degree to other parts the wool is then improved. It differs in quantity in different breeds. It is very abundant in the Merinos, and is sufficiently plentiful in most of the southern breeds, either to assist in the production of the wool or to defend the sheep from the inclemency of the weather. In the northern districts, where the cold is more intense, and the yolk of the wool is deficient, a substitute for it is sought by smearing the sheep with a mixture of tar and oil or butter." This artificial protection to the wool greatly increases the fineness of the staple as well as its strength and lustre. "Where there is a deficiency of yolk, the fibre of the wool is dry and harsh and weak, and the whole fleece becomes thin and hairy; while, where the quantity of yolk is abundant, the wool is soft and oily, and plentiful and strong. Precisely such, in a less degree, is the effect of the salving, in supplying, and increasing, and strengthening the wool."

This yolk is termed chemically *suint*, and consists in large part of various soluble salts of potassium which is derived from the soil, and after circulating in the blood is united with various animal acids, and secreted from the skin with the sweat, with which it remains attached to the fibres, or forms a layer near their roots. Formerly this suint was looked upon as a kind of soap, because it was soluble in water, and along with it the wool contained about 8 per cent. of fat, but this fat is usually associated with earthy matter, such as lime, and consequently forms a soap which is very insoluble in water. The soluble suint, however, appears to be a definite compound, and is known as sudorate of potassium, arising from the combination of potash with a peculiar animal oil of which very little is known. The recovery of the potash from the washings of sheep or wool has become a large industry in districts where large quantities of sheep or wool are washed. When derived from the wool, the wool is placed in casks, pressed down as much as possible and cold water poured over it. No greasy particles escape with the brown solution, and all the sand and dirt is retained by the wool, which acts as a filter. The solution obtained is boiled down to dryness, and the sudorate of potassium, which has the appearance of baked molasses, is broken into lumps and calcined in retorts. The residue is lixiviated, and the liquors boiled up to 30° or even 50° B. The chloride and sulphate of potassium crystallise out on cooling, while the mother liquid, when boiled down to dryness, yields carbonate of potassium free from soda. The production is generally 140 to 180 lbs. of dry sudorate of potassium, or from 70 to 90 lbs. of pure carbonate, and 5 to 6 lbs. of sulphate and chloride of potassium from every 1,000 lbs. of raw wool.

This suint also contains a substance which appears to have the composition indicated by the formula $C_{26}H_{44}O$, and which has received the name of *Cholesterin*. It may be obtained by boiling the grease with alcoholic potash, and crystallising the unsaponified residue from alcohol. When the chloride obtained by the action of phosphorus pentachloride on cholesterin is digested with alcoholic ammonia, a peculiar substance cholesterylamine, having the composition $C_{26}H_{43}NH_2$, is obtained. This substance, as obtained together with cholesterin, by the saponification of wool grease, consists chiefly of an isomeride of cholesterin, which separates from alcohol in white flocks. The portion of wool grease which does not dissolve in alcohol consists of ethers of cholesterin and isocholesterin, while the portion soluble in alcohol contains free cholesterin, and probably also free isocholesterin, together with fatty ethers of both these alcohols.

When wool is thoroughly washed in water so as to remove all the soluble suint, and is then treated with alcohol, the latter solvent extracts a solid and a more liquid fat or oil. The quantity of these two substances amounts to from 16 to 20 per cent. of the total weight of the washed and dried wool, and varies with different kinds of wool. When wool is washed in water, dried, and afterwards treated with alkaline liquids, a considerable quantity of these fats are given up, but not in anything like the same quantities as when treated with alcohol. These two fats may be separated from each other by their different degrees of solubility in alcohol, and were examined by Chevreul and named by him respectively, Stearerin (wool-suet), and Elairerin (wool-oil).

Stearerin is a solid fat at ordinary temperatures, but melts at 140° F. It is quite neutral, and is apparently free from both nitrogen and sulphur. It does not form an emulsion when boiled with water, but by boiling with two parts of hydrate of potash and water an emulsion is formed without the saponification of the fat. It dissolves in 1,000 parts alcohol of sp. gr. 0·805 at 60° F.

Elairerin melts at 60° F., and, like stearerin, is neutral, and free from nitrogen and sulphur. When boiled with water it forms an emulsion, and is saponified by the addition of hydrate of potash. At the melting point it dissolves in 143 parts alcohol of sp. gr. 0·805. When the two fats are treated together with water and hydrate of potash for 125 hours, in contact with air, no solution is obtained, but the fats appear to be completely altered. On mixing the alkaline liquid with phosphoric acid, and separating the acid solution from the precipitated fat, the latter is found to consist of one or two neutral substances and two fatty acids of different melting points. The alkaline salts of these acids seem to resemble resin soaps. The acid solution yields by distillation a volatile acid which has the odour of valerianic acid, and probably possesses a somewhat similar composition $C_5H_{10}O_2$.

We have already seen that, along with the other constituents of wool, there is always a considerable variety of mineral matter, and which, although it does not probably amount to more than from 1 to 2 per cent. of the whole, is of considerable importance when viewed in relation to the reactions of colouring matter upon the fibre, because the combinations of these mineral constituents, to a certain extent, undoubtedly act the part of feeble mordants with many dyestuffs. I made a considerable number of analyses of the ash obtained by the incineration of various kinds of wool, both English and foreign, and checked my own results by an exhaustive analysis made for me by Mr. W. H. Wood, F.I.C., F.C.S., which may be taken as a typical example.

ANALYSIS OF ASH OF LINCOLN WOOL.

	Whole Ash.	Soluble Ash.	Insoluble Ash.
Potassium oxide K_2O	31·1	42·3	trace
Sodium oxide Na_2O	8·2	17·3	trace
Calcium oxide CaO	16·9	4·5	51·2
Alumina Al_2O_3 Ferric oxide Fe_2O_3	12·3	3.6	37·7
Silica SiO_2	5·8	4·1	11·1
Sulphur trioxide SO_3	20·5	24·8	trace
Carbon dioxide CO_2	4·2	3·4	—
Phosphorus pentoxide P_2O_5	trace	trace	trace
Chlorine	trace	trace	—
	100·0	100·0	100·0

The wool was scoured with hard white curd soap, and thoroughly washed with pure water and dried before burning. One per cent. of ash was obtained by the burning. On treating the ash with water 75 per cent. dissolved, leaving 25 per cent. insoluble. The quantity of any of the above constituents corresponding to 100 parts of the wool may be obtained by moving the decimal point two places to the left in the figures given under the column "Whole Ash." In some of my own analyses I found a much larger proportion of ash, in one case at least double, or 2 per cent., but as the excess was chiefly alumina, potash, and silica, I am not quite sure whether a more perfect washing would not have removed much of this excess in the form of sand and clay, which was probably firmly attached beneath overlapping edges of the epidermal scales. In one analysis I also found as much as 2 per cent. of the ash to consist of magnesium oxide, in which case the sheep may have pastured in a district rich in magnesian limestone.

It is impossible, of course, to conjecture in what exact forms of combination or relation these various mineral constituents are built up into the organic structure of the fibre, because the whole is broken up by the application of the red heat, but as they form in less or greater degree a necessary concomitant of all wool fibres, they must influence the relation of the fibre in a chemical sense to other substances.

When dealing with the mineral constituents of the cotton fibre, we pointed out how they probably formed one of the chief reasons why any reaction between unmordanted cotton and colouring matter was possible, since the pure fibre itself consists of cellulose, which is a perfectly neutral and impassive body. The presence, however, of such salts as the carbonate, chloride and sulphate of potassium, as well as the carbonates and phosphates of lime and magnesia, together with alumina and peroxide of iron, rendered reactions possible, as these being in chemical union with the fibre enabled them to play the part of mordants in certain cases, and thus enable the fibre to unite with colouring matter, or have the colouring matter produced within the fibre walls.

I made a considerable number of experiments with the purest cotton fibre which I could obtain after the removal of the cotton wax, but, in all cases, when brought into contact with reagents, I could never, by any process at my command, entirely free the cotton fibre from them, because, whenever liquid transfusion took place, a portion of the reagents always remained united with the fibre, and from many of the reactions I formed the opinion that this resulted from some attraction between the mineral constituents rather than the organic parts of the fibre.

In the same way, but to a much less extent than in the case of cotton, I am of opinion that these mineral constituents do play a part in chemical changes within the wool fibre, quite independent of the great affinity which some of the albumenoids which compose it themselves possess.

Even when wool is only heated to a moderate degree, say above 150° F., it gives off an odour of sulphur, and the same is perceptible when wool is boiled in water, which clearly indicates that considerable quantities are held in feeble affinity by the constituents of the fibre. Sheep's wool dried at 100° F. contains about 1·5 to 3·5 per cent. of sulphur, of which it gives up none on boiling with distilled water, but spring or river water takes up some of it, because they usually contain small quantities of alkaline salts in solution.

This sulphur cannot indeed be entirely removed even by dilute alkaline solutions, such as soda-ley, but requires prolonged boiling with strong alkalis which, however, destroy the texture of the wool. On this point Chevreul remarks that since the wool disengages sulphur and hydrosulphuric acid, without losing its characteristic properties, he is of opinion that sulphur, in its elementary condition, enters into the composition of a body distinct from the filamentous material proper. This sulphur is very difficult to remove entirely, and necessitates great care to prevent discoloration from the formation of dark coloured sulphides when the wool is allowed to come either in contact with metallic surfaces, or with salts of lead, copper, or iron. This can easily be demonstrated by treating wool washed with water with a solution of plumbite of soda, which can be obtained by dissolving oxide of lead in caustic soda, when the wool will become black owing to the formation of sulphide of lead by the reaction of the sulphur in the wool upon the oxide of lead. This is very important when the wool is to be dyed bright colours.

Chevreul, in the treatment of the wool used at the Manufacture de Gobelins, near Paris, removes the sulphur by soaking the fibre for 24 hours in milk of lime at the ordinary temperature of the air, and then washing the wool with dilute hydrochloric acid and afterwards with water. He found that even when this treatment was repeated 48 times, for 48 hours each time, the sulphur was not entirely removed, although it ceased to give any reaction with the plumbite of soda. He estimated that the remaining sulphur amounted to as much as 0·46 per cent.[*]

We have already seen that wool is almost identical

---

[*] "Dyeing and Calico Printing," W. Crookes, F.R.S., p. 85.

in composition with the other epidermic tissues, such as horns, hair, or feathers, and like these there is often associated with the wool fibre a colouring matter which exists as a cell content, and is more especially abundant in the nucleated cells which are often present in the central axis of the fibre. Of the character of this colouring matter comparatively little is known, and yet we know that in various kinds of wool, as in hair, we have every shade represented, from a light straw colour up through brown and red to black. Vauquelin found that fair hair contained salts of magnesia in place of oxide of iron, and manganese, which exist in dark hair, and in black hair he was able to distinguish as many as nine different substances, including a greenish black oil. In red hair he found a red oil present in place of the latter. Some physiologists are of opinion that it is not clearly determined how far the colour of the hair is dependent upon chemical composition, or upon the nature and quantity of the fluid which bathes it, or upon the ultimate molecular arrangement of the hair substance itself.*

When colourless hair or feathers are treated with dilute sulphuric acid by boiling they yield a colourless solution, but when they are black or brown they yield a black or brown solution, and leave a black or brown amorphous substance which approximates in composition to albumen. This substance appears to have a composition something like the following:—

* Kingzett Animal Chem., p. 340.

STRUCTURE OF THE WOOL FIBRE.

Composition of Colouring Matter.

Carbon	55·40 per cent.
Hydrogen	4·25 ,,
Nitrogen	8·50 ,,
Oxygen	31·85 ,,
	100·00

and may be represented by the formula $C_9H_8NO_4$. The substance is probably a derivative of albumen and possesses a composition of much greater complexity than this formula indicates.

When we come to consider the action of various reagents upon wool, we must assign the first place to the caustic alkalis, because of the very important part which they usually play in the washing of the wool preparatory to the manufacturing processes.

Like all the horny tissues and animal fibres, strong alkaline solutions easily dissolve wool, eliminating ammonia, especially with the aid of heat, and forming a yellow solution, which, when treated with acids, gives off sulphuretted hydrogen, and yields a white gelatinous precipitate. When fused with hydrate of potassium, wool gives off hydrogen and forms acetic, butyric, and valerianic acids, also leucine, tyrosine, &c. Even when the solutions are not strong, all these fibres suffer partial decomposition by the action of carbonated alkalis, especially when assisted by the action of an elevated temperature.

In using any alkalis or alkaline salts of any kind as a cleansing agent, it is, therefore, specially important that the greatest care should be taken in regard to both the strength of the solution and the temperature at which the solution is applied. The latter point, viz., the temperature of the solution, is a most important matter, and is one which must never be overlooked in our washing processes. We have already seen that the real base of the wool fibre is a body which very closely resembles, and is allied to, the albumenoids, and all these bodies are subject to very great changes in molecular condition when subjected even to moderate degrees of heat. The wool fibre, probably, in the natural state contains, as the largest element in its composition, a series of several albumenous bodies which form the walls of the constituent cells and the covering membranes of the epidermal scales, and it is difficult to understand how a very slight change in the temperature, even without the presence of any alkali, can be made without affecting these. I made a series of experiments with a bright haired wool with a view to determine how far the lustre and strength were affected by the application of different degrees of heat without the presence of any alkali whatever. So far as the brightness of the hair was concerned, it is somewhat difficult to estimate exactly the changes which occur, even over a considerable range of temperature, because, as the results have to be measured by the comparison with small quantities, there is a wide margin for error arising from the difficulty of presenting them under the same illumination, but if the range is a wide one, say 100° F., there is no difficulty in seeing how serious the question of temperature becomes.

Wool which looked quite bright when well washed with tepid water was decidedly duller when kept for some time in water at a temperature of 160° F., and the same wool when subjected to boiling water, 212° F., became quite dull and lustreless. When examined under the microscope the cause was quite apparent. The scales of the wool when only treated with tepid water had a smooth horny appearance, with an almost metallic lustre when seen by oblique light. When treated for some time at 160° F. the lustre was decidedly less, and the scales had more the appearance of a smooth paper which was unglazed. When treated with boiling water the lustre was still further diminished, and the appearance like that of dull white blotting paper, with a more or less fibrous structure apparent. If the boiling is continued long enough, when the water contains even very small quantities of an alkali, the whole of the surface of the wool, and indeed the substance of the wool itself is dissolved into a jelly-like mass. We can also easily see how important the question of the quality of the water becomes, because many spring waters contain considerable quantities of alkaline salts which react upon the free sulphur in the wool, and at elevated temperatures these chemical changes tend to set up a partial dissolution of the covering surfaces of the fibres.

When tested for strength, the same fibres which

carried on the average 500 grains before boiling, only carried 480 grains afterwards. The matter is still more serious when the liquid used contains caustic alkalis, because these have a direct action on the fibres even in the cold. Alkalinity is, indeed, in most cases unfavourable for the treatment of wool, and although absolutely necessary in some cases, as the dyeing of indigo, which can only be applied in the alkaline state, this should be reduced as far as ever possible so as to prevent injury to the fibre. Extract of indigo may, however, be used in dyeing from an acid solution.

Borax, soaps of good quality, and as neutral as possible, carbonate of ammonia and caustic ammonia, and stale urine, which contains carbonate of ammonia, are the substances which act upon the wool fibre the least, and can therefore be best used as detergents; but both soda and potash, especially the latter, can also be used without injury if the quantities and temperature are properly regulated.

Disulphide of carbon dissolves the suint and fat of wool very easily and completely, without injuring the fibre. The disulphide may then, when removed from the wool, be driven off at a steam heat, leaving the unchanged fats behind as a residue.

That these conditions are not attended to by the majority of our manufacturers, and indeed hardly ever receive a thought, is a matter of our common experience. A thermometer is seldom used, and most of the soaps are strongly alkaline, and literally as well as metaphorically *scour* the wool. If we use a soap for our own skin which contains a large quantity of free alkali we soon suffer from its effects and the tender epithelial scales of the wool fibre are quite as delicate as the surface of our own body, and no wonder that they are injured, especially when subjected to an elevated temperature. How few, however, of the manufactured soda soaps approach to a neutral character and do not contain a large amount of free alkali, and the same may said of the potash soaps, which for the treatment of wool are much better than soda, as is shown by the fact that the natural grease on the skin of the sheep, which feeds and sustains the wool, is largely composed of this substance. When cheap soaps are used we have all kinds of unknown elements introduced,—resin, silicate of soda, china clay, and other bodies,—and large quantities of free alkali to enable them to clear a large quantity of wool from grease without any thought of the deterioration of the fibre.

In the washing of wool the greatest attention ought also to be paid to the character of the water used, and the softer it is, that is to say the less mineral salts which are contained in the water, the better will it be for the character of the wool and the economy of the operation. As a rule the use of spring waters is risky, because they almost always contain more or less carbonate and sulphate of lime. The latter is the most objectionable, because it is very difficult to remove; whereas the former can be removed, partially at any rate, by prolonged exposure to the air or to a boiling temperature. If, however, the water contains very large quantities of soluble salts, it ought not to be used unless it is previously softened by some process, such as the Hyde-Clarke or other methods. If a hard water is used the salts immediately decompose the soap, the sulphuric and carbonic acids contained in them uniting with the alkali, while the fats and oils unite with the lime to form an insoluble lime soap, which is deposited on the surface and within the meshes of the fibre, and fixes all the grease and other impurities which the washing was intended to remove. Nor is this all, for the insoluble lime soap which is fixed into the fibre attacks all the dyestuffs which may be afterwards used in dyeing the yarn, and renders it quite impossible to obtain either fast or even colours, while it is almost impossible to remove it by any number of subsequent washings when once deposited on the fibre. In the washing of wool we ought also to remember that the fats associated with the wool are of two kinds. Those which are only mechanically adherent, and those which are chemically constituent, and probably form an integral part of the fibre cells. We can remove the former without any deterioration in the quality of the fibre; but it is very doubtful whether if we trench upon the latter we do not injure both the strength, brilliancy, and elasticity of the fibre.

On the continent the washing of the wool is usually more attended to with a view to leaving the constituent fats within the fibre undisturbed, and this enables a softer and more pliable fibre to be obtained, as well as a far better condition of both the surface and interior for the reception of colouring matter.

In my lectures upon the cotton fibre, I pointed out that strong alkaline solutions above 50° Tw. had been discovered by Mercer not to injure but strengthen the fibre; but if the solution is weak the fibre is tendered, especially if the alkaline solution is at a boiling temperature. Unlike cotton, strong or weak alkaline solutions deteriorate wool, because even when sufficiently weak not to decompose the organic structure of the cells of which the fibre is composed, they act on the fatty contents of these cells, and by the removal render the cell walls more brittle and less elastic, as well as more unable to withstand flexure by the removal of that which assisted the sliding of the cellular surfaces over each other. When I treated a sample of wool with an alkaline solution of caustic soda which contained 5 per cent. of soda, I found that the same fibres which on an average carried 500 grains before treatment only carried 440 grains afterwards, which gives a diminution of 12 per cent., and shows how serious the deterioration is.

This ought always to be remembered whenever we are treating wool for the removal of the grease which is mechanically associated with it, since, if there is an excess of free alkali, this excess, whenever the adhering grease has been removed, immediately attacks the surface of the wool, and penetrating within the fibre removes the constituent fats which are a necessary part of the cell contents, and thus deteriorates its strength and lustre, and no after process of oiling can so well and intimately reassociate grease with the fibre. Even when it is necessary that the constituent fat should be removed in order to facilitate the action of certain colouring matters upon it, it requires to be done by the use of weak reagents, and I have frequently thought that many of these cleansing processes could be much better performed within vacuous vessels, so as to assist the passage of weak reagents into the interior of the fibres, which usually contain considerable quantities of air, and thus resist the passage of fluids into the interior at the ordinary pressure.

Under certain conditions the action of alkalis upon wool fibre produce a characteristic acid known as Languinic acid, the composition of which may be represented by the formula $C_{38}H_{60}N_{10}O_{20}$. This acid is best produced by treating the wool with alcohol, ether, and boiling acetic acid, which removes all sulphur and impurities. The purified wool is then boiled with concentrated baryta water, the excess of baryta being removed by carbonic acid, the filtrate precipitated by lead nitrate, and the copious precipitate washed and decomposed by hydrogen sulphide. The solution on evaporation leaves Languinic acid, as a yellow, translucent, and uncrystallisable mass. This acid gives salts, with both baryta and lead.

The reaction of alkalies upon wool fibre give a

ready means of distinguishing it when mixed with vegetable fibres, as the wool completely dissolves when boiled for some time in potash or soda ley of a specific gravity 1·04 to 1·05, while the vegetable fibres remain entirely unattacked. Silk, however, dissolves in this solution the same as the wool.

The action of acids upon wool is very similar to their action upon all the horny structures, but very different to their action upon cotton. We saw that strong acids and alkalis acted upon cotton in such a manner as to strengthen it, while weak acids, especially with the aid of heat, rapidly destroyed the fibre; but destroyed it in a peculiar way, by a process of disintegration, which, while it permitted the component cells to be separated from each other, really left their mechanical structure unchanged, and that upon this peculiarity one of the most successful methods of separating wool from mixed fabrics is based. The treatment of the wool along with acid for the removal of the burrs or vegetable fibres associated with it, and which are very great sources of annoyance in the process of manufacture, does not injure the structure of the wool fibres although it entirely destroys the others; and, indeed, some experimenters are of opinion that the action of the acid rather tends to strengthen the wool than otherwise. Herr Weisner, of Vienna, found that when horsehair and mohair were treated with acid which did not exceed 4 per cent. in quantity, or the heat above 150° F., fibres which before treating with the acid broke with a strain of 480 grains, afterwards carried as much as 568 grains. When, however, the strength of the acid solution was raised to above 7 per cent. the fibres were weakened. I made a series of experiments with a view to test these results with the longer English wools, but was not able to detect any strengthening influence, as when treated with acid (sulphuric) up to even 10 per cent. the average strength of the fibres remained unchanged; but I found that the temperature was a very important point as with solutions not exceeding $2\frac{1}{2}$ per cent. of acid and a prolonged temperature of under even 150° F. the fibre was weakened.

In the case of wool the action is the reverse of with cotton, for the action of weak acids upon the wool is very little indeed, while even weak alkalis, with the aid of heat, destroy it more or less, and strong alkalis completely. The action of alkalis upon wool seems indeed to be like the action of acids upon cotton; they destroy the bonds between the individual cells while the cell structure remains unchanged, and hence strong solutions of caustic soda or potash are the best reagents for bringing out the cellular structure of all the epidermal substances. When wool is heated along with strong sulphuric acid, the fibres swell out and partially dissolve, and the solution when diluted with water becomes turbid when neutralised with an alkali or mixed with the ferrocyanide of potassium. When wool is boiled for a length of time with weak sulphuric acid the solution yields tyrosine, leucine, ammonia, and other compounds.

When wool or any of the horny tissues are heated along with nitric acid, the fibre swells up and becomes yellow in colour, and ultimately dissolves in it. When ammonia is added so as to neutralise the acid, the yellow solution acquires a darker colour, and at last becomes an orange tint. Van Laer is of opinion that in the first instance xanthoproteic acid is formed, then saccharic acid, and finally oxalic acid. The fact that nitric acid, even when dilute, colours wool yellow, is taken advantage of in the printing of patterns upon woollen fabrics, especially those which have previously been dyed blue with indigo, because in destroying the indigo the nitric acid gives a deeper yellow stain which is quite permanent. The action of nitric acid upon wool and silk is not thoroughly understood, but many chemists are of opinion that the surface is partially converted into picric acid. Acetic acid produces little action upon wool beyond destroying the lustre of the fibre, but it causes it to swell up, and when aided by heat and long continued application will disintegrate it.

Strong hydrochloric acid produces along with wool the same blue or violet colour which is characteristic of all the albuminous substances when treated with the same acid, and when the action is intensified by heat the wool gradually dissolves. When the acid is very strong its continued application, even when cold, will dissolve the fibre. Dry hydrochloric acid gas carbonizes the fibre and completely disintegrates it when the action is continued long.

Closely allied to the action of strong acids upon wool is the effect produced by chlorine gas. All the horny tissues when subjected to chlorine, in an aqueous solution, appear to undergo no change in external appearance, but they become more harsh to the touch, and dissolve completely in ammonia with the evolution of considerable quantities of nitrogen.

When in a concentrated state, chlorine has such a powerful effect upon all fibrous matters that it completely destroys them; but when used in a diluted form it only acts upon them in such a way as to increase their susceptibility to receive colouring matter. In the case of chlorine acting upon cotton, we saw that its action was in all probability increased by the tendency which the cotton fibres possessed to absorb large quantities of gas within the substance of the fibre, in the same way as spongy platinum or bone charcoal. Wool possesses this property of condensation in a marked degree, as we have no doubt all had experience in the length of time which woollen clothes will retain the scent of various aromatic substances, such as tobacco smoke. It will even attach itself to the hair of the head and beard, as in the case where a non-smoker has been with others who have been smoking in the same room or railway carriage.

The discovery that chlorine increased the power of wool to absorb colouring matter by printing was discovered by Mercer, who was also the discoverer of the singular action in the same direction of strong alkalis upon cotton known as the Mercerising process. This action of chlorine upon wool has been very largely used in the printing of mousseline-de-laine, which is prepared for the process by passing the goods through a dilute solution of bleaching powder (chloride of lime), and then through an acid which liberates the chlorine within the meshes of the goods, and but for this discovery the printing of these goods by machinery would have been impossible.

About twenty years ago Lightfoot took out a patent for preparing wool and other animal fibres to be dyed aniline black by treating them with chlorine. For this purpose, woollen or mixed goods require stronger chlorining than for ordinary colours, and it is recommended to test the completion of the process by ascertaining that the wool does not destroy the colour of a solution of permanganate of potash.*

In consequence of the action of chlorine and hypochlorous acid, which attack wool even at ordinary temperatures and turn it yellow, it is quite impossible to use chlorine for the purpose of bleaching wool, but notwithstanding this it is much easier to bleach than either cotton or linen. It is, however, quite impossible to employ either the same materials or the same elevated temperature which is used in the two latter cases, and hence whenever a dead white is not required the process of bleaching wool is only a prolonged and gentle treatment with soap and alkaline carbonates.

---

* "Dyeing and Calico Printing," by C. O'Neill, F.C.S., vol. ii., p. 45.

When, however, a brilliant white is required, such as is rendered necessary when the wool or goods are to be dyed or printed brilliant colours, advantage is taken of the action of sulphurous acid upon the fibre, which removes all colouring matter. This may be effected by hanging the moist yarn or pieces in a close chamber filled with sulphurous acid gas, either produced within the chamber by the burning of sulphur, or admitted from some outside source, or else by passing the goods over a series of rollers working within enclosed chambers filled with the gas. The goods always require washing after sulphuring, because during the process a small quantity of sulphuric acid is formed within the fabric which, if not removed, will ultimately act upon the fibres and thus tender them in course of time. No doubt the same cause which enables wool to concentrate large quantities of chlorine or ammonia within the fibre increases the intensity of the action of the sulphurous acid. Excellent results in the bleaching of wool and cloth may also be obtained by employing a solution of sulphite of soda, acidified with hydrochloric acid as the bleaching liquid, and when the necessary whiteness is obtained, washing well with water to remove any sulphuric acid which may be remaining within the fibre.

In the lectures upon the cotton fibre we saw that the inert nature of the cellulose was not favourable to the action of reagents upon it, and that with the exception of certain vegetable substances, such as

tannin, it was probable that no real union in a chemical sense took place when the cotton was immersed in solutions of various salts; and further, that it was not improbable that when any real reaction occurred it might be traced to the presence of certain unchanged cell contents of a more or less astringent nature, or the presence of some of the mineral constituents of the fibre. With the wool fibre the case is altogether different, and its action upon certain salts is remarkable. M. Chevreul made a number of experiments to determine the action of wool, silk, and cotton upon solutions of salts of various kinds, so as to determine to what extent these salts were decomposed. On this point and the related matter, I cannot do better than read the digest of these experiments, which is contained in O'Neill's work on "Dyeing and Calico Printing." He says:—
"The method consisted in taking a saline solution of known strength, immersing the fibres in phials of the solutions for a certain length of time, withdrawing them, and then by analysis determining what change had taken place in the composition of the liquid, both quantitatively and qualitatively. The fibres were then washed with water until the water used ceased to remove or dissolve any of the salt used, and they were analysed to ascertain whether any of the salt or part of the salt remained in a state insoluble in water, and lastly, the washed fibres were dyed in various dyestuffs and their appearances noted in comparison with the appearance acquired by untreated fibres.

"The solutions experimented upon were those of common salt, bichloride of mercury, sulphuric acid, hydrochloric acid, lime water, baryta water, alum, nitrate of baryta, nitrate of lead, and yellow prussiate of potash. In nearly every case there was found some disturbance in the composition of the liquid; either the fibre had left the solution stronger or weaker by the withdrawal of water or by the withdrawing of salt. With common salt all the fibres took up more water than the proportion present in the solution, leaving it stronger than before. In bichloride of mercury the reverse was the case with both wool and silk, which took up a considerably greater quantity of the salt than the proportion dissolved and retained it very stubbornly. Cotton did not disturb the proportions of salt and water, but retained some of the mercury after long washings. With lime water and baryta water also more solid was removed than liquid. With alum, cotton absorbed water and rejected the salt, leaving the solution stronger; while wool and silk acted in the contrary manner, absorbing more salt than water, and leaving the solution weaker; but in each case after washing with water until the reagents showed no sulphates present, the dyeing experiments showed that alum or something else remained which enabled fibres to dye distinctly different colours from untreated fibres."* It would be extremely difficult even if it were desirable to give a satisfactory condensation of all the experiments, but it is perhaps not

---

* Mem. de l'Acad. des Sc., xxiv., p. 449.

even desirable, because the application of the results or their relevance to the phenomena of dyeing is not direct or clear. The salts experimented upon are rather unusual, they are seldom or never used alone in dyeing, and the condition of leaving them in the cold presents very little resemblance to the conditions under which they are applied in practice.

Some years later M. Bolley took up the research upon nearly the same principles, and by the same methods as M. Chevreul, but with different salts. He experimented with cotton, silk, and wool upon dilute sulphuric acid, sulphate of indigo, yellow prussiate of potash, cream of tartar, neutral acetate of lead, and alum.

He found that except in the case of yellow prussiate of potash, where no action was observable, all the other salts were more or less changed in composition, except in one or two cases where the action of cotton was negative or doubtful. In the case of sulphuric acid, some of the acid had been attracted by wool and silk, but none by cotton. Sulphate of indigo gave up indigo and a small quantity of acid; cream of tartar lost acidity, but no potash was absorbed; while upon acetate of lead cotton had no action, but silk and wool took up oxide of lead. Alum gave up a sub-salt, leaving the solution more acid than before. Along with these fibrous matters, Bolley ascertained that charcoal had almost the same action, a fact which confirmed him in his opposition to Chevreul's theory of chemical affinity having anything to do with these partial decompositions of chemical compounds. The French chemists, Thénard and Roard, long previous to Chevreul's experiments, stated that when wool was put into contact with a solution of alum it absorbed, and so to speak, fixed a portion of the alum without any decomposition of the salt. This alum cannot be removed by any practicable washing in cold water, but when treated with boiling water it yields it up. It, however, requires twenty successive washings to remove it entirely. When wool is boiled with a solution of alum, a portion of the substance of the wool is dissolved in the alum liquor; but it also appears that undecomposed alum is absorbed by the wool. With acetate of alumina these chemists say that wool absorbs the unchanged salt. If the wool is dried some acetic acid escapes, and if the dried wool is boiled with water it yields up some acetate of alumina, but the alumina from that portion of the acetate which was decomposed remains firmly attached to the fibre. They also state that wool boiled with cream of tartar takes up tartaric acid, leaving in solution a neutral tartarate of potash. What really takes place when wool is boiled with a mixture of alum and tartar is only a matter of conjecture. It is supposed that there may be existing at the same time in the wool, alum, tartarate of alumina and potash and free tartaric acid.*

"I give these conclusions, extraordinary as they seem to a modern chemist, because in most of the details

---

* "Dumas sur la Teinture," Sec. 4,326, p. 143.

these authorities are confirmed by Chevreul and Bolley. There is no ground for rejecting them, but as the experiments were made at a time when methods of chemical analysis were much less accurate than they are now, it will be well to receive them with some reserve. Bolley's statement that alum taken up by wool contains more alumina than common alum, seems more credible than that unchanged alum should be assimilated.

"M. Paul Havrez, of Verviers, in writing upon the subject of wool mordanted with alum, found that a weak alum liquor acted as if it were alkaline, while a strong alum liquor acted like an acid upon the wool when tested by dyeing. He endeavoured to explain this double and opposite action by supposing the accidental constituents in the wool or the water, such as traces of soda left in the wool after scouring, or lime in water, or ammonia resulting from the fibre itself, were influencing the results. M. Stas, the well known Belgian chemist, suggested that a simple explanation of the phenomena might be found in the dissociation or separation of the constituents of the alum. M. Havrez found that this was the true cause, and proved it by numerous experiments. He found that if the quantity of alum be small compared with the wool, say 1 part to 200, the alum undergoes dissociation, hydrate of alumina being deposited upon the fibre. The colours which such mordanted wool dyes up in various colouring matters are what are called of the alkaline sort, that is, as if dyed in an alkaline liquor. If, on the other hand, the proportion of alum be large when compared to the wool, the colours dyed up of an acid character, or as if an acid had been present in the dyeing liquor. If the proportion of acid be small, and free acid added to it, the mordant deposited upon the wool is less in quantity, but still has the basic or alkaline character. The conclusions of a very lengthy memoir may be stated as follows :—

(1) Strong doses of mordants of aluminum, iron, chromium, tin or copper, act upon wool by depositing an acid salt.

(2) Weak doses of the same mordants act upon wool by depositing upon it a metallic hydrate of an alkaline or basic character.

(3) The wool is the cause of the dissociation of the alum, and its absorption into the fibre with unequal amounts of acids and base.

(4) Additions of acids or acid salts, as bisulphate, bitartrate, or binoxalate of potash to the alum, is equivalent in the character of the mordanting to the addition of more alum.

(5) An increase in the quantity of the water favours the precipitation of the mordant as hydrated oxide.

(6) In judging of the nature of the mordanting by the colours dyed upon the wool, it must be noted that the colours taken by pure wool itself disguise the effect

of the acid or alkaline hydrate to a certain extent."*

More recently a paper has appeared in the Chemical Journal, by Dr. Mills, F.R.S., and Jokichi Takamine, of Tokio, Japan, on the absorption of weak reagents by cotton, silk, and wool. The object of these researches was to obtain a quantitative measurement of such absorption, and then to ascertain whether the absorption is amenable to the laws already established in other fields of chemical investigation. The researches were divided into two distinct parts, viz., (1) the rate and amount of absorption of individual reagents, and (2), the ratio of absorption of mixed reagents. The wool employed in the experiments was fine cashmere; the silk, a plain pure silk, free from Prussian blue; and the cotton, a pure calico—all in the piece. They were all washed previous to the experiment with weak sodic hydrate water, very weak hydric chloride, and distilled water, successively in the cold. In the first case the acids and alkalis used as the reagents were hydric sulphate, hydric chloride, and hydric tartarate. The results show clearly that both wool and silk absorb these reagents, and that the greater part of the effect is completed, at the ordinary temperature, in a week's time. Cotton absorbed much less than either silk or wool of the individual acids, and was not, therefore, treated for the mixtures. The reagents used to determine the

---

* Technologiste, xxxii., p. 345. Moniteur Scientifique, xiv., p. 598. O'Neill, "Dyeing and Calico Printing," vol. ii., p. 49.

second question were three mixtures of hydric sulphate and hydric chloride. The proportion of the hydric sulphate remaining the same while the hydric chloride was in the proportion of 1, 2, and 4. The ratios of absorption appeared from the experiments in the case of silk to be very similar in all the reagents, and wool and silk tend to resemble each other in the weight they absorb of sodic hydrate, but wool takes up much more from acid solutions than is the case with silk. The quantities of hydric chloride and sodic hydrate were used in the proportion which HCl bears to NaHO, and when the wool was treated with weak solutions the absorption was nearly in the ratio of 2HCl to 3NaHO. The corresponding results for silk and cotton are as 3HCl to 10NaHO in both cases. There is, therefore, a very intimate relation between silk and cotton—a relation which, whatever it may be in part, is shown by these changes to be to a great extent of a strictly chemical nature.*

Although wool, cotton, and silk, have certain reactions in common with various reagents, they are easily distinguished from each other chemically.

Wool and silk are easily distinguished from cotton or linen by drawing out a thread and setting it on fire. The animal fibres shrivel up and leave a shining, tumefied, difficultly combustible cinder, which leaves a large quantity of ash when completely burnt. The smoke has a smell of burnt horn, and turns turmeric brown. The vegetable fibres leave a cinder having

---

* Jour. Chem. Soc., Lon., Mar., 1883, p. 142.

the form of the thread, and only a small quantity of ash, while they burn with a smoke which has an empyreumatic smell and reddens litmus.

Wool and silk are also easily distinguished from cotton and linen by the yellow colour which they assume when treated with nitric or picric acid, as the vegetable fibres are not coloured.

Wool and silk also dissolve by boiling with potash or soda ley of sp. gr. 1·04 to 1·05, whereas the vegetable fibres remain unchanged. When treated with cuprate of ammonium the reverse is the case, as the cotton, linen, and silk dissolve while the wool is insoluble.

Wool and silk can be distinguished from each other by a solution of sodic plumbate, which can be prepared by adding caustic soda to acetate of lead till the resulting precipitate redissolves. When wool or hair are treated with this solution they turn brown in consequence of the sulphur which they contain, forming the dark plumbic sulphuret, while the silk, which is free from sulphur, remains unchanged.

Grothe gives the following as the best methods of distinguishing wool and silk :—

(1) Wool, cautiously heated to 130° C., gives off the odour of carbonic disulphide and ammonia, assumes a golden-yellow colour and curls up, while silk becomes coloured only at 140° to 145° C., and does not curl up.

(2) When the fibres, moistened with potash ley, are dipped in a solution of cupric sulphate,

and then exposed to the air, the wool quickly turns brown in consequence of the formation of cupric sulphide, whereas the silk remains unchanged.

(3) On mixing the solution of wool in caustic potash with tartaric acid, and then with cupric sulphate, a large quantity of cupric sulphide is formed, and the filtered liquid exhibits a dark brown-red colour. Silk treated in the same manner yields a somewhat viscid solution, having a fine violet colour.*

---

* Zeitschr. Anal. Chem., iii., p. 153.

LECTURE IV.

IN our last lecture we investigated the mechanical and chemical nature of the structure of the wool fibre. We saw that the fibre itself consisted mechanically of a bundle of spindle-shaped cells, united together at their surfaces by some animal substance which permits of their free motion over each other when subjected to longitudinal strain, and upon which depends the elasticity of the fibre; and that this inner or cortical part is held together externally by a sheath of more inspissated and flattened cells, of a horny nature, which constitute on the external part of the fibre a series of imbricated plates, which overlap each other in the direction of the free end of the fibre. These plates, which were originally more rounded and hollow cells, were formed by the flattening of the cells on the external surface as the fibre passed upwards within the generating follicle, and are capable of being acted upon and swelled out by the use of certain reagents. Upon the form and arrangement of these plates, as well as the nature of their surface, depend the suitability of the wool for use in textile manufactures and the degree of lustre which the fibres will exhibit, and upon the structure of the cortical cells and their reaction with various dyestuffs depend the softness, pliability, and power to retain any colour which may be imparted to it. We also saw that chemically the composition of wool exhibits a strong resemblance to that of hair, hoof, and other horny substances, which are generated in the same manner as an appendage of the epidermal tissues of animals, but differs from them in always having associated with it a considerably larger amount of structural fat, colloidal albumenoids, and water, and therefore forms a compound substance which is peculiarly liable to decomposition and change when acted upon by weak alkalis, and even hot water when above moderate temperatures.

We have already seen that all the epidermal structures are liable to variation and change under varying conditions, and especially those which are occasioned by alterations in food, soil, and climate; but, in addition to this, they are also subject to modification by causes which are at present obscure, and which may be exhibited in animals which are otherwise subject to the same conditions, and even in different parts of the same animal. When looking at the structure of the cotton fibre, we saw that there were variations in the nature of the fibre, even in cases where the fibres were taken from the same boll, and that these differences seemed to depend upon the position of the fibre in the boll, and the varying amount of nourishment and light which was received.

The same variation occurs in regard to the wool fibre, and when we come to compare the extent of these variations from the typical fibre we are brought to the second part of our inquiry, viz.,—

II.—*What variations from this type structure are presented to us?*

C. In fibres from the same animal and grown at the same time.
D. In fibres from the same animal grown in different years.
E. In fibres from the same animal grown under different climatic and other conditions.
F. In fibres from different breeds of sheep grown in different countries.

C.—In looking at the variation in the nature of the wool fibres when taken from the same animal, we can best consider the question by looking at the general variation which occurs in the distribution, strength, and length of different fibres in the same fleece. As in the case of all animals, the length and strength of the hair differs materially in different parts of the fleece, the finest and shortest wool being found as a rule in the region of the shoulders and neck, while the longest and strongest is situated on the hind quarters round the region of the tail. Hence when the wool is to be used for textile purposes, it is quite necessary that the different parts of the fleece should be separated from each other, in order that the various qualities of hair may be used together, because, as we shall afterwards see, it is quite essential that in order to have uniformity in the quality of the yarn we must have something like a general uniformity in the raw material, so far as the length and strength of the fibre is concerned.

In the first place we must remember that the character of the wool is to some extent changed over the whole surface of the sheep by the process of shearing, because it causes the lambs' wool to be removed, and hence in the second growth the terminal character of the fibres is changed.

This causes a distinction to be made in the wool of the first and subsequent clips. In the case of lambs' wool, or the first clipping from a one-year-old sheep, the character of the staple is more or less pointed, and the same distinction is exhibited in the individual hairs. The hairs themselves are also more or less attached at the bottom end so as to be less free in drawing out, and this wool is called hog wool, from the name which is usually given to the one-year-old sheep, a hog or hogget. After the first clip the ends of the wool staples are more or less square, and the individual hairs which compose the lock are the same. This fleece is called a wether fleece, and the sheep after its first shearing is called a wether. The topping of the fibres by the process of shearing causes them to grow stronger and firmer, and hence the character of the wether wool is usually coarser and less pliable than the hog, as well as more wanting in the waved and curly structure which is so valuable a feature in first-class wool. The first clip, therefore, from a sheep is the most valuable in a technical point of view, and can be applied to the production of a higher series of counts and a better quality of yarn than the subsequent clippings. The separation of the various qualities of wool in a fleece is accomplished by the process of "sorting," which consists in tearing off each quality separately with the hand. It is unnecessary to say that long practice is required to enable this to be done with precision and accuracy.

It is well known that the quality of the mutton derived from the carcase of the sheep varies in different parts, and is more delicate and finer in the grain on the fore than the hind part of the animal, and on the shoulders than on the legs. In the same way the character of the flesh seems to be transmitted to the wool which grows upon the different parts of the animal, since we find the finest and best grown wool covering those parts which are finest and best flavoured when prepared as food. This general indication points to the fact that in all sheep the finest wool is found on the forepart of the animal, and it grows coarser and generally inferior as we descend downwards towards the under part of the belly and backwards towards the tail and flanks. The habits and requirements of the animal also tend to increase these distinctions, since the under parts and flanks of the sheep are subject to greater attrition and fouling than those higher up and more forward.

We can best understand the different qualities of wool which are to be found in a single fleece if we refer to Plate XXI., which gives us a representation of a fleece of English wool, laid out flat upon the sorting board or ground, so that the various qualities of which it is composed can be clearly seen. The fleece itself roughly represents the general features of the body of the sheep—the ridge or back which follows the course of the spine being in the centre, and dividing the fleece into two equal halves from the head to the tail.

The distinction in quality between fibres from one part of the fleece and another is so great that a large number of different "sortings" can be made, and of course the number will depend upon the general character of the fleece and the purposes to which the wool is afterwards to be applied. As we might naturally expect, the range of qualities in any individual fleece varies according to whether the fleece is of a fine or coarse breed of sheep. This variation in the quality of different breeds has been compared to "the keyboard of a piano, where each sheep has its octave of qualities; but the octave of the Merino is very high, while the octave of the Lincoln is very low." In the same way the names which are given to different qualities of wool, even out of the same fleece, are very various in different localities, and even amongst different firms in the same neighbourhood, where special names are given to different classifications, and it is a pity that some general rule is not adopted so as to avoid confusion. In the finer classes of wool the various qualities are often named after the highest counts into which they will spin, and such division has the merit of having a definite basis for classification.

The diagram, Plate XXI., shows the position of the various qualities of wool on a fleece of Leicester hog; but the same relative positions hold good in all kinds of fleeces. The finest and most even grown wool is always found on the two shoulders about the positions marked AA. In some fleeces this quality extends more into E and BB and F than in others, and the quality of the wool at BB is not very much inferior, although rather stronger and coarser. These two qualities would be called in the woollen trade picklock and prime or choice, while the wool found in the position C is frequently finer in the staple but shorter than AA or BB, and apt to be more defaced by irregular or coloured hairs. When free from these defects it forms a super quality. The qualities D and E shade into those on each side of them, and as they form the apex of the neck and shoulders they are less deep grown or close in the staple than A or C. The quality F closely resembles BB, into which it shades, and for many purposes, especially for spinning down, A, B, E, and F are frequently used as one quality. In Bradford the wool from the shoulders and neck is usually called "blue" or "fine" matching, according

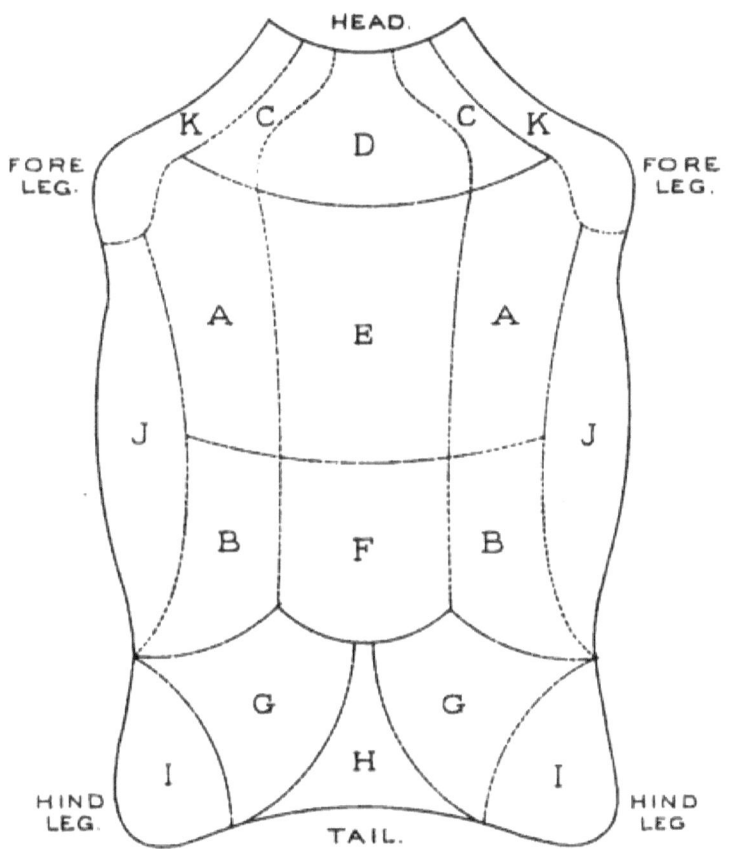

FLEECE OF LEICESTER WOOL.

Showing the position of the various qualities of Wool

as the quality of the fleece may be. In an ordinary Leicester fleece it would be "blue" matching, and would spin to 40's. If, however, the fleece was of a superior quality, such as a fine Kent selected for quality, it would make "fine" matching, and would spin to 42's or even 44's. If, however, the fleece was a strong Lincoln or Gloucester, it would probably only be classed as "neat" matching, and would in that case spin no further than 36's. When we pass beyond F backwards on to the flanks of the sheep the wool becomes long and coarse, the best being found in the positions marked GG, and this would make what is called "brown" matching or drawing, which would not spin higher than 32's, even in fine selected fleeces of English wool, and in many not so high. At H and H the coarsest part of the fleece is reached, where the wool grows in large locks with long coarse hairs. The latter is called the "breach" or "britch," and can only be used for very coarse yarns and low numbers, not spinning higher than 26's, even when the fleece is comparatively fine in the other parts. Sometimes it is also called "say cast." From the extremities of H there is often taken a lower quality still, which is called "tail" or even "cow-tail," from the resemblance which the hair possesses to the strong tuft growing at the end of the cow's tail, and of course this can only be used for the very lowest numbers. There are usually also a quantity of hard lumps, consisting of matted fibre and dirt, which have to be cut off with the shears by the sorter and are called "toppings." These are smaller in proportion as the flock is well tended and the seasons fine. In the ordinary English fleeces all these qualities are long enough to be combed; but just round the edges of the fleece in the positions marked JJ and KK, and at the furthest ends of D and CC nearest the head, we have a very short stapled wool, which grows in small tufts or staples called "shorts" or "brokes," and which are used for carding. In quality they correspond to the longer wools with which they are associated in the different positions on the body. They are usually divided into three qualities, which correspond to the blue or fine matching, the neat matching, and the britch. The finest, which are derived from the extremities of D, CC, and the position K, are often called "super" or "downrights." Those which grow on the position JJ, especially the forward part, are called "middle" or "seconds;" and those from the extremities of JJ nearest to I are called "common" or "abb." When the fleece is cross-bred, and even in some cases where it is not, there is always a tendency to the production of "kemps" along the skirt, but specially at the parts marked KK and the extremity nearest the head. Where the kemps occur in the combing wool is most frequently in the region of the tail, in the part marked H.

As we have already observed the difference between the qualities of wool, both in position and quantity, differs very much even in sheep of the same breed and feeding in the same field, as each sheep and fleece has its own "individual" characteristics with its own special "octave" to refer to the former figure. When I was engaged in the worsted trade we usually divided the fleeces from the same farmer into three qualities, "super," "fine," and "common," the names indicating the relative fineness of the average wool which they contained, and only those who have "cased" or classed large quantities of wool know how wide this variation frequently is.

When we come to look at the differences which exist in the hairs grown on the various parts of the same sheep, we are struck with the fact that the hair follicles, and consequently the hairs, are most numerous on those parts where the wool is the finest in quality, and, as we might also naturally expect, there is on these parts the largest production of the suint or grease which is exuded from the glands for the nourishment and support of the hair. We saw, when looking at the human hair, that there were about an average of 600 to 700 hairs growing upon every square inch of the head, a quantity which differs considerably in different individuals. On an ordinary English Leicester sheep the numbers are about as follow: 1,500 to 1,900 on the shoulder, and 800 to 1,200 on the flanks, so that they are nearly twice as rank in the one case as the other. In many cases, as in the human subject, there are more than one hair contained within the follicle, and as this varies with different individuals, the numbers of hairs will probably vary even more than these figures express in different sheep. The growth of double hairs also seems to be more numerous in some sheep than others, and also they are more numerous where the fibres are most rank—that is to say, where the wool is the finest in quality. Although I have not had the opportunity of observing the rankness of the growth of wool on the finest qualities of sheep, such as the Merino, still, from the seemingly universal rule on the English sheep, I have no doubt but that the same proportions in the relative quantities of wool fibres growing upon the different parts of the sheep will probably hold good.

We have already remarked that there are considerable differences in the character of the wool fibres on sheep which are of the same flock, but the differences existing in the structure of the fibres from different parts of the same sheep are frequently greater than those on the corresponding parts of different sheep. As we might naturally expect where the wool is the best in quality, as on the shoulders of the animal, we find all the best qualities of the wool, such as evenness of length, soundness of fibre, softness, and curl, reach their maximum, and as we depart from this region all these qualities fall off. Wherever the breed of the sheep is true and pure, we find all these characteristics more extensively over the fleece than in those cases where the breed is untrue or mixed; and when we come to look at the microscopical character of the fibres on the different parts of the same sheep, we are struck with the fact that those peculiarities in the structure and arrangement of the scales, and the general uniformity of diameter of the fibres, which render the finest qualities and varieties of wool the most valuable, are always found on the fibres grown in those regions of the fleece where the best qualities are found. At first sight it might appear that this is simply the utterance of a truism, much the same as saying that the best wool fibres always grow where the best wool is found; but if we consider the matter, we shall see that this is not the case, because we know of no necessary connection existing between some of these qualities. Thus, although there always seems to be some relation between the number of epidermal scales per linear inch, and the number of waves or curls in the fibre, we do not know of the same universal relation between these characteristics and the uniformity of diameter or the soundness and softness, since we frequently find wool fibres in various classes of sheep which possess numerous scales and curves, and yet are both wanting in uniformity of length and soundness of staple. Notwithstanding this, however, it fortunately happens that whatever care is taken to cultivate the sheep so as to improve its best qualities in one part has apparently a reflex action on the other parts, and affects them beneficially also; and the same care and attention bestowed on any one sheep so as to increase the length of the average staple increases also all the other qualities which are most valuable, and tends to diminish the production of abnormal fibres, and increase the microscopic likeness of the fibres to each other. We can, perhaps, best understand this if we examine the fibres taken from two sheep of the same Lincoln breed, and notice the difference between the fibres from the shoulder and britch of each of them.

Plate XXII. gives a fair representation of four fibres, two of them, A and B, taken from the best part of the fleece, and two of them, C and D, from the britch. In the case of this sheep it has evidently been well bred and cultivated, and the fibres, although showing great strength of shaft, as compared with fine Southdown or Merino wool, are fairly uniform and equally scaled on the epidermal surface. Although the difference between the two classes of fibre are distinctly marked, yet there is even in the case of the coarser hairs, C, D, a considerable likeness to the finer ones, A, B. The greatest difference seems to be that the britch hairs are larger in diameter, and the scales themselves stand out more boldly, but there would be, however, no difficulty in at once identifying the whole of the fibres as of the same class.

If, however, we examine Plate XXIII. we see a marked difference. The fibres which are marked with the same letters, as on the previous plate, indicate that the fibres have been taken from corresponding parts of another sheep of the same breed, but in this case the sheep has been poorly bred and only indifferently cared for. Even the fibres A and B, which are taken from the shoulder, are much more irregular in their epidermal scales and in the average diameter,

Plate XXII.

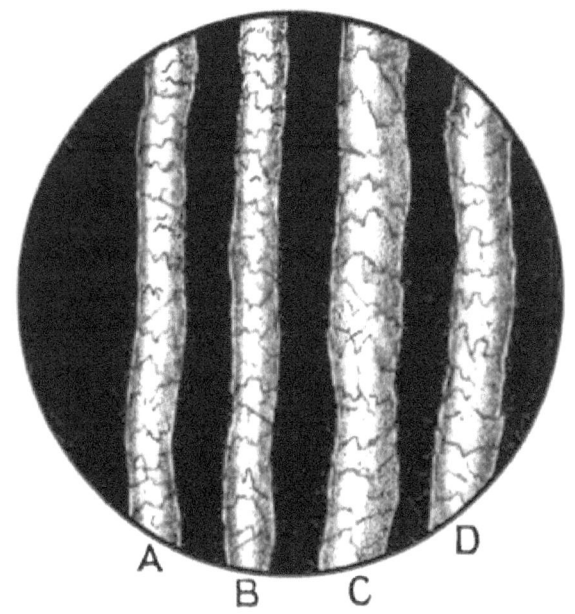

100 DIAMETERS.

FIBRES OF FINE LINCOLN WOOL.

A & B. Fibres taken from the Shoulder

C & D. Fibres taken from the Britch.

and indeed they almost differ from each other as widely as the fibres from different parts of the better bred sheep in the last plate. Neither the strength nor general good qualities will be present either. The two fibres C and D, taken from the britch of this sheep, differ very widely even from A and B, much more widely indeed than the fibres taken from the same part of the last sheep do from those taken from its shoulder. It seems as if indeed these coarse fibres had lost many of the characteristics of wool and were reverting to coarse hair, except for the serrated scales, and the difference between the fibres on different parts of this sheep is quite as great and distinct as we shall afterwards find to exist between fibres taken even from different breeds of sheep.

From this it seems certain that purity of breed and general good management in the cultivation and pasturage as well as the feeding of sheep tend to produce uniformity of characteristics in the fibres of the wool grown on all parts of the body. While, however, the fibres differ in length and diameter, and the number of serrations or epidermal scales per linear inch, on different parts of the body of the same sheep, it is also wonderful what a variation there is even in contiguous fibres, especially in regard to the diameter.

Remarking on this point Mr. N. Burgess* says: "The size of the fibre is very irregular, scarcely any two from the same staple being found alike, and each varying in its own length. In a fibre of Southdown

---

* Journal Queckett Microscop. Club, vol. i., p. 30.

wool, a comparatively uniform species, I have found the size to vary in $\frac{1}{312}$ of an inch, as much as one-fifth of the whole diameter. The finest Saxon wool I have ever seen gave a remarkable result on being measured. Five hairs in one staple were selected. The finest gave the extremely small diameter of $\frac{1}{3489}$ of an inch, while another fibre lying by its side measured the $\frac{1}{1749}$ of an inch. The mean of the fine fibre gave $\frac{1}{2134}$ of an inch. Another sample of Saxony wool gave $\frac{1}{2075}$ of an inch.

"Amongst Saxon wools shown in the grease two of the fibres were measured, and one gave $\frac{1}{1562}$ of an inch, while the other was $\frac{1}{1250}$ of an inch. Probably this sample could not be exceeded for beauty or symmetry. It was taken from one of Steizer's celebrated ewes.

"The Southdown sample shown gives for one fibre $\frac{1}{890}$ of an inch, and another $\frac{1}{520}$ of an inch. The Lincoln wool gives for one part of the fibre $\frac{1}{625}$ of an inch, and another $\frac{1}{520}$ of an inch. The coarsest fibre gives $\frac{1}{460}$ of an inch.

"The fibre of the Northumberland wool measured in its thinnest part gave $\frac{1}{600}$ of an inch, and in its thickest part $\frac{1}{400}$ of an inch. These examples will suffice for showing the relative degrees of size and the variations which occur in the same fibre."

In my own experience I have found even greater variations than these, although I have also noticed that this tendency to variation in the diameter of individual fibres, as well as parts of the same fibre,

Plate XXIII.

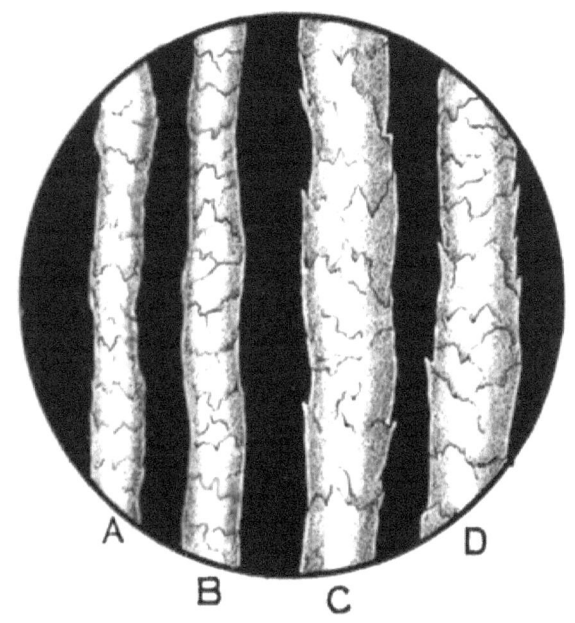

100 Diameters.

FIBRES OF COARSE LINCOLN WOOL.

A & B. Fibres taken from the Shoulder.

C & D. Fibres taken from the Britch.

differs in different sheep. This may be shown by a number of examples which I have measured and tabulated below, and which represent the variation in diameter in different parts of the same fibre :—

VARIATION IN DIFFERENT FIBRES FROM THE SAME PART OF THE SAME SHEEP.

Kind of Wool.	Greatest diameter in decimals of an inch.	Least diameter in decimals of an inch.	Difference.
Lincoln Hogs, No 1	·00210	·00192	·00018
,, 2	·00180	·00135	·00045
,, 3	·00166	·00143	·00023
Average	·00185	·00157	·00028
Irish Hogs, No. 1	·00125	·00100	·00025
,, 2	·00183	·00130	·00053
,, 3	·00174	·00124	·00050
Average	·00161	·00118	·00043
Southdown, No. 1	·00111	·00073	·00038
,, 2	·00125	·00092	·00033
,, 3	·00100	·00041	·00059
Average	·00112	·00068	·00014
Australian Merino, No. 1	·00053	·00014	·00039
,, ,, 2	·00047	·00011	·00036
,, ,, 3	·00041	·00011	·00030
Average	·00047	·00012	·00035

In each of these cases the whole of the samples seemed to be fair examples of the different kinds of wool, and they were not deformed by effects which could be traced to bad breeding. They must not, however, be taken as representing the average differences existing in the same locks of their respective wools, but only as instances to show something like the variations occurring, because I have found many specimens which differ much more than these do, although taken at random from locks which happened to be in my possession at the time when measuring. If we come to coarse and bad bred wool, such as some of the Russian or Central Asian wool, or even some of our own mountain sheep, we find a range of variation which is almost incredible. Of course it is not possible on a large scale, in the ordinary processes of manufacture, to take into account the variations in every hair and fibre of the fleece; but the prevalence or otherwise of considerable variations must always be considered, and as there is a great difference in this respect in different classes of wool, it may not be uninteresting to give a series of experiments which I made at the time when I was practically engaged at the "sorting board," and which were undertaken with the view of determining the relative quantities of the various classes of wool which were to be obtained out of different kinds of fleeces. These analyses were made not with single fleeces, but with a considerable number, since 240 lbs., or one pack of wool, was taken for each experimental sorting, and these tables are the average of a number of such trials of each kind of wool:—

Analysis of Lincoln Hogs.

Qualities.	1st Experiment. Weight in lbs.	2nd Experiment. Weight in lbs.	3rd Experiment. Weight in lbs.
Fine Matching ⎫	15·85	17·01	13·21
Blue ,, ⎬ Combing	160·00	140·00	154·14
Neat ,, ⎭	40·00	52·00	38·21
1st Brokes ⎫	3·24	4·22	8·65
2nd ,, ⎬ Carding	5·58	9·04	7·42
3rd ,, ⎭	1·06	2·75	3·00
Britch or Say Cast	9·68	11·64	8·75
Cow-tail	1·70	1·00	2·31
Cots	·50	·08	1·00
Grey	·01	·12	......
Toppings	1·33	2·14	1·24
Dead Waste	1·05	......	2·07
	240·00	240·00	240·00

Qualities.	4th Experiment. Weight in lbs.	5th Experiment. Weight in lbs.	Average weight in lbs.
Fine Matching ⎫	22·36	19·41	17·57
Blue ,, ⎬ Combing	144·03	150·00	149·03
Neat ,, ⎭	50·11	46·53	45·37
1st Brokes ⎫	5·60	7·31	5·80
2nd ,, ⎬ Carding	6·36	8·14	7·31
3rd ,, ⎭	4·21	2·34	2·67
Britch or Say Cast	5·55	4·36	7·99
Cow-tail	·03	1·50	1·31
Cots	......	......	·31
Grey	......	......	·03
Toppings	2·01	·55	1·45
Dead Waste	......	......	1·16
	240·26	240·14	240·00

This table of the sorting of five packs of Lincoln hogs will serve to show the nature of the variation in the different qualities out of five different parcels of this wool, and the average at the end of the table shows something like what we may expect to obtain as an average out of any lot of the same class of wool. The loss which I have called dead waste consisted of small sweepings and dust which it was impossible to gather up, and as will be seen in some cases there was a gain instead of loss, probably arising from a slight over-weighing in all the various qualities, or some one of them, as the wool was weighed on ordinary warehouse beam scales.

No endeavour was made in any of these lots of wool to allow for the moisture which might be present over a normal quantity. The wool was undried and exactly in the condition in which it was taken out of the sheets as received from the wool-stapler. The experiments may, therefore, be taken to represent the various quantities of the different qualities, under the ordinary conditions which exist in the wool warehouse. It is quite possible that a part of the dead waste registered in some of the experiments may have resulted from the drying in of the wool consequent on the opening and sorting of the fleece.

The following analysis of Leicester hogs may be compared with the Lincoln hogs just given, and we shall then see the difference in somewhat similar classes of wool:—

ANALYSIS OF LEICESTER HOGS.

Qualities.	1st Experiment.	2nd Experiment.	3rd Experiment.
Fine Matching ⎫	24·13	20·40	46·85
Blue ,, ⎬ Combing	155·36	140·65	125·21
Neat ,, ⎭	38·51	58·41	45·00
1st Brokes ⎫	6·44	5·58	4·31
2nd ,, ⎬ Carding	7·71	6·83	4·14
3rd ,, ⎭	1·31	2·30	3·00
Britch or Say Cast	5·27	4·21	7·11
Cow-tail	......	1·00	......
Cots	......	......	3·14
Grey	......	......	......
Toppings	1·00	·50	1·00
Waste	·27	·12	·24
	240·00	240·00	240·00

Qualities.	4th Experiment.	5th Experiment.	Average.
Fine Matching ⎫	38·74	39·40	33·90
Blue ,, ⎬ Combing	138·21	140·21	139·93
Neat ,, ⎭	40·44	38·64	44·18
1st Brokes ⎫	5·25	4·40	5·19
2nd ,, ⎬ Carding	3·64	2·83	5·03
3rd ,, ⎭	3·21	3·40	2·68
Britch or Say Cast	6·11	7·30	6·00
Cow-tail	......	·80	·36
Cots	3·21	2·44	1·76
Grey	......	·11	·02
Toppings	·64	·14	·65
Waste	·55	·33	·30
	240·00	240·00	240·00

It will be noticed that in the Leicester hogs the proportion of fine matching is larger than in the Lincoln hogs, but that the blue matching is proportionately less, and there is an entire absence of grey wool.

Analysis of Northumberland Hogs.

Qualities.	1st Experiment.	2nd Experiment.	Average.
Fine Matching ⎫	38·5	36·7	37·6
Blue ,, ⎬ Combing	135·3	140·4	137·8
Neat ,, ⎭	42·9	43·8	43·4
1st Brokes ⎫	5·5	4·3	4·9
2nd ,, ⎬ Carding	4·1	3·8	3·9
3rd ,, ⎭	3·2	5·7	4·5
Britch or Say Cast	5·4	4·2	4·8
Cow-tail	3·1	1·0	2·1
Cots	……	……	……
Grey	……	……	……
Toppings	1·1	……	·5
Waste	·9	·1	·5
	240·0	240·0	240·0

The experiments with the Northumberland hogs are only made out of two parcels of this wool, and the average is not therefore so reliable as where five experiments were made, but they will serve to show the general character of the wool. In these two instances the wool was rather coarser than usual at the britch, and hence the large proportion of cow-tail.

Analysis of Irish Hogs.

Qualities.	1st Experiment.	2nd Experiment.	3rd Experiment.
Fine Matching ⎫	32·41	40·30	26·75
Blue ,, ⎬ Combing	142·31	150·50	149·10
Neat ,, ⎭	42·50	30·10	46·00
1st Brokes ⎫	4·28	5·31	6·25
2nd ,, ⎬ Carding	6·50	5·11	5·40
3rd ,, ⎭	3·90	4·28	2·31
Britch or Say Cast	5·70	4·40	3·14
Cow-tail	......	......	1·60
Cots	·50	......	......
Grey	......	......	......
Toppings	1·30	......	......
Waste	·60	......	......
	240·00	240·00	240·55

Qualities.	4th Experiment.	5th Experiment.	Average.
Fine Matching ⎫	40·40	30·90	34·15
Blue ,, ⎬ Combing	140·10	140·65	144·53
Neat ,, ⎭	38·40	45·31	40·46
1st Brokes ⎫	4·90	3·61	4·87
2nd ,, ⎬ Carding	6·30	5·40	5·76
3rd ,, ⎭	3·21	4·00	3·54
Britch or Say Cast	5·10	4·13	4·49
Cow-tail	1·00	·50	·60
Cots	1·30	4·40	1·24
Grey	......	......	......
Toppings	......	1·20	·50
Waste	......	......	·12
	240·71	240·12	240·26

All these Irish hogs were of a very good quality, and were free, clean wool; the only exception was in the fifth lot, when there were two fleeces which contained a much larger proportion of cots than was found in the other lots, and which brought up the average considerably.

ANALYSIS OF IRISH WETHERS.

Qualities.	1st Experiment.	2nd Experiment.	Average.
Fine Matching ⎫	34·51	30·13	32·32
Blue ,, ⎬ Combing	120·40	125·41	122·91
Neat ,, ⎭	66·31	67·50	66·90
1st Brokes ⎫	6·40	5·32	5·86
2nd ,, ⎬ Carding	4·30	5·15	4·72
3rd ,, ⎭	5·15	3·80	4·47
Britch or Say Cast	2·10	2·69	2·40
Cow-tail	......	......	......
Cots	......	......	......
Grey	......	......	......
Toppings	......	......	......
Waste	·83	......	·42
	240·00	240·00	240·00

When compared with the Irish hogs it will be noticed that these wethers, which were from the same parcel, yield very similar results in the fine matching, but they have a larger proportion of neat and less blue matching. Like the hogs, they were of good quality, and free, clean wool. They were classed by the writer as Irish Leicesters, and may be compared with the next analysis of Leicester hogs.

Analysis of Half-bred Leicester Hogs.

Qualities.	1st Experiment.	2nd Experiment.	3rd Experiment.
Fine Matching ⎫	17·01	20·40	16·71
Blue ,, ⎬ Combing	100·00	120·00	105·32
Neat ,, ⎭	91·10	68·40	87·14
1st Brokes ⎫	4·22	5·20	4·32
2nd ,, ⎬ Carding	9·04	7·11	8·21
3rd ,, ⎭	2·75	3·65	8·03
Britch or Say Cast	9·75	8·30	7·56
Cow-tail	2·00	3·11	1·20
Cots	·08	1·00	......
Grey	1·12	1·31	......
Toppings	2·14	1·40	1·00
Waste	·79	·13	·51
	240·00	240·00	240·00

Qualities.	4th Experiment.	5th Experiment.	Average.
Fine Matching ⎫	24·50	19·35	19·59
Blue ,, ⎬ Combing	114·12	113·94	110·90
Neat ,, ⎭	71·71	80·40	79·75
1st Brokes ⎫	5·26	6·10	5·02
2nd ,, ⎬ Carding	8·31	7·31	7·99
3rd ,, ⎭	4·00	2·80	4·25
Britch or Say Cast	6·50	5·30	7·50
Cow-tail	2·00	1·90	2·04
Cots	·50	......	·31
Grey	·80	......	·64
Toppings	2·00	2·30	1·77
Waste	·30	·60	·24
	240·00	240·00	240·00

In these half-bred hogs it will be noticed that the average of the fine matching is less than any of the other full-bred wools except the Lincoln, while the blue matching is less than in any of the other examples. All these wools were specially sorted for the manufacture of 30's super, for export. Out of the fine matching in the hogs 40's super were spun. I have never had the opportunity of sorting any of the fine English or foreign wools, and therefore cannot give any analyses of these; but from these examples and what I have seen of these wools casually, I am of opinion that they will run somewhat similar in quantities of the various kinds, bearing in mind always that the classification will be much finer all through, and in all probability the very coarsest classes, and the grey, cots, and toppings being omitted almost entirely.

As I have before remarked, the classification of the sorting will vary with each individual firm, and it would be difficult to find even two sorters who could agree as to the exact line at which the division of the fleece should take place. As a check against my own analyses I give below a table taken from the Supplement to Ure's Dictionary, page 983, in which a series of sortings are given from various classes of English wool, and these are given in percentages, or lbs. per 100 lbs. of each sort. As they include some of the finer varieties, such as Kent and Norfolk wools, and wethers as well as hogs, they are additionally valuable:—

Analysis of English Wools.

Name.	Fine Drawing.	Blue Drawing.	Neat Drawing.	Brown Drawing.	Britch or Say Cast.	First Brokes.	Second Brokes.	Third Brokes.	Toppings or Shirlings.
Lincoln ... Hogs	0	24	50	15	7	1	1	1	1
Yorkshire ,,	5	30	38	15	7	2	1	1	1
Leicester ,,	8	34	30	15	5	2	3	2	1
Northum'lnd. ,,	9	25	36	15	7	3	3	1	1
Nottingham ,,	7	24	35	20	7	2	3	1	1
Norfolk ,,	30	25	10	10	7	3	$2\frac{1}{2}$	1	$1\frac{1}{2}$
Lincoln Wethers.	0	12	50	25	7	2	2	1	1
Yorkshire ,,	0	36	40	12	6	2	2	1	1
Warwick ,,	4	31	40	12	5	3	2	2	1
Somerset ,,	4	35	29	18	6	2	3	2	1
Kent ,,	56	20	10	7	4	$\frac{1}{2}$	$\frac{1}{2}$	$\frac{1}{2}$	$\frac{1}{2}$

These examples, however, will serve to show something like the proportionate weight of the range of qualities which are to be found in the deep-grown wools. The various experiments in each table show the variation in different lots of wool taken out of different parcels in the same year.

I cannot pass from the consideration of the character of the fibres on the same sheep in the same year, without pointing out how very greatly this character is influenced by the health of the sheep. In sorting any parcel of wool the sorter often comes across some special fleece, the very handle of which is different from the others—the fibre seems leaner and softer, and often seems to have lost both its elasticity and tenacity. When the strength of the staple is tried the locks are readily broken, as if the staple was rotten. When examined under the microscope, the fibres are seen to be generally finer or smaller in diameter than the usual run of the fibres in the same lot of wool, and often this fineness only extends to a part of the fibre, as if the sheep had been temporarily indisposed, and during that time the vitality of the animal was so much lowered that the usual growth of the wool fibres could not be maintained—the wool sharing in the weakness of the animal. Plate XXIV. is an illustration of a number of such fibres, and here we see the nature of the variations. Sometimes the whole texture of the fibre becomes finer, and while the same proportion of lorications is maintained the diameter of the fibre is much diminished, as in fibre A; while in other cases the number of scales in the same length seems to be diminished also, and the scales are less prominent as though finer in texture, as though fewer epidermal cells were grown in the same time, as seen in fibre B. Sometimes these variations occur at frequent intervals, as though the animal experienced alternate periods of health and sickness, as in fibres C and D. But in all these cases a permanent weakness is introduced into the structure of the fibre which is very deleterious to its use in yarn, as being entirely wanting in evenness of strength and texture. These variations in individual fleeces always occur most frequently in bad seasons, when food is scarce and the surroundings unfavourable.

D.—Great as are the differences in fibres of wool

Plate XXIV.

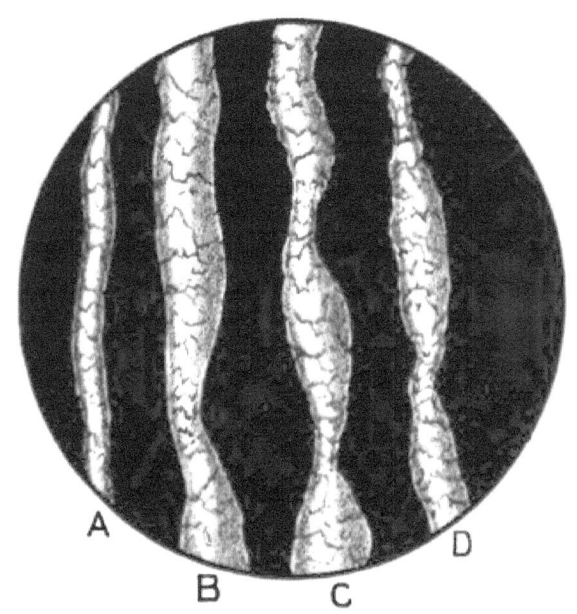

120 Diameters

FIBRES OF DISEASED WOOL.

A. Attenuated Fibre.

B. Fibre with diminished number of epidermal scales.

C & D. Fibres with alternate attenuation and diminished epidermal scales.

growing upon the same sheep in the same year, there are also great differences in the wool of the same sheep in different years, because the wool and its character depend very largely not only on the health of the sheep but also upon climatic and other influences. The mildness or severity of the season and the plenty or scarcity of food very largely affect the character of the wool. In very severe seasons there is a tendency to a thickening of the fibres, with greater irregularity in the length of the general staple, and a greater rankness of the fleece, with undergrowth of short fibres, and a greater irregularity in the diameters of the individual fibres and the different parts of the same fibre. The general character of the wool is also affected, because from constant wetting and drying in the bad seasons the wool becomes tender and rotten, and loses its brilliancy and lustre. This may also arise from the fact that a part of the suint or yolk is soluble in water, and in very wet seasons much of this is dissolved out. When examined under the microscope, the individual fibres are found to be injured in their structure by the want of proper nourishment and the deficiency in the natural suint or grease, a large part of which is soluble in water, and when removed leaves the fibres dry and hask. Of course, amongst well-tended flocks these variations are reduced to a minimum, because they are supplied with suitable shelters from the storms, and fed artificially when there is a scarcity of pasture; but amongst those sheep which occupy less favoured positions, and are more dependent upon the character of the seasons for everything which they require, there is a much larger variation than would really be suspected without actual observation. Those who have cased or classified considerable quantities of the highland and mountain wools know how much lower is the general classification of the fleeces in stormy than mild seasons. I have noticed a marked variation in the structure of the scales on the surface of the wool fibres from the same sheep in different years. Whatever tends to improve the general health and condition of the sheep, increases the number of the serrations and causes them to be more regular.

These last observations relate to the variation which arises in the character of the wool where the sheep remains really stationary, and the greatest variation which occurs in its surrounding conditions arises from the difference in the meteorological changes taking place at its area of residence; but there are also very important variations which are introduced into the character of the wool when the same sheep is removed from one district to another. These changes may be considered under our next division.

E.—These variations are the result of an entire change in the surrounding or environment of the sheep both in regard to climate and food. In some instances this variation may be only slight, because the conditions only vary in a small degree; but as a rule, if there is very great difference in the character of the two districts, there will be equal results produced

Plate XXV.

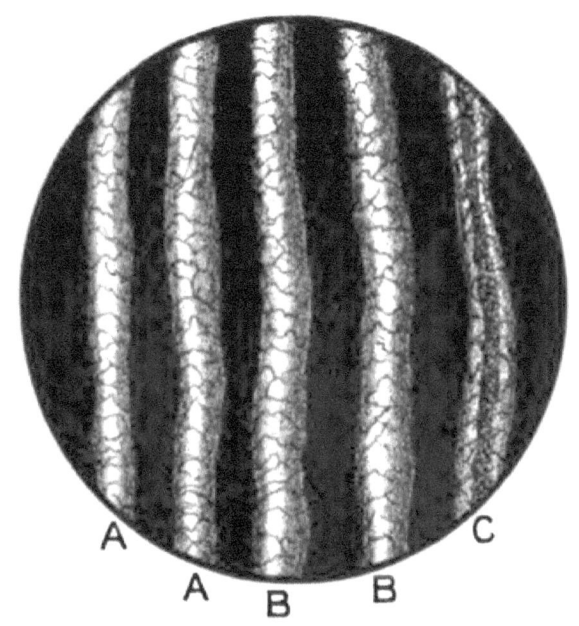

400 Diameters.

FIBRES OF ALPACA.

A.A. Fibres of Ariquepa Alpaca
B.B. Fibres of Chala Alpaca.
C. Fibre of Brown Alpaca.

in the character of the wool. When a mountain sheep is brought down into the valleys it soon begins to change the character of its fleece. The long coarse hair which is mixed with coarser parts of the fleece of wool diminishes in number, and the general character of the wool becomes finer: even the general appearance of the sheep changes, since it requires less exertion in the procuring of its food, and therefore accumulates more flesh and of a finer quality.

This change in the character of the wool and even of the sheep themselves, by simple removal from one district to another, was very distinctly marked in the early history of sheep farming in New South Wales. As the colony had no native sheep a flock was introduced from Bengal, which was the nearest place where they were found, and which had regular communication with the colony. The sheep first imported, however, were of a very poor class: they are described as having "large heads, with Roman noses and slouch ears. They were extremely narrow in the chest, with plain and narrow shoulders; high curved backs; tremendously long legs, and covered with a coarse hairy fleece."* This was an accumulation of bad qualities which seemed to augur ill for the future of the sheep in Australia, since they were almost more like goats than sheep. The change, however, in the surroundings and food of the sheep worked wonders, and the alteration which was produced seemed to be an exception to the generally recognised fundamental

---

* Widowson's "Van Diemen's Land," p. 142.

principles of the paramount influence of blood and breed, and showed how largely even these two important considerations might be modified by the far more subsidiary ones of soil and climate. In two or three years the sheep were scarcely recognisable: even the general form of the sheep was improved, and the hairy covering was replaced by a comparatively fine woolly fleece. The individual fibres of which the fleece is composed improve in the same way as the general character of the fleece. The uniformity in the length and diameter, and the silkiness and general tendency to curl becomes greater, while the scales on the surface become more numerous. The serrations also become more distinct, and thus the wool is rendered better adapted for textile purposes.

When the Merino was introduced, the third or fourth cross with these earlier sheep produced an animal whose fleece was equal to that of the pure Merino in Europe, and indeed the wool of the pure breed seemed to improve as much as that of the primitive sheep had done.

We have already mentioned the remarkable case of the Angora goats which, when removed from their native district in Asia Minor, where they yield the long lustrous Mohair, to other climates, immediately alter the character of the fleece, so much so that for a considerable length of time it was thought that they could not be cultivated elsewhere; but recent experience has shown that when these creatures are introduced into favourable situations, such as Cape

Colony and the United States, and crossed with native goats, they not only yield an equal quality of fibre but are actually much improved by the care and attention of scientific farming as compared with oriental neglect. In the same way when other sheep are introduced into the Angora district the fibre of the fleece increases in length and lustre: indeed the district conditions seem peculiarly favourable to the growth of long silky hair, for it even extends to the cats, rabbits, and rats of the district, and when removed these also tend to deteriorate.

This alteration of the character of the wool with change of conditions is even more strikingly illustrated in its deterioration when sheep yielding good and fine wool are neglected or permitted to run wild. The general quality of the fleece deteriorates at once, the tendency to produce hair and coarse wool increases, and the general symmetry of the sheep becomes lost and reverts back to the ungainly form of its primitive ancestors.

The same causes which affect the character of the wool in the same sheep when removed to other conditions are also at work in varying the character of the wools on the various sheep which are found scattered over different parts of the earth's surface; and in addition to these we have the variety of race which has probably resulted from the continuous operation of these external forces. These peculiarities will be best considered under our next division, viz.:—

F.—The variation in fibres from different sheep and grown in different countries.

As we have already seen, the wool fibre is liable to great variation and modification in structure, until on the one hand it passes into true hair, and on the other into such unlike structures as the feathers of birds. It is indeed very difficult to find any classification of the sheep which in all its varieties can be based upon any general likeness in the structure of the wool fibre, in the same way that fishes have been classified according to the nature of their scales. We may, however, generally consider them as ranged into three classes.

(1) Those sheep the fibres of whose wool most nearly approach to a true hair, where we have the nature of the epidermal covering scales most horny and attached most firmly to the cortical structure. This class includes all the lustrous varieties of wool, besides Alpaca and Mohair.

(2) Those where, although the epidermal scales are more numerous than in the first class, they are less horny in structure and less adherent to the cortical substance of the fibre—that is to say, in proportion to their length. This class includes most of the middle woolled sheep and half-breds.

(3) Those where the characteristics of a true wool are most highly developed—where we have greatest suppleness of fibre, fineness of texture, and where the epidermal scales are attached to the cortical substance through the smallest part of their length. This class

includes the wools of all the finest classes of sheep, such as the Merino and crosses with it.

Of course, as we shall shortly see, it is quite impossible to draw any distinct line of demarkation between these various classes, as they insensibly shade into each other, and we can only see the real differences when we come to examine the fibres which stand furthest apart in the different classes. I am, however, of opinion that along with the mechanical differences there is also a chemical difference indicated in these variations, and one which we shall afterwards see influences the relation of colouring matters to them.

(1) Amongst the fibres most nearly allied to a true hair we must class Alpaca, and indeed, strange as it may appear to some, Mohair is far more allied to wool than this fibre, although we call it a hair. When examined under the microscope many of the fibres of Alpaca indicate not only an external but an internal likeness to true hairs also, for there is in a large number of the fibres, especially the coloured ones, a distinct central portion composed of large nucleated cells with considerable quantities of coloured pigment. When the external surface of the fibre is examined, like an ordinary hair the scales are scarcely visible, and only reveal themselves by the transverse and anastomosing lines which indicate the edges of the plates. When treated with a caustic alkali, sufficiently strong to remove all the fatty matter from the surface and beneath the free edges of the scales

they are more distinctly seen, and Plate XXV. gives an illustration of a number of these fibres from different districts: A, is Arequipa Alpaca; B, Chala Alpaca; and C, Brown Alpaca. When we examine the nature of the surface of the Alpaca fibre, we notice the very great brilliancy of the surface of the epidermal scales, which, when perfectly clean and viewed with light reflected from the surface, shine almost like polished metal. When carefully compared with the scales on the surface of a true wool, the Alpaca scales are more robust, and dense, and wanting in translucency, having a sort of ivory consistency rather than a glassy appearance. This is of considerable importance to note, because it lies at the root of some of the difficulties which are experienced in the dyeing of Alpaca as compared with the truer wools, and is one of the causes which render it more difficult to fix the colour permanently upon Alpaca. There are of course great varieties in the appearance of fibres even from the same animal, and greater still in different animals; but as a rule we may assume that the structure of the Alpaca fibre as a whole is denser than the truer wool fibres, and offers a greater resistance to the penetration of dyes, more especially those which require the aid of a mordant to fix them.

Nearly allied to the Alpaca fibre are many of the coarser wools which are derived from the mountainous districts of Asia, although these are frequently much more defaced by the prevalence of long coarse and kempy hairs than the Alpaca. We may mention a

Plate XXVI.

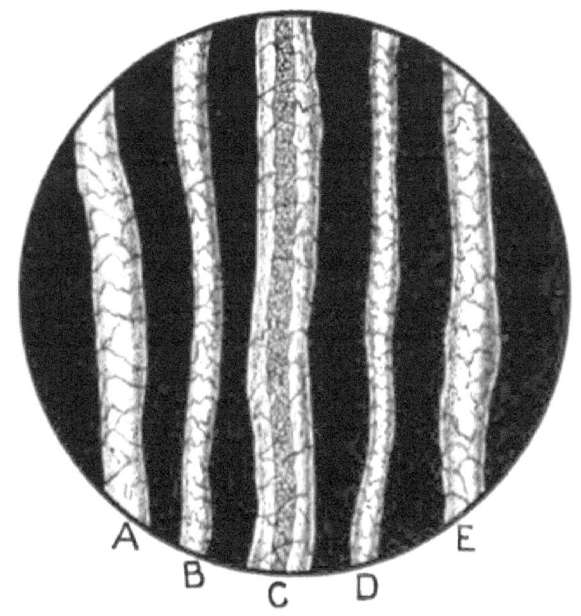

100 DIAMETERS.

FIBRES OF PACPATHIAN WOOL.

A & E. Fibres of Coarse Wool closely resembling Alpaca

B & D. Fine fibres with all the characteristics of true Wool

C. Coarse hair with central core of dark pigment cells.

few of them, although they are very numerous, but these will serve as examples to illustrate what we mean. In the grey Vicaneer and yellow Pacpathian wools we have large horny scales which very closely resemble the Alpaca scales, but they are not quite so regular and not quite so lustrous, though they differ very much in this respect. These wools are, however, always defaced by the coarse hairs which grow along with them, and mixed with a finer undergrowth of a much more true wool. Plate XXVI. gives an illustration of the yellow Pacpathian, where we see fibres of all these different kinds. The fibres A and E will be seen closely to resemble Alpaca in general appearance, and in the structure of the epidermal scales. C is a coarse hair with large rough scales and dark pigment cells, while B and D are fibres which exhibit all the characteristics of fine true wool. The same general features which are found in these wools extend to all the coarser wools of Asia and Northern Europe, but when we pass into the east of Asia we come in contact with another breed of sheep, where we have all the characteristics of true wool exaggerated in large coarse fibres. In this Chinese wool we have the surface covered with a series of plates which possess high lustre, but where the fibre seems to be composed of distinct segments, the various scales being in each instance not distinct but coalesced into separate rings, which fit into each other like cups or crowns, and the serrations being large and distinct. A few fibres of this wool are exhibited in Plate XXVII. At A we have one of the finer fibres where the cup-like structure is distinctly visible, but with serrated scale edges. In B and C we have coarse large-scaled fibres, and in D a coarse fibre exhibiting a finer structure at the upper end. The same general remarks which apply to the ordinary run of the coarser wools in Asia also apply to the Russian and other nomadic wools of Northern Europe. We have amongst them all classes of fibre, varying from hair which cannot be distinguished from the goat's down to a fine short wool. In many districts within recent years very great improvements have been introduced: indeed some of the very finest and purest Merino wools are exported from Russia.

When we come to Mohair we have another distinct step towards true wool. The scales become less numerous than in the Alpaca, but are more decided and show a more definite edge, and we find a much greater variation in the general structure of the surface of the fibre when taken from different parts of the same fleece. The illustrations given in Plate XXVIII. are taken from a pure-bred ram and magnified 300 diameters. The fibres were very fine and wavy, and of a pure, transparent, lustrous white. A and D are fibres taken from the finest part of the fleece, while B and C are from the britch. The length of some of the fibres was nearly twelve inches, and the diameters varied from $\frac{1}{850}$ of an inch to $\frac{1}{1520}$ of an inch. In the coarser fibres the scales are the largest, and seem to be more irregularly disposed on the

Plate XXVII.

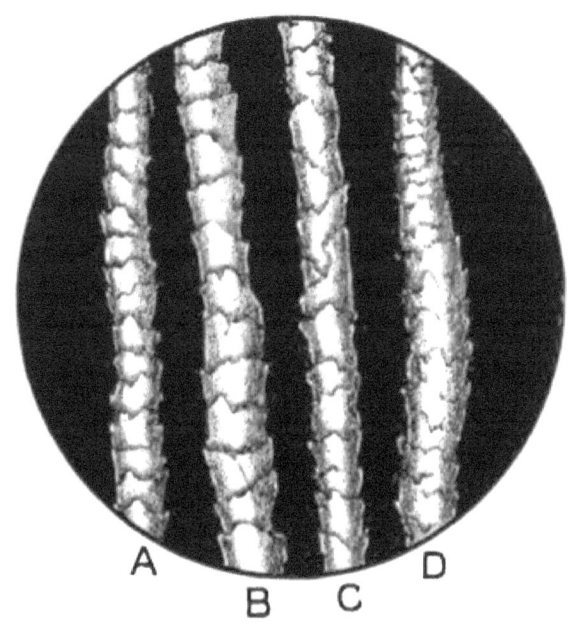

100 DIAMETERS.

FIBRES OF CHINESE WOOL

A. Fibre most closely resembling true Wool.

B & C. Coarse fibres from the flank of the sheep

D. Coarse fibre running into fine at the extremity.

surface, and in the finer fibres the scales and general structure seem to become very closely allied to the longer varieties of deep-grown lustrous wool. These finer fibres may with advantage be compared with those taken from a well-bred Lincoln hog given in Plate XXII., and the general likeness will be easily recognised. In all the deep-grown English wools we have the same general type as given here, the only variation being that as we approach the finer character of staple we distinctly increase the tendency to greater distinctness of the covering scales and greater number of them. Thus in the fine-bred Leicesters we have them generally more numerous than in Lincoln wools, and more so again in the best deep-grown Irish and Northumberland. I have, however, seen in more than one sample of pure-bred Leicester, fibres which could scarcely be distinguished from some of the longer Australian wools, although not so fine in the staple; and this may serve to mark the persistence of the new Leicester type even when crossed with the Merino after a few generations. Closely allied to the Mohair is the fine Cashmere wool of India, which is the produce of a goat which abounds in the mountains of Tibet. The hair is even longer than that of the Angora goat, some specimens reaching even 18 inches in length, but it is not so curly, and indeed in many specimens has hardly any curl whatever. The finest parts of the fleece only are used, of which a single goat does not yield often more than 3 oz., and the produce of ten goats is required for a single shawl not more than 1½ yard square. The surface of the fibres, which are even more like true hair than the Mohair, is not, however, so brilliant in the samples which I have seen, and the scales are rather more numerous, and in many places so thin as almost to be invisible or only revealed by the very faintest surface markings.

A mixed breed produced by crossing the Tibet with the Angora goat has been found to possess the most valuable properties by increasing the best properties of each of the parent stock, and also the abundance of the best fibre, but even in this cross the peculiar goat-like arrangement of the scales is still visible.

When we come to deal with

(2) The middle class of wools, where we have the artificial introduction of fresh blood for the special purpose of modification of the wool, so as to obtain the lustre and length of the deep-grown with the softness and fineness of the Southdowns and other short-woolled sheep, we can see at once the influence of this crossing in the structure of the fibre.

I was particularly struck with this in a sample of Mohair which I examined some time ago, and which was marked "first cross, half-bred wether." This example, which is figured in Plate XXIX., may be compared with the pure Mohair given in the last Plate XXVIII., and the difference will be at once apparent. This difference is specially noticeable in the coarser fibres C and D, where the scales are much more serrated at the edges. A and B closely

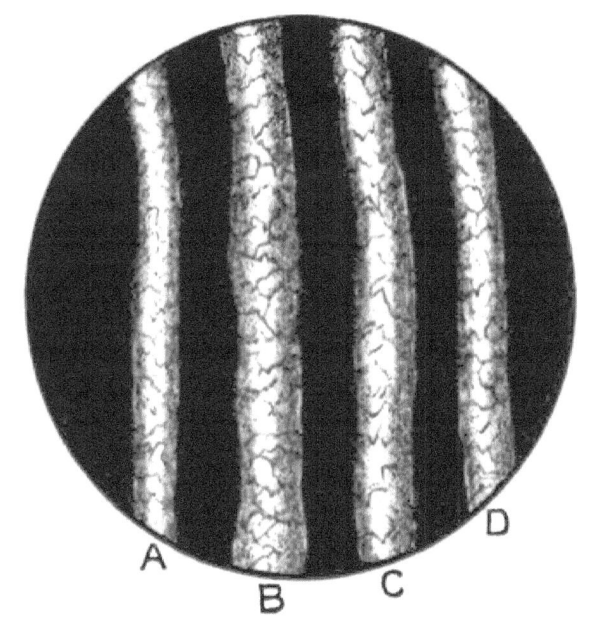

300 DIAMETERS.

FIBRES OF MOHAIR.

A & D. Fibres taken from the finest part of the fleece.

B & C. Coarse fibres with large irregular scales.

resemble wool. I do not know what class of animal the Angora was crossed with, but we see at once the much more close approximation of the fibres to true wool than even in the finest fibres of the pure Mohair. The general length of the fibres was not more than 4 inches, and the average diameter not more than $\frac{1}{1500}$ of an inch, so that I think the cross must have been with some pure, well-bred goat which is not native to America, from whence I received the sample. It is probable that it was a Cashmere goat or some derivation. In the half-bred English wools we have another step towards the perfection of the true wool fibre, and this increases just in proportion as we advance towards the pure Southdown. There is a continual tendency to shorten the length of the wool, but to increase all its most typical qualities by an increase in the tendency to curl, in the number of serrations or scales to the inch, and the looseness with which they are attached to the cortical substance, as well as a decrease in the average diameter of the fibres.

All these properties vary with the degree of pureness in the breed of the sheep, and the degree of care to which they have been subjected. Although the Merinos have ceased to exist as a separate breed in England, the influence which they have exerted on he Southdowns is quite perceptible in the general structure of many of the fibres, which in the finest classes closely resemble the pure Merino.

Plate XXX. may be taken as a fair illustration of pure Southdown wool, where we have the typical characteristics of this class well exhibited. All the fibres, A, B, C, and D, are splendid examples of this famous wool. The scales are transparent and loose with fine serrated edges, and a tendency to run into each other so as in many parts to form a series of ring-shaped scales like the coarser Chinese wool, only of course very much finer. The colour is pearly white, and the fibres quite transparent, so that the internal structure scarcely shows under any illumination. This class of wool approaches very closely to the

(3) Highest type of wool fibre, where we have all the best qualities exhibited. These high-class fibres are all the result of the cultivation of the Merino sheep and its judicious crossing with the new Leicester and other first-class long-woolled breeds, so as to increase the length of the staple and render the wool fit for combing purposes as well as for carding. We need only give two illustrations of these fibres. The first, Plate XXXI., where we have a number of fibres of the finest American Merino, which even exceed in beauty and fineness of fibre the best Saxony or Australian wool. Some of these fibres were not more than $\frac{1}{3000}$ of an inch, and the scales so numerous that they were not further apart than half the distance of the diameter of the fibre, so that these must have been about 6,000 to the inch. The whole structure of the fibre was so beautifully delicate and silvery that it was quite a picture to look at. The fibres A and B are the perfection of wool, and even C and D from the coarser part of the fleece, leave nothing to

Plate XXIX.

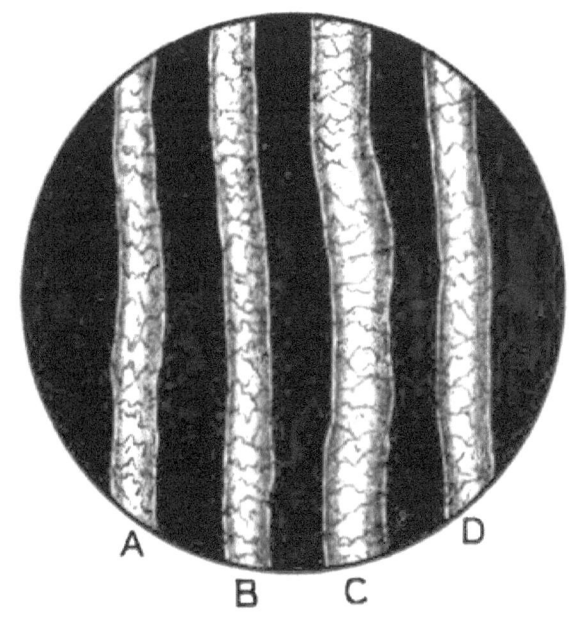

300 DIAMETERS.

FIBRES OF HALF BRED MOHAIR.

A & B. Fine fibres closely resembling true Wool.

C & D. Coarse fibre showing the serrated edges of the scales.

be desired. The length of the fibre was about 2 inches. This was the finest sample of wool I ever saw. Of course when we cross these fine-fibred wools with the long-woolled breed of sheep we increase the lustre of the fibre, because we increase the size of the reflecting surfaces which diminishes the dispersion of the light, but we also increase the diameter of the fibres and their general coarseness. We gain, however, the length of staple which enables these fine wools to be used for worsted spinning, and at the present time such has been the improvement in these wools derived from some of our colonies, that all classes of English bright wools can now be replaced by some of these long-woolled foreign varieties, and even where not replaced the yarns are much improved by an admixture with them.

Plate XXXII. gives a typical illustration of this class of wool—the Leicester Botany. Here we have the curl and softness of the Merino united with the length and lustre of the best deep-grown English wool. The diameter of the fibres is reduced from an average of about $\frac{1}{800}$ of an inch, as in the pure Leicester, to $\frac{1}{1000}$ of an inch, and the number of scales per inch also increased in about a like proportion; while, with the purity of the climate and the care and attention bestowed on the sheep, the fibres become wonderfully uniform, and the lustre bright and silvery, some of the fibres approaching in brightness even the lustre of the Mohair.

Having now shortly looked at the various modifications which are introduced into the wool fibre by variation in the condition of the sheep as far as food, climate, cultivation, and race are concerned, we are now in a position to consider the last part of our inquiry, viz.,—

III.—*How far these variations in the ultimate fibre may affect its use in the manufacturing process.*

G. Mechanically.

H. Chemically.

This, of course, is really the most important part of our subject, and the one which demands our closest attention, because it really involves any practical results which may flow out of our previous investigations. All the changes through which the raw material is passed in the manufacturing process is either mechanical or chemical, or a combination of the two, for though in some cases they cannot be separated they are nevertheless of a different order.

G.—In regard to the mechanical effect of the various differences in the nature of the fibres with which we have to work, I can only repeat what I said in my previous lectures on the "Structure of the Cotton Fibre," that we can only expect to arrive at better results by an intelligent adaptation of all the knowledge which we possess, both in regard to the nature of the material with which we are working and to the use of right methods in the manipulation—that is to say, methods which are founded on a correct *rationale* of the principles involved in the transforming

Plate XXX

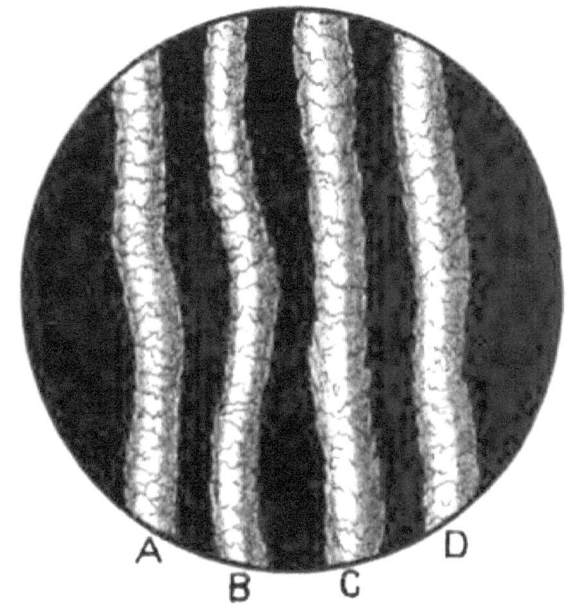

350 DIAMETERS.

SOUTHDOWN WOOL.

A & B. Fibres taken from the Shoulder.

C & D. Fibres taken from the Flanks.

---

process. All our machines and processes are only a means to an end, and the correct method of proceeding is ever to have the *end* in view from the beginning. Strange as this may appear, such is not always the case in our manufactures, and especially in those where the materials pass through many hands in different works before reaching the final stage. How often do we find the farmer, for example, quite careless in regard to the nature of the dips, and washes, and smears which he uses for his sheep, in utter forgetfulness of the fact that although he may gain a temporary advantage he is spoiling the wool for future use in spinning and dyeing. The manager of a very large wool-combing establishment once said to me, "Nothing bothers us more than the ignorance and stupidity of some farmers. If they would let the wool alone, and send it to us as it grows on the sheep, we should have far less difficulties to contend with. The fibre is spoilt before it comes to us." How often in detaching the wool from the skin at the felmonger's, or even in careless sorting and packing, do we find the fibre needlessly injured, not to speak of the after washing and drying of the wool, when temperature is guessed, and soaps and scouring solutions used, with an utter disregard either to the spinning, or manufacturing, or dyeing. How often do we find in the spinning of the yarn an utter want of proper adaptation, either in the machines used for the raw material which is being worked, or, what is quite as bad, in the wrong setting of the various parts of the machine to do the work even when they are capable of it when rightly managed. I know that the exigencies of trade have often compelled manufacturers to endeavour to use their machines for purposes for which they were not strictly designed by· the greater variety and character of yarns which are now required; but I also know that until recently, at any rate, there has been less attention paid in the worsted than in the cotton trade to the exact adaptation of every process, and every machine to the exact raw material which it was designed to work, and the machines themselves were less automatic. This is, however, now passing away, and in consequence of these defects, there have been many failures in the endeavour to produce certain results which are attainable if the right machines and the right use of them are only applied. The future of manufactures seems to me like the future of scientists, to point to *specialists*, and we already see this in the fact that certain individuals and even certain districts obtain a special name, which the necessary adaptation in every respect alone can give, and it will be more so in the future as a continually higher standard of perfection will be required. What shall I say in regard to the neglect of all consideration in the mechanical processes which is often evinced in respect to after chemical processes, such as dyeing and finishing, where unsuitable soaps, unsuitable oils, unsuitable temperatures, both moist and dry, are frequently used in absolute forgetfulness that the delicate fibres are afterwards intended to receive various shades of colour,

Plate XXXI.

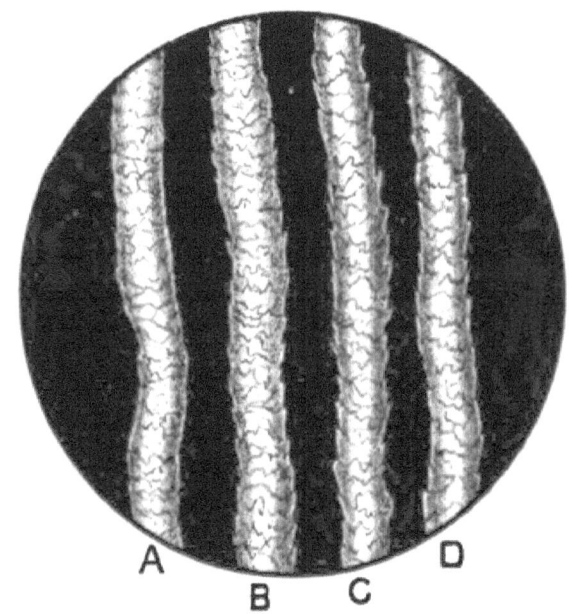

450 DIAMETERS.

MERINO WOOL.
(AMERICAN.)

Showing the delicate Serrated edges of the epidermal scales and their great regularity.

and need all the porosity of the fibre, and all the original surface lustre of the epidermal scales, if they are to give the full effect to the beauty with which they were originally endowed? Then we wonder how it is that certain goods come up wrong, or certain parts of the warp or weft are not alike, or certain shades are fugitive or change their colour, and every one concerned blames every one else in a "vicious circle."

It is beyond the scope of our lectures to deal with the nature of the machinery which is employed in the mechanical processes of manufacture, either in spinning or weaving, and for such information I can only refer you to such a work as the little treatise issued by my friend Mr. W. S. B. McLaren, M.A., on "Spinning Woollen and Worsted," in Cassell's Series of Manuals of Technology; Ashenhurst's "Treatise on Weaving;" or Barlow's "History and Principles of Weaving." Our intention here is to treat of the principles which underlie these processes. The treatment of cotton in the process of manufacture into yarn is much more purely mechanical than that of wool, because the cotton needs no previous process of washing, which is one of the essentials previous to either worsted or woollen spinning, at any rate so far as grey yarns are concerned, and indeed all yarns which are made in the first instance from the fleece; for we know that many kinds of woollen yarn are now made from materials which, to say the least of it, possess only a very small quantity of original wool in them. No process is more important than this preliminary washing, and indeed the more attention which is paid to this part of the manufacture the better will be the results which are obtained.

We have already seen how delicate is the structure of the fibre, and how easily the fine enamelled surface of the epidermal scales can be injured, either by too great heat in the water, or the use of alkaline leys, which remove not only all the suint and free fats which are associated with it, but also attack the fatty constituents of the structural cells, and thus not only tend to render the fibre hard, unpliable, and hask, but also deteriorate the strength and destroy the lustre. The results of our inquiries in regard to these various points, which we have already considered in their proper places, mechanically and chemically, would lead us to the following conclusions in regard to the rules which should guide us in this preliminary cleansing of the wool :—

RULES TO BE FOLLOWED IN WASHING WOOL.

(1) Never permit the temperature of the washing liquor to exceed 100° F.

The practice of turning steam direct into the vessels which contain the wool is most reprehensible, because when the steam, in the act of condensation, comes into contact with the fibres of the wool they may be subjected to a much higher temperature than they can stand without injury, since the mass of wool in the water prevents the free formation of currents, and

350 Diameters.

AUSTRALIAN WOOL.

(BOTANY.)

A & B. Fibres taken from the best part of the fleece.

C & D. Fibres taken from the coarser parts.

thus causes one part of the liquid to be at a much higher temperature than another. My own experiments in regard to this matter have shown that in a bowl of water and wool the temperature of the water in some parts may almost approach the boiling point, 212° F., while in other parts of the same bowl it may not be more than 90° F., or even less. The best way is to have the water heated in a separate tank or cistern, and draw the water into the washing machines from this cistern, where the temperature can be kept comparatively constant.

(2) Nothing but perfectly neutral soaps should be used, at any rate when the wool is in any degree clean, and potash in preference to soda as the base of the soaps.

When the wool is very dirty and the grease hard and stiff, it may sometimes be necessary to use a slightly alkaline soap, and thus remove the adhering grease more rapidly, but the greatest care should be exercised to prevent the surface of the fibre from being injured. The suint, which is the natural grease of the wool, as we have already seen, is composed in the larger part of sudorate of potash, which really assists in the washing of the wool without in any way deteriorating it. The higher lustred fibres, such as alpaca and mohair, are even more sensitive to temperature and free alkali than wool, and hence in washing all fibres when lustre is important, the lowest temperature above 60° F. and the perfect neutrality of the soaps are most important.

(3) The less agitation and mechanical action in the form of squeezing or pressure which can be used the better.

We have already seen that when wool fibres are exposed to the action of hot water they are more liable to felt than when in the dry state, and especially, when the wool is intended for worsted rather than woollen spinning, ought the greatest care to be exercised in the manipulation of the wool so as to cause the least felting action.

(4) The greatest care should be exercised in the drying of the wool, after washing, so as to prevent too high a temperature, which should not exceed 100° F. at the most, but the lower the better.

This is also a most important matter, because if the wool is too much dried it becomes desiccated and loses its natural kindness and suppleness, and tends to become brittle. In addition to this, when unduly dry the wool fibre becomes electrified, and the fibres then are mutually repellant, so that they resist the natural order in which they should be placed by the action of the machinery, and the yarn becomes uneven and rough.

We have already seen that the suint or fatty matter associated with the wool is soluble in disulphide of carbon, and some time ago it was suggested to use this substance as a detergent in place of soap and water, because the temperature need not be high like hot water; but great difficulty was experienced in the practical working of the plan on account of the volatile and explosive nature of this substance when mixed with air. Recently, however, the use of this substance has again been tried, and with some success as regards the kindness with which it treats the fibre; but other difficulties have supervened, and although Messrs. Isaac Holden and Sons, along with the patentees of the process, have spent a considerable sum of money on the experiments, I understand they are not now using it. The uncertainty attending this method is much to be regretted, because so many undoubted advantages are gained, not the least of which is the fact that wool cleansed by the disulphide works with considerably less waste, and can be spun into finer counts than the same wool when washed with soap and water.

When the process of washing is completed, it becomes necessary to determine the special character of the process of spinning which is to be adopted in order to change the fibre into yarn. Wool may be changed either into worsted or woollen yarn according to the processes to which it is subjected. These two different classes of wool threads are essentially different. Formerly it was considered a sufficient definition between the two to say that worsted was made from long wool, and woollen yarn from short wool; or the difference was frequently expressed by saying that worsted yarns were made from combed, and woollen yarns from carded wool. These distinctions were generally true, because formerly nothing but long wools could be spun into worsted, and short wools into woollen yarn, and the usual process was combing for the worsted and carding for the woollen yarns; but neither of these definitions expressed the essential difference between the two which is really determined by the method in which the fibres are arranged in the two threads.

The improvements in machinery, especially in combing, have rendered it possible to comb short wools which at one time could only be carded, and many wools are now treated by carding preparatory to combing, as well as many short wools being spun into worsted. The real difference lies not in the method of preparation, but in the difference of mechanical constraint which is put upon the fibres in the two different classes of yarn. In the worsted thread the fibres are arranged parallel to each other, and the twist which is put into the yarn is simply a general twisting of all the parallel fibres round the central axis of the thread, the longer and shorter fibres being intermixed with each other equally throughout the whole cross-section. In the woollen thread this is not the case: the parallelism of the fibres is purposely prevented, and the method employed in spinning determines that all the longer fibres shall arrange themselves more or less along the central axis of the thread, while the shorter are thrown upon the surface, so that in cross-section the longer fibres occupy the centre and the shorter the circumference. The strength of the two threads, also, in the case of the worsted thread depends more upon the strength derived from the mechanical arrangement of the fibres, and their mutual resistance to longitudinal strain derived from their parallelism and twist; while in the woollen thread it is derived from the matting and entanglement of the fibres one with another, like links in a chain, arising from the interlocking action of the epidermal scales. The characteristic of worsted yarn is therefore great smoothness and hardness of thread, while that of woollen is roughness and fulness, and the greatest perfection of each of these respective yarns is reached just in proportion as these two characteristics are most prominent. Worsted yarn is therefore best adapted to display the best strength and lustre of wool, while woollen yarn best exhibits the softness and pliability. These respective features are easily seen when a worsted and woollen thread are examined with a low magnifying power, such as the ordinary piece-glass used for counting the number of picks in cloth.

In the process of worsted spinning, therefore, the greater the uniformity of the fibres, both in regard to length and diameter, the greater will be the chance of arriving at the best results in the finished yarn; while in the woollen thread the same regularity will not be necessary—indeed, the highest character will be attained where there is a considerable but not too great difference in the dimensions of the separate fibres.

We have already seen that in all wools there are considerable differences in regard to both these dimensions, and it becomes important to see how far these differences affect the regularity and perfection of the spinning, as regards the uniformity of strength, regularity of twist, and evenness of diameter, especially in the worsted yarns, because all these desiderata are less important in the woollen thread.

It will be seen from this how very important it is that the proper class of wool be selected from which to spin the various kinds of yarn which are required in textile manufactures, because upon this suitability of the raw material will depend the success of the results in the manufactured state. Nothing indeed in the whole range of technical knowledge requires greater judgment and experience than the selection and blending of the various wools, and where this preliminary is neglected it is impossible to spin good yarn.

The counts to which wool can be spun depends upon the diameter of the fibres of the wool, because if we get less than a certain number of fibres in a cross-section of the thread, we cannot have either uniformity in the spinning or tenacity in the yarn. The fineness of the wool differs very much in different classes of wool, but the following table, taken from Leroux's "Treatise on the Manufacture of Worsted and Carded Yarns," will give some idea of this relation between fineness and spinning power. In this table I have translated the French numbers into English counts, and the diameters from millimetres into inches :—

COMPARISON OF WOOLS FROM DIFFERENT SOURCES, WITH THEIR DIAMETER AND THE COUNTS INTO WHICH THEY CAN BE SPUN.

Sorting Number.	Silesia.	Saxony.	WOOL FROM Australia.	Champagne.	Spain.	North of France.	Algeria.	Counts.	Diameter of fibres in decimals of an inch.
1	Extra fine.	....	....	....	....	....	....	199·35	From ·0059
2	Superfine.	Extra fine.	....	....	....	....	....	159·48	
3	Fine.	Superfine.	Extra fine.	....	....	....	....	141·76	to
4	Semi-fine.	Fine.	Superfine.	Extra fine.	....	....	....	128·47	
5	Medium.	Semi-fine.	Fine.	Superfine.	Extra fine.	....	....	115·18	·0098
6	Coarse.	Medium.	Semi-fine.	Fine.	Superfine.	....	....	106·32	From ·0098
7	Very coarse.	Coarse.	Medium.	Semi-fine.	Fine.	....	....	93·03	
8	....	Very coarse.	Coarse.	Medium.	Semi-fine.	Extra fine.	....	84·17	to
9	....	....	Very coarse.	Coarse.	Medium.	Superfine.	....	7·531	
10	....	....	....	Very coarse.	Coarse.	Fine.	Extra fine.	62·02	·0177
11	....	....	....	....	Very coarse.	Semi-fine.	Superfine.	48·73	From ·0177
12	....	....	....	....	....	Medium.	Fine.	26·58	
13	....	....	....	....	....	Coarse.	Semi-fine.	22·15	
14	....	....	....	....	....	Very coarse.	Medium.	17·72	to
15	....	....	....	....	....	....	Coarse.	13·29	
16	....	....	....	....	....	....	Very coarse.	8·86	·0295

To determine the degree of regularity in the strength, counts, and twist in yarns, I made a large series of experiments with different classes and counts of worsted yarns, under similar test conditions to those which I have already given in my work on the structure of the cotton fibre, and to these I must now call your attention.

EXPERIMENTS ON WORSTED YARNS.

In making the experiments upon the strength and regularity in counts of cotton yarn, I always operated upon one wrap or lea, which is 120 yards, or $\frac{1}{7}$th part of the hank of 840 yards; and when this lea is reeled upon a reel $1\frac{1}{2}$ yard or 54 inches in diameter, it represents the average strength of 160 threads, or 80 threads on each side of the wrap subjected to tension. The worsted hank is only 560 yards, in place of 840 yards in cotton, and therefore, in order that we may compare the relative strength of worsted and cotton yarns, we must reel the worsted on a 36-inch reel in place of a 54-inch, and then the hank will consist of 7 leas of 80 yards each, in place of 120 yards in the cotton lea, while we have the same number of threads to carry the strain. This is the general method of reeling single worsted yarns, and the worsted table will stand thus :—

WORSTED TABLE.

```
1 yard    =  1 thread
80 yards  =  80 threads  = 1 wrap or lea
560  ,,   = 560   ,,     = 7 wraps or leas = 1 hank
```

WEIGHT AND COUNTS OF YARN.

The counts are determined in worsted in the same way as in cotton yarns—that is to say, that 1 hank of 1's, or 560 yards of 1's, weighs exactly 1 pound avoirdupois or 7,000 grains, and 1 lea of 80 yards therefore weighs exactly 1,000 grains. If, therefore, W represents the weight of the lea in grains, and C the counts of the yarn, we have—

$$C \times W = 1,000$$

$$\text{therefore } \frac{1,000}{C} = W$$

$$\text{and } \frac{1,000}{W} = C$$

In this way we can easily determine the counts of any worsted yarn if we know the weight of 1 lea or 80 yards, or the weight of 80 yards of any yarn if we know the counts. The same table of counts and weight for any number of leas of cotton yarn will serve equally for worsted yarns, if we use the 36-inch wrap reel in place of the 54-inch, because we shall then have only 80 yards in the lea in place of 120 yards. Although the 36-inch reel is the one usually employed it is not universal, as the length sometimes varies from 1 yard up to 12 yards, and the forms of making up, leasing, and tying are endless. The following table, therefore, which appeared in my work on the structure of the cotton fibre, will be useful to worsted spinners, remembering that the length of the lea is 80 yards :—

Table of Weights of Various Counts of Worsted Yarn.

Counts.	Weight of 1 lea = 80 yds. in grains.	Weight of 2 leas = 160 yds. in grains.	Weight of 3 leas = 240 yds. in grains.	Weight of 4 leas = 320 yds. in grains.
1	1,000·000	2,000·000	3,000·000	4,000·000
2	500·000	1,000·000	1,500·000	2,000·000
3	333·333	666·666	1,000·000	1,333·333
4	250·000	500·000	750·000	1,000·000
5	200·000	400·000	600·000	800·000
6	166·666	333·333	499·999	666·666
7	142·857	285·714	428·571	571·428
8	125·000	250·000	375·000	500·000
9	111·111	222·222	333·333	444·444
10	100·000	200·000	300·000	400·000
11	90·909	181·818	272·727	363·636
12	83·333	166·666	250·000	333·333
13	76·923	153·846	230·769	307·692
14	71·428	142·857	214·285	285·714
15	66·666	133·333	199·999	266·666
16	62·500	125·000	187·500	250·000
17	58·823	117·647	176·470	235·294
18	55·555	111·111	166·666	222·222
19	52·631	105·263	157·894	210·526
20	50·000	100·000	150·000	200·000
21	47·619	95·238	142·857	190·476
22	45·454	90·909	136·363	181·818
23	43·478	86·956	130·434	173·913
24	41·666	83·333	124·999	166·666
25	40·000	80·000	120·000	160·000
26	38·461	76·923	115·384	153·846
27	37·037	74·074	111·111	148·148
28	35·714	71·428	107·142	142·857
29	34·482	68·965	103·447	137·931
30	33·333	66·666	99·999	133·333
31	32·258	64·516	96·774	129·032

WEIGHT AND COUNTS OF YARN.

Table of Weights and Counts.—*Continued.*

Counts.	Weight of 1 lea = 80 yds. in grains.	Weight of 2 leas = 160 yds. in grains.	Weight of 3 leas = 240 yds. in grains.	Weight of 4 leas = 320 yds. in grains.
32	31·250	62·500	93·750	125·000
33	30·303	60·606	90·909	121·212
34	29·411	58·823	88·234	117·647
35	28·571	57·142	85·713	114·285
36	27·777	55·555	83·332	111·111
37	27·027	54·054	81·081	108·108
38	26·363	52·727	79·090	105·263
39	25·641	51·282	76·923	102·564
40	25·000	50·000	75·000	100·000
41	24·390	48·780	73·170	97·560
42	23·809	47·619	71·429	95·238
43	23·255	46·511	69·766	93·023
44	22·727	45·454	68·181	90·909
45	22·222	44·444	66·666	88·888
46	21·739	43·478	65·217	86·956
47	21·276	42·553	63·829	85·106
48	20·833	41·666	62·499	83·333
49	20·408	40·816	61·224	81·632
50	20·000	40·000	60·000	80·000
51	19·607	39·215	58·822	78·431
52	19·230	38·461	57·691	76·923
53	18·867	37·735	56·602	75·471
54	18·518	37·037	55·555	74·074
55	18·181	36·363	54·544	72·727
56	17·857	35·714	53·571	71·428
57	17·543	35·087	52·630	70·175
58	17·241	34·482	51·723	68·965
59	16·949	33·898	50·847	67·796
60	16·666	33·333	49·999	66·666
61	16·393	32·786	49·179	65·573
62	16·129	32·258	48·387	64·516
63	15·873	31·746	47·619	63·492
64	15·625	31·250	46·875	62·500

TABLE OF WEIGHTS AND COUNTS.—*Continued*.

Counts	Weight of 1 lea = 80 yds. in grains.	Weight of 2 leas = 160 yds. in grains.	Weight of 3 leas = 240 yds. in grains.	Weight of 4 leas = 320 yds. in grains.
65	15·384	30·769	46·153	61·538
66	15·151	30·303	45·454	60·606
67	14·925	29·850	44·775	59·701
68	14·705	29·411	44·116	58·823
69	14·492	28·985	43·477	57·971
70	14·285	28·571	42·856	57·142
71	14·084	28·169	42·253	56·338
72	13·888	27·777	41·665	55·555
73	13·698	27·397	41·095	54·794
74	13·513	27·027	40·540	54·054
75	13·333	26·666	39·999	53·333
76	13·181	26·363	39·544	52·727
77	12·987	25·974	38·961	51·948
78	12·820	25·641	38·461	51·282
79	12·658	25·316	37·974	50·632
80	12·500	25·000	37·500	50·000
81	12·345	24·691	37·036	49·382
82	12·195	24·390	36·585	48·780
83	12·048	24·096	36·144	48·192
84	11·904	23·809	35·713	47·619
85	11·764	23·529	35·293	47·058
86	11·627	23·255	34·882	46·511
87	11·494	22·988	34·482	45·977
88	11·363	22·727	34·090	45·454
89	11·235	22·471	33·706	44·943
90	11·111	22·222	33·333	44·444
91	10·989	21·978	32·967	43·956
92	10·869	21·739	32·608	43·478
93	10·752	21·505	32·257	43·010
94	10·638	21·276	31·914	42·553
95	10·526	21·052	31·578	42·105
96	10·416	20·833	31·249	41·666
97	10·309	20·618	30·927	41·237

TABLE OF WEIGHTS AND COUNTS.—*Continued.*

Counts.	Weight of 1 lea = 80 yds. in grains.	Weight of 2 leas = 160 yds. in grains.	Weight of 3 leas = 240 yds. in grains.	Weight of 4 leas = 320 yds. in grains.
98	10·204	20·408	30·612	40·816
99	10·101	20·202	30·303	40·404
100	10·000	20·000	30·000	40·000

If this table is required to be used for higher counts than 100's, it is best to double the number of leas, and then double the counts which the weight represents. Thus 8 leas of 120's will weigh 66·666 grains, which corresponds to 60's on this table, and double this number is 120's, which is the counts required. For twofold yarns, 2 leas will correspond to 4 on this table, as, for example, 2 leas of 2/40's will weigh 100 grains, which is the weight of 4 leas of single 40's. In any case it is better to use 8 leas in place of 4 leas when the yarn is above 100's, because the difference in weight between one count and the next is so small that they can only be distinguished by very accurate weighing, whereas by increasing the number of leas we increase the difference, so as to make it more readily appreciable and less liable to be mistaken for any other count.

In making the experiments on worsted yarns I used the same precautions and methods which I so fully described to you in my work on the cotton fibre, and the same class of machines for the work, except that the reel was 36 in place of 54 inches in diameter, and it is not, therefore, necessary for me to repeat them.

The room in which the operations were performed is kept at a uniform temperature by a steam stove, and all the samples of yarn were exposed in the room for twenty-four hours before testing, so as to permit them to acquire as far as possible the same conditions in regard to temperature and moisture, both of which have an effect on the strength of the yarn.

The samples of yarn themselves were selected from various makers, and were fair averages of a large production, and not picked samples, my intention being to arrive at the degree of perfection attainable in the ordinary yarns of commerce; but all the yarns were made by spinners who have a good name in the market for their respective productions.

My experiments extended over a much wider range of counts and samples than are here recorded, but the general results were the same as given by these examples, and I have therefore chosen only those which are generally used in the Bradford trade, and they may be taken as types of all other similar counts of yarn.

In all cases five experiments were made with the same thread, and four threads taken out of each sample promiscuously, and the results in the following tables may therefore, from the care which I took in the experiments, be relied upon as a basis for generalization, and they may also be taken as a fair representation of what may be expected in the degree of perfection to which ordinary good commercial yarns usually attain.

SAMPLE A.
24's Single, 8·5 turns, spun from Leicester Botany Wool.

Number of experiments.	Breaking weight per lea in lbs.	Weight in grains.	Average weight.	Counts.
No. 1	60 48 64 42 60	40·12 41·32 41·48 40·25 41·83	41·000	24·34
No. 2	52 60 40 64 60	41·20 41·00 40·38 42·00 42·12	41·340	24·18
No. 3	44 50 65 60 52	41·30 40·15 40·22 41·00 42·11	40·956	24·41
No. 4	45 61 52 62 54	41·11 42·00 42·00 41·80 40·66	41·514	24·08
	54·75		41·202	24·25

This is a good commercial yarn. The counts are ¼ of a count on the fine side. The greatest variation in strength is in No. 2, from 40 to 64 lbs. = 24 lbs., or 43 per cent. of the average strength. The greatest variation in weight is in No. 3, from 40·15 to 42·11 grains, or 1·96 grains, which is about 5 per cent. of the average weight.

T

SAMPLE B.

30's Single, 9·75 turns, spun from Irish and Leicester Botany Wool.

Number of experiments.	Breaking weight per lea in lbs.	Weight in grains.	Average weight.	Counts.
No. 1	30	34·20		
	42	33·60		
	40	34·12		
	28	34·24		
	25	34·00	34·032	29·38
No. 2	38	34·50		
	36	34·12		
	40	34·20		
	44	34·15		
	26	34·11	34·216	29·22
No. 3	40	33·81		
	28	33·40		
	34	33·75		
	36	34·12		
	40	34·00	33·816	29·57
No. 4	25	33·12		
	29	33·40		
	39	33·62		
	37	33·04		
	27	33·21	33·278	30·05
	34·2		33·835	29·55

This is a good yarn. The counts are rather coarse on the average. The greatest variation in strength is in No. 2, from 26 to 44 lbs. = 18 lbs., or 53 per cent. of the average strength. The greatest variation in weight is in No. 3, from 33·4 to 34·12 grains = ·72 grains, or 2·1 per cent. of the average weight.

SAMPLE C.

36's Single, 12 turns, spun from Irish and Leicester Botany Wool.

Number of experiments.	Breaking weight per lea in lbs.	Weight in grains.	Average weight.	Counts.
No. 1	32	26·55		
	30	27·80		
	28	27·84		
	24	27·13		
	21	27·95	27·454	36·42
No. 2	30	26·83		
	21	27·81		
	28	27·24		
	27	28·13		
	24	28·25	27·652	36·16
No. 3	32	27·50		
	30	27·83		
	22	28·12		
	25	28·12		
	30	27·90	27·894	35·85
No. 4	28	27·40		
	26	27·93		
	30	27·21		
	20	27·60		
	32	27·80	27·588	36·24
	27		27·647	36·16

A good commercial yarn. The counts are slightly on the fine side. The greatest variation in strength is in No. 4, from 20 to 32 lbs. = 12 lbs., or 44 per cent. of the average strength. The greatest variation in weight is in No. 2, from 26·83 to 28·25 grains = 1·42, or 5 per cent. of the average weight.

SAMPLE D.

40's Single, 12·25 turns, spun from Leicester Botany Wool.

Number of experiments.	Breaking weight per lea in lbs.	Weight in grains.	Average weight.	Counts.
No. 1	25 24 20 28 20	24·87 24·88 24·31 24·90 24·25	24·642	40·58
No. 2	26 17 24 25 16	24·60 24·75 24·83 25·12 24·60	24·780	40·35
No. 3	28 25 19 20 21	24·80 25·12 25·00 25·12 24·75	24·958	40·06
No. 4	20 18 15 22 24	24·60 24·50 24·33 25·12 25·25	24·760	40·38
	21·8		24·785	40·34

This is a good yarn. The counts are about ⅓ of a count on the fine side. The greatest variation in strength is in No. 2, from 16 to 26 lbs. = 10 lbs., or 41 per cent. of the average strength. The greatest variation in weight is in No. 4, from 24·33 to 25·25 grains = ·92 grains, or 3 per cent. of the average weight.

SAMPLE E.

40's Single, 16·5 turns, spun from Leicester Botany Wool.

Number of experiments.	Breaking weight per lea in lbs.	Weight in grains.	Average weight.	Counts.
No. 1	27	25·84		
	29	25·67		
	26	25·04		
	22	24·75		
	28	25·26	25·312	39·56
No. 2	26	25·42		
	28	25·13		
	28	25·20		
	24	24·31		
	21	24·84	24·980	40·00
No. 3	25	25·12		
	28	25·31		
	27	25·00		
	22	25·43		
	29	25·12	25·196	39·68
No. 4	26	25·14		
	26	25·31		
	30	24·74		
	21	25·18		
	24	25·04	25·082	39·86
	25·8		25·142	39·77

This is a first-class yarn. The counts are rather coarse. The greatest variation in strength is in No. 4, from 21 to 30 lbs. = 9 lbs., or 35 per cent. of the average strength. The greatest variation in weight is in No. 2, from 24·31 to 25·42 grains = 1·11 grains, or 4·4 per cent. of the average weight.

SAMPLE F.

50's Single, 17·22 turns, spun from Leicester Botany Wool.

Number of experiments.	Breaking weight per lea in lbs.	Weight in grains.	Average weight.	Counts.
No. 1	21	20·13		
	19	20·84		
	20	20·21		
	19	21·01		
	20	21·41	20·720	48·26
No. 2	22	20·01		
	21	20·31		
	18	20·13		
	20	20·34		
	21	20·53	20·264	49·34
No. 3	18	20·31		
	17	19·85		
	24	19·75		
	20	20·12		
	22	20·00	20·006	50·00
No. 4	23	20·10		
	20	20·31		
	18	20·00		
	21	19·75		
	20	19·81	19·994	50·00
	20·2		20·24	49·40

This is a very good yarn. The counts are heavy, rather more than ½ a count. The greatest variation in strength is in No. 3, from 17 to 24 lbs. = 7 lbs., or 34 per cent. of the average strength. The greatest variation in weight is in Nos. 3 and 4, from 19·75 to 20·31 grains = ·56 grains, or 2·7 per cent. of the average weight.

SAMPLE G.

60's Single, 15·37 turns, spun from Botany Merino Wool.

Number of experiments.	Breaking weight per lea in lbs.	Weight in grains.	Average weight.	Counts.
No. 1	16	16·84		
	16	17·24		
	15	16·93		
	17	17·04		
	16	17·00	17·010	58·78
No. 2	16	16·64		
	13	16·51		
	17	16·40		
	14	17·10		
	16	16·64	16·658	60·03
No. 3	14	16·60		
	15	16·31		
	17	16·40		
	17	16·64		
	12	16·25	16·440	60·82
No. 4	16	17·14		
	15	16·84		
	14	16·80		
	17	17·00		
	17	17·14	16·984	58·88
	15·5		16·773	59·63

This is a first-class yarn. The counts are on the coarse side. The greatest variation in strength is in No. 3, from 12 to 17 lbs.= 5 lbs., or 33 per cent. of the average strength. The greatest variation in weight is in No. 1, from 16·84 to 17·24 grains= ·4 grains, or 2·4 per cent. of the average weight.

SAMPLE H.

70's Single, 17·93 turns, spun from Botany Merino Wool.

Number of experiments.	Breaking weight per lea in lbs.	Weight in grains.	Average weight.	Counts.
No. 1	10 11 10 9 10	14·58 15·12 14·93 15·30 14·75	14·936	66·92
No. 2	6 9 11 10 8	13·42 13·85 14·12 14·14 13·80	13·866	72·11
No. 3	12 10 8 11 10	14·21 14·36 13·88 14·41 14·36	14·244	70·20
No. 4	13 12 9 8 13	14·34 14·21 14·00 14·12 15·18	14·370	69·58
	10		14·354	69·71

This is a first-class yarn. The counts are rather coarse. The greatest variation in strength is in No. 2, from 6 to 11 lbs. = 5 lbs., or 50 per cent. of the average strength. The same variation occurs in No. 4, from 8 to 13 lbs. The greatest variation in weight is in No. 4, from 14·00 to 15·18 grains = 1·18 grains, or 8 per cent. of the average weight.

SAMPLE I.

80's Single, 18·71 turns, spun from Botany Merino Wool.

Number of experiments.	Breaking weight per lea in lbs.	Weight in grains.	Average weight.	Counts.
No. 1	8 10 11 9 10	12·84 13·12 13·00 12·50 12·14	12·720	78·61
No. 2	8 9 10 10 9	13·12 13·41 12·82 13·01 13·40	13·152	76·02
No. 3	11 12 9 10 8	12·42 12·63 12·75 12·31 12·21	12·464	80·23
No. 4	10 10 9 10 7	12·33 12·52 12·48 12·56 12·84	12·546	79·70
	9·5		12·720	78·64

This is a first-class yarn. The counts are coarse, and vary considerably between Nos. 2 and 3 = 4·2 counts. The greatest variation in strength is in No. 3, from 8 to 12 lbs. = 4 lbs., or 41 per cent. of the average strength. The greatest variation in weight is in No. 1, from 12·14 to 13·12 grains = ·98 grains, or 7 per cent. of the average weight.

SAMPLE J.

Twofold 30's, 11 turns, spun from Irish and Leicester Botany Wool.

Number of experiments.	Breaking weight per lea in lbs.	Weight in grains.	Average weight.	Counts.
No. 1	140	66·70		
	144	66·82		
	138	66·67		
	142	66·93		
	140	66·82	66·788	14·97
No. 2	146	66·80		
	137	66·71		
	135	66·54		
	140	66·80		
	143	66·20	66·610	15·00
No. 3	144	66·70		
	138	66·50		
	140	66·83		
	136	66·54		
	138	66·31	66·576	15·02
No. 4	140	66·24		
	141	66·36		
	136	66·80		
	142	66·75		
	140	66·51	66·532	15·03
	140		66·626	15·00

This is a good commercial yarn, and the counts are correct. The greatest variation in strength is in No. 2, from 135 to 146 lbs. = 11 lbs., or 8 per cent. of the average strength. The greatest variation in weight is in No. 2, from 66·2 to 66·8 grains = ·6 grains, or ·9 per cent. of the average weight.

SAMPLE K.

Twofold 36's, 13 turns, spun from Irish and Leicester Botany Wool.

Number of experiments.	Breaking weight per lea in lbs.	Weight in grains.	Average weight.	Counts.
No. 1	124	55·94		
	130	55·60		
	122	55·21		
	124	55·62		
	124	55·64	55·602	17·98
No. 2	128	55·80		
	132	55·76		
	125	55·24		
	127	55·40		
	124	55·35	55·510	18·00
No. 3	126	55·40		
	127	55·33		
	130	55·61		
	131	55·70		
	122	55·50	55·508	18·00
No. 4	124	55·50		
	126	55·62		
	124	55·40		
	130	55·43		
	127	55·70	55·530	18·00
	126·3		55·537	17·99

This is a good yarn. The counts are correct. The greatest variation in strength is in No. 2, from 124 to 132 lbs. = 8 lbs., or 6·2 per cent. of the average strength; the same variation occurs in No. 3, from 122 to 130 lbs. The greatest variation in weight is in No. 1, from 55·21 to 55·94 grains = ·73 grains, or 1·3 per cent. of the average weight.

SAMPLE L.

Twofold 40's, 12·25 turns, spun from Leicester Botany Wool.

Number of experiments.	Breaking weight per lea in lbs.	Weight in grains.	Average weight.	Counts.
No. 1	90 100 95 99 100	50·25 50·14 49·73 50·00 49·71	49·966	20·00
No. 2	95 98 100 96 100	50·12 49·80 49·87 50·00 50·14	49·986	20·00
No. 3	99 100 100 94 95	50·23 50·40 49·75 49·66 50·00	50·008	20·00
No. 4	93 95 95 100 88	50·40 49·80 49·60 49·75 50·20	49·950	20·00
	96·6		49·975	20·00

This is a first-class yarn. The counts are correct. The greatest variation in strength is in No. 4, from 88 to 100 lbs.=12 lbs., or 12·5 per cent. of the average strength. The greatest variation in weight is in No. 4, from 49·6 to 50·4 grains=·8 grains, or 1·6 per cent. of the average weight.

SAMPLE M.

Twofold 40's, 12·2 turns, spun from Leicester Botany Wool.

Number of experiments.	Breaking weight per lea in lbs.	Weight in grains.	Average weight.	Counts.
No. 1	93 95 100 92 90	50·14 50·40 49·73 49·50 49·75	49·904	20·00
No. 2	94 95 96 98 95	49·80 49·75 50·12 50·15 49·83	49·930	20·00
No. 3	99 97 99 96 95	50·00 50·14 50·38 49·73 50·10	50·070	20·00
No. 4	99 100 95 95 101	50·30 49·75 49·95 50·13 49·87	50·000	20·00
	96·2		49·976	20·00

This is a first-class yarn. The counts are quite correct. The greatest variation in strength is in No. 1, from 90 to 100 lbs. = 10 lbs., or 10·4 per cent. of the average strength. The greatest variation in weight is in No. 1, from 49·5 to 50·4 grains = ·9 grains, or 1·8 per cent. of the average weight.

SAMPLE N.

Twofold 50's, 15·3 turns, spun from Leicester Botany Wool.

Number of experiments.	Breaking weight per lea in lbs.	Weight in grains.	Average weight.	Counts.
No. 1	65 70 71 64 63	40·12 40·00 39·80 40·12 40·00	40·000	25·00
No. 2	70 66 60 65 68	39·84 39·90 39·75 40·12 40·21	39·964	25·00
No. 3	69 68 70 70 66	40·12 39·81 39·90 40·24 40·00	40·014	25·00
No. 4	65 70 72 74 71	40·21 40·10 40·14 40·30 39·75	40·100	24·94
	67·8		40·019	24·98

A first-class yarn. The counts are correct. The greatest variation in strength is in No. 3, from 60 to 70 lbs. = 10 lbs., or 14·7 per cent. of the average strength. The greatest variation in weight is in No. 4, from 39·75 to 40·3 grains = ·55 grains, or 1·3 per cent. of the average weight.

SAMPLE O.

Twofold 60's, 19·6 turns, spun from Botany Merino Wool.

Number of experiments.	Breaking weight per lea in lbs.	Weight in grains.	Average weight.	Counts.
No. 1	55 58 54 57 52	34·12 33·21 33·75 33·30 33·22	33·520	29·83
No. 2	50 54 52 58 50	33·14 32·86 32·91 32·88 33·20	32·998	30·30
No. 3	48 55 57 50 56	33·20 33·12 33·40 32·84 32·75	33·062	30·24
No. 4	54 58 58 50 49	33·15 32·86 32·94 33·00 32·91	32·972	30·32
	53·75		33·138	30·17

This is a first-class yarn. The counts are almost correct. The greatest variation in strength is in No. 4, from 49 to 58 lbs. = 9 lbs., or 16·6 per cent. of the average strength. The greatest variation in weight is in No. 1, from 33·22 to 34·12 grains = ·9 grains, or 2·7 per cent. of the average weight.

SAMPLE P.

Twofold 70's, 23·3 turns, spun from Botany Merino Wool.

Number of experiments.	Breaking weight per lea in lbs.	Weight in grains.	Average weight.	Counts.
No. 1	44	28·62		
	40	28·32		
	46	28·53		
	38	28·34		
	48	28·51	28·464	35·13
No. 2	40	28·75		
	44	28·55		
	36	28·62		
	45	28·44		
	42	28·38	28·548	35·03
No. 3	37	28·88		
	38	28·62		
	40	28·31		
	44	28·35		
	39	28·44	28·520	35·06
No. 4	42	28·77		
	48	28·82		
	47	28·55		
	39	28·62		
	42	28·50	28·652	34·91
	41·95		28·546	35·03

This is a first-class yarn. The counts are correct. The greatest variation in strength is in No. 1, from 38 to 48 lbs. = 10 lbs., or 23·8 per cent. of the average strength. The greatest variation in weight is in No. 3, from 28·31 to 28·88 grains = ·57 grains, or 2 per cent. of the average weight.

SAMPLE Q.

Twofold 80's, 28·8 turns, spun from Botany Merino Wool.

Number of experiments.	Breaking weight per lea in lbs.	Weight in grains.	Average weight.	Counts.
No. 1	40	25·12		
	38	24·88		
	42	24·90		
	36	25·10		
	40	25·00	25·000	40·00
No. 2	36	25·00		
	38	24·87		
	35	24·82		
	40	25·14		
	41	24·90	24·946	40·08
No. 3	35	25·12		
	40	24·80		
	40	24·95		
	42	24·90		
	36	25·20	24·994	40·00
No. 4	38	24·80		
	40	25·14		
	41	25·25		
	34	24·75		
	35	24·88	24·964	40·05
	38·35		24·976	40·03

This is a first-class yarn. The counts are correct. The greatest variation in strength is in No. 3, from 35 to 42 lbs. = ·7 lbs., or 18 per cent. of the average strength. The greatest variation in weight is in No. 4, from 24·75 to 25·25 grains = ·5 grains, or 2 per cent. of the average weight.

In looking at the general results obtained from these experiments, we are struck with the great variation in the strength of the single yarns, ranging from 33 per cent. in sample G to 53 per cent. in sample B. The average variation in the whole of the samples is 42·1 per cent. The variation in counts is very much less, viz., from 2 per cent. in sample B to 8 per cent. in sample H. When compared with the results of similar counts in single cotton yarns the worsted yarns are very much more variable, since cotton yarn varies in strength only from about 7 to 22 per cent., while the variation in weight is from 2 to 10 per cent., which is very similar to worsted yarn. No doubt the great variation in the strength of the single worsted yarn as compared with cotton arises from the fact that the samples of single cotton yarn tested were all twist yarns and not weft, while the worsted yarns have much less proportionate twist, and so correspond with weft yarns. We may also note that in most of the worsted yarns, except those spun from the finest Botany, there is a much greater variation in the size and elasticity of the component fibres, which causes the various parts of the thread to resist the torsion unequally, and thus force the twist, even when regularly put in by the machine, to adjust itself unequally in the final equilibrium which takes place in the thread.

When we examine the twofold yarns we find less variation in the strength, but still more than we should have expected in twofold yarns. The variation is from 6·2 per cent. in sample K to 23·8 per cent. in sample P. The average variation is 13·8 per cent., and we notice it increases as the counts become finer. The variation in counts is very small, only 1·6 per cent. on the average—varying from less than 1 per cent. in sample J to 2·7 per cent. in sample O. When compared with the average strength of similar twofold cotton yarns the variation in strength is still more marked, but there is not so great a difference as in the single yarns. Twofold cotton yarns vary in strength from about 8 to 19 per cent., and in counts from $1\frac{1}{2}$ per cent. to about 8 per cent.

Undoubtedly the great cause of the irregularity in strength is the unevenness with which the twist is finally distributed in the thread, and this is much greater than any one who has not examined the subject would think possible. Of course, as in the case of single cotton yarns, it is very difficult to test the regularity in twist in single worsted yarns, because, if we take any length to test beyond a few inches which cover the length of the staple, the yarn will not sustain itself until the twist is determined. We can, however, easily see the great variation by a casual examination of the yarn with a small magnifying glass, and then our wonder is not that the yarn is so irregular in strength, but that it is not even more so than our experiments prove.

To determine the regularity in twist in twofold yarns is a comparatively easy matter, and in doing so I used the same machine that I employed in testing the cotton yarns, and the testing was done under similar conditions, 5 inches being taken as the standard in the second column, and 1 inch in the fourth column. I also use the same letters in the twofold samples which denote the same sample when the yarn is tested for strength, so that any further comparisons which may be required may be easily made from the data which the experiments furnish. Thus, sample J in the twofold, tested for twist, is the same yarn as sample J which was tested for strength and regularity of counts in the former tables.

I might have very much extended these tables by giving those founded upon experiments made with other counts and classes of yarn. This would have much extended the work, but I thought that for our present purpose it would be best to confine myself to the range of yarns which are mostly in use in Bradford and the neighbourhood. The experiments which I made, however, extended over a much wider range, and exhibited some very interesting results. I found, for example, that in low slack-twisted carpet yarns the variation from the theoretical twist was on the average not greater than in some of the finer yarns—a result which I had hardly anticipated. I found also that the variation was not so great in slack-twisted as in hard-twisted yarns, because in the slack-twisted yarns the strain put upon the component fibres was less, so that in the final equilibrium the twist is more evenly distributed throughout the length of the thread.

SAMPLE J.

Twofold 30's, 11 turns, spun from Irish and Leicester Botany Wool.

Number of experiments.	Twist taken 5 inches together.	Average twist per inch.	Twist taken inch by inch.	Average twist per inch.
No. 1	40 50 60 52 55	10·28	15 10 9 8 11	10·60
No. 2	56 54 42 58 59	10·76	14 12 10 7 9	10·40
No. 3	48 46 52 54 49	9·96	8 15 10 12 9	10·80
No. 4	58 44 49 56 42	9·96	9 16 11 10 10	11·20
		10·24		10·75

The greatest variation in twist taken 5 inches together occurs in No. 1 thread, from 40 to 60 turns = 20 turns, or nearly 40 per cent. of the average number. The greatest variation when taken inch by inch is in No. 1 thread, from 8 to 15 turns = 7 turns, or 65 per cent. of the average number. The same variation also occurs in No. 2, from 7 to 14 turns; and in No. 4, from 9 to 16 turns.

SAMPLE K.

Twofold 36's, 13 turns, spun from Irish and Leicester Botany Wool.

Number of experiments.	Twist taken 5 inches together.	Average twist per inch.	Twist taken inch by inch.	Average twist per inch.
No. 1	60 68 52 64 60	12·16	13 9 11 18 12	12·60
No. 2	64 68 55 55 60	12·08	11 11 16 15 10	12·60
No. 3	64 64 58 57 48	11·64	10 15 9 14 14	12·40
No. 4	66 61 58 60 55	12·00	10 8 9 13 14	10·80
		11·98		12·1

The greatest variation in twist taken 5 inches together occurs in No. 1 thread, from 52 to 68 turns = 16 turns, or 27 per cent. of the average number. The same variation occurs in No. 3, from 48 to 64 turns = 16 turns. The greatest variation when taken inch by inch occurs in No. 1 thread, from 9 to 18 turns = 9 turns, or 74 per cent. of the average number.

SAMPLE L.

Twofold 40's, 14 turns, spun from Leicester Botany Wool.

Number of experiments.	Twist taken 5 inches together.	Average twist per inch.	Twist taken inch by inch.	Average twist per inch.
No. 1	66		12	
	74		14	
	62		9	
	69		16	
	78	13·96	14	13·00
No. 2	80		11	
	74		10	
	65		18.	
	66		15	
	69	14·16	10	12·80
No. 3	68		8	
	66		15	
	64		12	
	67		12	
	72	13·48	13	12·00
No. 4	69		15	
	74		10	
	78		18	
	68		14	
	66	14·20	13	14·00
		13·95		12·95

The greatest variation in twist when taken 5 inches together occurs in No. 1 thread, from 62 to 78 turns = 16 turns, or 23 per cent. of the average number. The greatest variation when taken inch by inch is in No. 2, from 10 to 18 turns = 8 turns, or 61 per cent. of the average number.

SAMPLE M.

Twofold 40's, 12·2 turns, spun from Leicester Botany Wool.

Number of experiments.	Twist taken 5 inches together.	Average twist per inch.	Twist taken inch by inch	Average twist per inch.
No. 1	60 50 63 55 58	 11·44	11 12 9 14 11	 11·40
No. 2	66 63 52 48 56	 11·40	13 13 10 11 8	 11·00
No. 3	69 55 56 50 58	 11·52	12 7 14 14 10	 11·40
No. 4	70 72 66 54 55	 12·68	13 13 8 13 9	 11·20
		11·76		11·25

The greatest variation in the number of turns taken 5 inches together is in No. 3, from 50 to 69 turns = 19 turns, or 32 per cent. of the average number of turns. The greatest variation when taken inch by inch is in No. 3 thread, from 7 to 14 turns = 7 turns, or 62 per cent. of the average number.

SAMPLE N.

Twofold 50's, 15·3 turns, spun from Leicester Botany Wool.

Number of experiments.	Twist taken 5 inches together.	Average twist per inch.	Twist taken inch by inch.	Average twist per inch.
No. 1	66		14	
	72		16	
	70		12	
	68		18	
	74	14·00	10	14·00
No. 2	77		20	
	75		13	
	60		17	
	78		16	
	74	14·56	12	15·60
No. 3	55		11	
	75		18	
	75		20	
	78		10	
	68	14·04	21	16·00
No. 4	80		13	
	82		16	
	74		15	
	70		11	
	69	15·00	17	14·40
		14·40		15·00

The greatest variation in turns taken 5 inches together is in No. 3 thread, from 55 to 78 turns = 23 turns, or 32 per cent. of the average number. The greatest variation when taken inch by inch occurs in No. 3 thread, from 10 to 21 turns = 11 turns, or 73 per cent. of the average number.

SAMPLE O.

Twofold 60's, 19·6 turns, spun from Botany Merino Wool.

Number of experiments.	Twist taken 5 inches together.	Average twist per inch.	Twist taken inch by inch.	Average twist per inch.
No. 1	75 90 100 98 102	18·60	19 10 17 20 16	16·40
No. 2	80 95 100 100 96	18·84	24 21 13 17 11	17·20
No. 3	102 94 105 88 100	19·56	25 28 18 18 14	20·60
No. 4	104 100 89 88 95	19·04	15 24 28 28 20	23·00
		19·01		19·30

The greatest variation in number of turns when taken 5 inches together is in No. 1 thread, from 75 to 102 turns = 27 turns, or 28 per cent. of the average number. The greatest variation when taken inch by inch is in No. 3, from 14 to 28 turns = 14 turns, or 72 per cent. of the average number.

SAMPLE P.

Twofold 70's, 23·3 turns, spun from Botany Merino Wool.

Number of experiments.	Twist taken 5 inches together.	Average twist per inch.	Twist taken inch by inch.	Average twist per inch.
No. 1	104		20	
	100		24	
	123		14	
	103		20	
	120	22·00	18	19·20
No. 2	125		21	
	100		27	
	114		24	
	118		22	
	128	23·40	13	21·40
No. 3	130		10	
	128		30	
	117		25	
	111		24	
	122	24·32	20	21·80
No. 4	103		13	
	118		25	
	100		26	
	99		28	
	101	20·84	17	21·05
		22·64		21·55

The greatest variation in turns when taken 5 inches together is in No. 2 thread, from 100 to 128 turns = 28 turns, or 25 per cent. of the average number. The greatest variation when taken inch by inch is in No. 3 thread, from 10 to 30 turns = 20 turns, or 95 per cent. of the average.

SAMPLE Q.

Twofold 80's, 28·8 turns, spun from Botany Merino Wool.

Number of experiments.	Twist taken 5 inches together.	Average twist per inch.	Twist taken inch by inch.	Average twist per inch.
No. 1	160		20	
	130		32	
	148		29	
	128		35	
	140	28·24	24	28·00
No. 2	150		25	
	166		22	
	170		29	
	122		33	
	135	29·72	26	27·00
No. 3	158		34	
	166		26	
	162		38	
	130		30	
	124	29·72	25	30·60
No. 4	147		27	
	125		22	
	135		34	
	158		35	
	130	27·80	22	28·00
		28·84		28·40

The greatest variation in twist when taken 5 inches together occurs in No. 2 thread, from 122 to 170 turns = 48 turns, or 33 per cent. of the average number. When taken inch by inch the greatest variation is in No. 1 thread, from 20 to 35 turns = 15 turns, or 53 per cent. of the average number.

In looking at the general results of these experiments we are struck with the great irregularity in twist, even when the tests are made in 5 inches, since they vary from 23 per cent. in sample L to 40 per cent. in sample J, the average variation in all the samples taken together being 30 per cent. of the average twist per inch. This is considerably greater than in cotton yarns, where in similar counts of twofold yarns the average variation is only about $18\frac{1}{2}$ per cent., with an extreme variation of from 11 to 26 per cent. When we come to the tests taken inch by inch in these worsted samples, we find the variation far greater—so great, indeed, as to excite our utmost astonishment, and especially when we recollect that all these yarns are by first-class spinners and high-class yarns. The extreme variation is from 53 per cent. in sample Q to 95 per cent. in sample P, and the average of all the tests gives 69·4 per cent. At the head of each test I have given the number of turns of twist which was aimed at by the spinners, and it will be noticed that in every case except the last the theoretical twist is in excess of the actual, showing the loss from the slip of the band on the wharve of the spindle. In the case of cotton yarns, the average variation in twist, when taken inch by inch, is about 38 per cent., which is only rather more than half that in worsted, and the extreme variation from 23 to 50 per cent. Any irregularity in the single yarn seriously affects the twist in twofold, because the thick place presenting great resistance to torsion throws the twist into the thinner part of the thread, and we may readily learn from this that it requires good single yarn to make good twofold. All my experiments—and those given in the foregoing pages are only samples of a considerably larger number taken both from fly, cap, and ring spinning and doubling—go to convince me that by far the greatest cause of variation, both in strength and twist, arises from the variation in the raw material itself. The greatest care should be exercised in the sorting of the wool if first-class results are to be obtained, so as to secure uniformity in the quality of the fibres to be used, because there is a singular tendency in worsted spinning for the thick fibres to associate with thick ones, and fine ones with fine, and the presence of these in the thread increases the difficulty of regularity in drawing and regularity in the putting in of the twist, or, at any rate, in the capacity of the thread to retain the twist in a regular manner, even if put in by perfect machinery. The law of averages gives wonderful results when taken over a series, but at present I am of opinion that our perfection in spinning is in excess of our perfection in preparing the fibres for spinning, and decidedly in advance of the present state of perfection in the raw material which we have to use. Nothing will more improve our manufacture than improvement in the growth of the wool itself, which will reduce the irregularities in the component fibres, and thus render them better fitted for making a comparatively good yarn. Careless sorting and preparation will render the best spinning in the world of no avail. These remarks apply specially to frame spinning, but also in a lesser degree to mule spinning, where, as we have already seen, the arrangement of the fibres within the thread is different. I am afraid that the present tendency in worsted spinning is in the direction of less careful sorting in the wool; and I would like to express a very strong opinion that this is a step in the wrong direction, as it may easily neutralize many of the improvements which have been introduced into machinery, and without this as a preliminary it is impossible to secure good and uniform yarn, even with the best plant which can be put down.

LECTURE V.

IN our lectures so far we have considered the structure of the wool fibre, both mechanically and chemically, without any direct regard to its relation to colouring matter. We have seen how the wool fibre is built up of a series of cells, which are arranged so as to secure lightness and strength, and enclosed within an epidermal sheath of similarly constituted cells, which are flattened out into more or less horny scales, arranged on the surface of the fibre in such a manner as to allow of the most perfect freedom of flexure in the fibre itself, while they present a series of reflecting surfaces, which in the lustre wools attain an almost metallic brightness. We have also seen that the chemical composition of wool is the same as that of the horny tissues generally, and consists of a series of more or less distinct albumenoid bodies, the whole of which are considered by some chemists to be represented by a definite chemical compound, Keratine, having the formula $C_{42}H_{157}N_5SO_{15}$. We have looked at the great variation which exists in the mechanical structure of fibres, not only taken from different races of sheep and different flocks, but also from different parts of the same sheep, and seen how these mechanical differences in the structure and magnitude of the wool fibre affect its use in the manufacture of yarn and goods. Not only so, but we have also seen the irregularities which these differences have introduced into the different classes of yarn, and we are now in a position to go a step further and inquire how far these differences, when taken along with the chemical composition of the wool, affect its use in the manufacturing process.

II. *Chemically.*

We must remember that there is a distinct difference between the relation which the chemical structure of the fibre bears to its mechanical structure, and that which both these qualities taken together bear to the external chemical treatment to which it may be subjected in the process of manufacture. While the ultimate analyses of different wool fibres seem to indicate that there are variations in the chemical composition which are co-extensive with mechanical variations, they do not indicate the exact position in the structure where these variations occur in the same way that the microscope reveals mechanical differences. Along with the matter which actually forms the structural part of the wool—that is, the various cell walls and their enclosing membranes—there are always

W

a number of cell contents, lubricating oils and fats, and mineral constituents, including endochrome, which, while they are not the wool itself, are so associated with it that they must be considered along with it; and as they vary from time to time, and in different wools, will also vary the reaction which the fibres will have with chemical reagents, whether the latter are dyeing materials or not.

In the manufacture of textile fabrics, we all know that, except in the case of the very coarsest materials, the element of colour and the process of dyeing play a very important part, and no consideration of the technical relations of the wool fibre would be complete without some consideration of that which it bears to the various colouring matters and dyestuffs to which it has to be subjected.

Just as we have not in these lectures in any way attempted to deal with the mechanical processes which are necessary in spinning and weaving the wool fibre, so we shall not trouble ourselves with the actual process of dyeing. We shall look at the effect which is produced when the process is finished, and endeavour to see what has been the actual change which has been produced, and the mechanical as well as the chemical manner in which the colouring matter and fibre are united.

When looking at the relation of the cotton fibre to colouring matter, and indeed to all chemical changes, we saw that cellulose was remarkably inert, so much so that its properties were almost best defined as a series of negative results. With the exception of very strong acids and alkalis its action with chemical reagents is almost *nil*, and when it is necessary to produce permanent colours upon it, or better still within it, this can only be accomplished by a series of secondary reactions in which the cellulose plays so unimportant a chemical part, that many chemists are of opinion that its action is as strictly mechanical as if the cotton fibre was a glass tube. This theory, which was strongly advocated by Mr. W. Crum, F.R.S., regards the colouring matters produced on cotton as simply an entanglement of the colouring matter within the successive envelope walls of the cotton fibre, in which the latter only serves the part of a containing vessel by holding the colouring matter within it. We ventured to differ from this theory, and gave our reasons for doing so, and for believing that while this might be true in regard to some classes of colouring matter it was certainly not so in regard to others. We also pointed out that while we might have to consider pure cellulose as one of the most inert of bodies it was never found in a perfectly pure state in the cottons of commerce, but always associated with oils, oily waxes, and unchanged cell contents, and with more or less mineral constituents in the form of metallic salts, which have an affinity for other chemical reagents and a distinct reaction with them. Recent researches have only confirmed our opinion, while those of Prof. Witz in France, and Messrs. Cross and Bevan[*]

---

[*] "Journal Society of Chemical Industry," No. 4, vol. iii., p. 206.

in this country, have shown how the cellulose molecule may be modified by oxidation and rendered capable of an affinity for various colouring matters which it did not possess before, and which opens up a wide field for future research and important applications.

We have already seen that animal fibres differ entirely from vegetable fibres in their chemical character, and that not only in the former is the molecule very much more complicated, but that it possesses direct affinities for various other bodies, both coloured and colourless. That the more complicated the molecule, the greater would be its range of affinities, we might naturally expect, because it offers, from its greater atomic heterogeneity, more points of attack in the presence of other substances, and so many more links in the atomic chain where attachments may be formed. Even this, however, does not explain the much greater readiness with which animal fibres unite with colouring matter; and there seems to be, from the very mechanical structure of the fibres, a greater adaptability to receive and retain the dyes which render wool better fitted than cotton for the reception of colour, for, after all, the power to reflect colour is dependent upon a mechanical arrangement of the molecular surface of the coloured body. This structure is too minute for us to examine it even with the best microscopical power at our command, but just as the molecular structure determines the nature of the system of rays which can be reflected from it, so the nature of the rays reflected enable us to gain some little insight into the nature of the surface from which they emanated, and whether that surface was uniform in its structure or not.

Strange as it may appear to some of you, there is really no such thing as colour as an attribute of any substance. The sense of colour is entirely derived from the nature of the undulations of the all-pervading luminiferous ether which are returned from the surface of the body to the eye, and it is there alone that the colour sense is manifest. It has merely a subjective existence, and is due to the triple constitution of nerves within the retina. Outside your eye the whole universe is dark, and what produces the sense of colour is only an undulation in the ether, in which the length of the undulating wave determines the specific character of the colours, and the amplitude of the wave the intensity. Undulations in the same ether which give no sensation of light, when falling upon the eye, are thrown off from the surface of the body along with the luminous undulations, and all these are so mingled together that they shade into each other, and some eyes which possess a greater range of sensibility can see the form of bodies which are almost invisible to others. When our eyes fail we have now the discerning power of chemically prepared surfaces, which far exceed in range the nervous surface of our own retina, and the faint impressions which are fixed can be chemically built up till they will throw off undulations discernible by our eyes, so that now we can photograph appearances invisible to our ordinary sense. I have myself taken photographs of objects in total darkness to the eye. The longer and slower undulations—that is to say, slower in the sense of a fewer number occurring in a second of time—give only the impression of a faint dull red, and as they increase in number the colour changes through brighter red to orange, yellow, green, blue, indigo, and finally violet, which in its most attenuated form marks the extreme limit of the sensibility of the eye to the most rapidly undulating waves. While we speak of slow and rapidly undulating waves in the etherial medium, we must remember that these terms are only relative. The slowest wave which will affect the eye undulates 392,000,000,000,000 times in a single second, and this gives the sensation of the faintest red, while the frequency of the extreme violet undulations at the other end of the range of sensibility is 757,000,000,000,000 per second. The mean length of these undulations is only about $\frac{1}{48000}$ of an inch.

Between these limits there is an indefinite variety of integral and fractional numbers, each of which represents the frequency of a particular kind of radiation—a particular kind or colour of light—so that there are as many kinds of colour possible as there are possible kinds of radiation between these limits, and in all sober truth, therefore, we may say the number of actual colours is almost infinite. From physical causes connected with the nature of the atmosphere of the sun and earth, many of these intermediate radiations are extinguished, and hence there are many colours which cannot be seen by daylight, and which are present in the light coming from other incandescent bodies, such as the lime ball oxy-hydrogen, or the electric arc, and hence the peculiar effect produced on the eye when coloured bodies are seen with these lights. If the light under which a body is seen only possesses in it one set of undulating rays, or is a one-coloured light—monochromatic, as it is termed—then all bodies, however varied in colour, when seen in ordinary daylight, cease to have any distinction except being darker or lighter varieties of the same shade. Take a box of coloured silk ribbons, the more varied in colour under ordinary conditions the better, or a set of samples of highly-coloured wall papers, or a dyer's most varied shade card, and illuminate them solely with the light of an alcohol flame in which common salt has been dissolved, and you will see how, though the form of the objects remain, the colour is all gone except a sort of yellowish grey. You cannot tell red from blue, or yellow from green. All colours except black and white seem very similar, and a painting or coloured design looks like an Indian ink sketch on a yellowish paper. Why have I told you this? Simply because I want you to understand that the appearance of colour on all bodies depends upon two circumstances and not one. It depends upon the nature of the surface of the body in regard to its molecular structure being such that when white light, which is really a mixture of all wave lengths, falls upon it, it shall suppress all undulations but those of one definite wave length, and return these alone to the eye. We then have a pure monochromatic colour. But it also depends upon the nature of the light which falls upon the reflecting surface, because if rays of the wave lengths which it is best fitted to return to the eye are absent, or few in number, the colour will be dim and unsatisfactory. Hence we know that many fabrics which when dyed look beautiful in daylight are anything but beautiful in gas light. If we wish to see perfectly pure monochromatic colours we must look at the band of light which is produced by passing the rays from an electric light through a prism. In passing through the prism the rays are bent or refracted, and this refraction sorts the rays out into their wave lengths in a definite order, producing the brilliant coloured band known as the "spectrum." We have already named these primary colours in their order, from the red to the violet, but between each definite colour the eye detects, at any rate in the brightest part of the spectrum, something like transitional colours—half shades intermediate between those which are perfectly definite and distinct. We may class them as follows:—

ANALYSIS OF THE SPECTRUM.

Definite shades.	*Half shades.*
Red.	
	Orange-red.
	Reddish orange.
Orange.	
	Orange-yellow.
	Yellowish orange.

Analysis.—*Continued.*

Definite shades.	*Half shades.*
Yellow.	
	Greenish yellow.
	Yellowish green.
Green.	
	Bluish green.
	Greenish blue.
Blue.	
	Ultramarine.
Indigo.	
	Blue-violet.
Violet.	

If we cut off all except a single part of the spectrum, these half shades become less distinct to the eye, because in the continuous spectrum they are intensified by the proximity of the two distinct colours on each side of them, but they are still visible, and the narrower the part of the spectrum which we observe the more distinctive the colour, which shows us that although intermediate they are monochromatic. We can obtain these intermediate colours in another way. The eye is not a perfect instrument, and indeed if it were more sensitive and discriminating it would serve its ordinary purpose less efficiently, and so we can produce, by the action of a series of independent wave systems upon the retina, effects which, although they differ in the method in which they are produced, are identical in the results so far as the sense of vision is concerned. For example, we can take a piece of greenish-blue glass, and the light transmitted through it will appear to the eye identical with the monochromatic light of the rays which form the half shade between the green and blue, and nearest to the latter; but if we analyse the light through a prism, we find the cause of the sensation is entirely different. The half shade of the same tint was in the spectrum purely monochromatic, and if again sent through a prism would be equally refracted; but the same apparent colour from the coloured glass, when analysed with a prism, is formed into a short and imperfect spectrum, consisting of green, blue, and yellow light, with perhaps several other colours more or less faintly represented, and sometimes with considerable gaps between the colours, showing that they are produced by distinctive wave systems. Many of our best dyed colours are of this character. They appear to the eye monochromatic, but are really not so. The dyed surface is not, therefore, homogeneous, but the molecules are arranged so that they throw off several systems of rays whose total effect has the same result on the sense nerves as if they were monochromatic; and since it is found that many such mixtures may produce the same apparently simple sensation, it shows us that there is a considerable latitude allowed in the molecular structure of our reflecting surfaces without injuring our results. If it were not for this our processes of dyeing would be still more difficult than they are, and far more uncertain.

When pursuing these investigations, I examined the surfaces of a large number of dyed fabrics with a powerful direct-vision spectroscope, and found that a number of colours which appeared almost similar to the eye differed very considerably in the nature of the spectrum which the reflected light yielded. As an example of these, I may instance a range of aniline shades dyed upon camlets, which gave the following results:—

Colour to the Eye.	*Nature of Spectrum.*
1. Light slate colour	More or less continuous spectrum, with bands of red, blue, and green.
2. Dark slate	Similar spectrum, but with extension of green into blue.
3. Bright orange	Short red spectrum, with extension into the yellow and green.
4. Scarlet	Bright continuous red and yellow spectrum, with slight extension into the green.
5. Emerald green	Continuous yellow, green, and blue spectrum about equal.
6. Sage green	Red, yellow, and green spectrum, the yellow being the longest.
7. Light blue	Short spectrum, yellow and green, with short extension into the blue.
8. Dark blue	Short blue spectrum, with extension into the green and yellow.
9. Violet	Short red spectrum, with yellow omitted but extending into green and blue.

In making these observations great care requires to be taken to exclude all light except that which is directly returned from the surface of the fabric, because at many angles with the spectroscope there is a certain amount of white light reflected from the surface of the fabrics, and this masks the true reflection from the dyed fibres, and gives a more or less continuous spectrum, in which all the colours are represented. I found, also, that two colours on similar fabrics which to the eye appeared almost identical gave a different spectrum when examined with the spectroscope. Thus, two pieces of similar cotton, one of which was dyed turkey red and the other an aniline red, but which were not distinguishable by the eye, were quite distinct in the spectrum. The turkey red gave a much shorter and distinct red spectrum, which in the case of the aniline was extended much further into the yellow and green.

I have been particularly struck with the fact that as a rule the aniline colours give a longer and more continuous spectrum than those derived from other sources. Thus, the spectrum reflected from the surface of an aniline blue of the same shade as another cloth dyed with indigo seems to be of a greater length. This may, perhaps, account for the greater brightness and brilliancy of the aniline colours, since the retina of the eye is affected by a wider range of vibrations, and in that respect the action is a nearer approach to that of white light. The difference is the same as between a solo and a chorus in music—the solo corresponding to the monochromatic spectrum, and the chorus to the effect produced by the system of different degrees of refrangibility. Those who are acquainted with recent chemical researches know that the examination of absorption spectra of saline and organic liquids, first by Gladstone, and afterwards by Bunsen and Russell, as well as by Hartley for the ultra-violet and Abney and Festing for the infra-red region, have led to interesting results in regard to molecular chemistry. Hartley found that in some of the aromatic compounds definite absorption bands in the more refrangible region are only produced by substances in which three pairs of carbon atoms are doubly linked, as in the benzene group; while Abney and Festing found that the radical of an organic body is always represented by certain well-marked absorption bands, differing, however, in position according as it is linked with hydrogen, a halogen, or with carbon, oxygen, or nitrogen. Indeed, it is not improbable that by this method of examination the hypothetical position of any hydrogen, which is replaced, may be identified, and this result has been rendered all the more probable by the recent researches of Perkin on the connection between the constitution and optical properties of chemical compounds.

An equally interesting field of observation is opened up by the examination with the spectroscope of the various dyes when in a state of solution, when we have a wonderful series of differences in the absorption bands, a study which some day may throw much light on the character of the molecular structure of the colouring matters themselves. In this case, we examine the rays which are transmitted through the dyes instead of reflected from the surface.

The best method of producing these artificial colours upon different textile materials constitutes the art or science of dyeing, and the most remarkable fact upon which the process of dyeing depends is the degree of facility with which various fibres, and especially those of animal origin, receive and retain the various colouring matters. From what we have seen regarding the nature of light, it follows that all our dyeing processes are simply the production of such a molecular condition on or within the surface of the fibres, that they will return certain luminous wave lengths to the eye and suppress or destroy others, till we have the effect so beautifully described in one of Tennyson's "Idylls of the King," in which the mother of Enid brought

> "A suit of bright apparel, which she laid
> Flat on the couch, and spoke exultingly—
> 'See here, my child, how fresh the colours look,—
> How fast they hold,—like colours of a shell
> That keeps the wear and polish of the wave.'"

Perfect dyeing must have these two attributes: *clearness of colour*, like the colour produced by diffraction from thin transparent films or closely-ruled lines, as in a diffraction grating; and *permanence*, so that the colours will remain fixed under all the conditions to which the fabrics are likely to be exposed in the uses to which they will be put.

The *rationale* or theory why and how this desired reflecting surface is obtained by what we term the fixation of various colours upon fibres or fabrics, is a matter of dispute and doubt even to the greatest authorities on these questions; and there is evidently a different solution to be given to the problems in the case of animal fibres, such as wool or silk, as compared with cotton or any vegetable fibre. There are really three theories which have been put forward.

(1) That the fixation of the colouring matter, however produced, is accomplished by an affinity or attraction between the colouring matter and the fibres in the same manner, but differing in degree from the ordinary chemical combination which occurs between unlike chemical bodies in which colour is produced.

(2) That the fixation of colour does not depend entirely upon any chemical affinity which may pertain between the fibres and the colouring matter, but also upon the mechanical structure of the fibres or fabric, which by absorption within the structure of these, fixes the colour and forms a reflecting surface, the fixity depending on the nature of the colouring matters themselves as well as on the degree of mechanical stability within the structure.

(3) That there is no chemical relation or reaction between the fibres or fabrics and the colouring matter, but that the layers or walls of the fibres simply form so many successive envelopes within which coloured pigments are deposited, and that the colour is entirely dependent upon the nature of these pigments themselves, which form the reflecting surface, and the permanency upon the degree of mechanical shielding which the structure of the fibre or fabric yields to the pigment.

My own opinion is decidedly in favour of the second of these theories, and I would give it the very widest interpretation, so that in its two extremes we may have on the one hand cases where the affinity between the colouring matter and the fibres exercises a most important part both in the production and fixation of the colour, while on the other hand we have a large series of cases where, from the nature of the colouring matter employed, they must exercise far more of the character of simple pigments, in which the affinities of the fibre are subordinated to their mechanical structure.

It must not, of course, be understood that in any case we suppose the reaction between the fibre and that of the colouring matter, even when we speak of their having a chemical affinity, to be of the same order and degree as that between oxygen and potassium. The whole reaction is much feebler, and we have not yet been able to detect any exact and definite proportions in which the combination takes place, and we must therefore remember that until this is proved, we can scarcely say that the dyeing of fibres is in any case a strictly chemical operation, and yet in the case both of wool and silk it is not certainly strictly mechanical. Speaking on this point M. Schützenberger, in his work on dyeing, says: "The cause of the absorption of colouring matter by wool does not reside simply, as might be thought, in the porous structure of the fibre, analogous to that of animal charcoal, for all the nitrogenized substances of the class of albumenoid protein compounds show the same character in a greater or less degree. Coagulated albumen, for example, approaches remarkably near to wool in respect of its powers of dyeing. It has been sought to explain the attraction which silk and wool have for soluble colours by supposing that these substances contain a peculiar organic mordant. Evidently it is the fibre itself which plays the part of a mordant. It combines chemically with the colour, since it causes it to lose one of its characters, its solubility. From this combination a true lake results, differing from the ordinary lakes in so far as the metallic oxide is replaced by an organic substance."* The question of the lakes is a difficult one, because we are by no means yet certain that any of the lakes even which have a metallic oxide for their bases are themselves true chemical compounds, especially the lakes which are of most importance to us, such as those formed with alumina, iron, and tin.

While the whole question is still involved in considerable doubt, so far as actual proof is concerned, there can be no question that in many cases there are instances of undoubted chemical combination, and we must always remember that all the wool fibres, as we have seen when treating in our last lecture on the chemistry of the wool, have always associated with them, as an integral part of their structure, a certain amount of metallic salts in the form of inorganic constituents, and even very small quantities of these diffused through the cell walls may act the part of mordants to the colouring matter, so as to fix and render them insoluble. Those who object to this

---

* "Traité de Matières Colorantes," i., p. 192.

theory, on the ground that these metallic salts are so small in quantity, must remember the exquisite sensibility of many of the colour tests of the various metals, such as iron with potassic ferrocyanide, where the blue colour is produced and visible to the eye, even when the dilution is enormously great. We may therefore expect to find both chemical and mechanical reactions.

This is really the theory of dyeing which was advanced by M. Chevreul, who believes that the matter which colours fibre is fixed in the fibre in three different ways :—

(1) By chemical affinity.
(2) By simple mixture with the fibres.
(3) By being in both states at once.

By the latter statement he means not that the same matter is in both states at once, but that the colour of the fibre is due partly to the union of the fibre with the colour chemically, and partly to a mechanical mixture of the same colouring matter in a state of mechanical mixture with the material forming the fibre cells.

In the case of wool we have a much greater number of substances which seem to have a direct affinity for the fibre than in the case of cotton, because the composition of the wool itself consists of a series of albumenoid bodies, all of which combine very readily with colouring matters, and the power of the fibre to absorb these, especially when properly cleared from all fatty matter, is very great, arising partly from its chemical and partly from its mechanical structure. This is an important matter, because before we can possibly dye any fibre we must have some means of introducing the dyestuff into the interior of the fibre. When speaking on this point in our lectures on the cotton fibre, we pointed out how important a discovery was the power of dialysis which is possessed both by vegetable and animal membranes, and there is no doubt but that these laws play an important part in the absorbent power of the cell walls in the wool fibre, and thus enable us to introduce the various chemical reagents within the fibre walls. Indeed, this appears to be the only solution which can be given, because I have found that perfectly washed wool, when placed in solutions which contain both "crystalloids" and "colloids," will absorb the former in far larger quantities than the latter, and thus renders the process of mordanting, which is usually accomplished by some metallic salt which is a crystalloid, much easier than it would otherwise be.

Of course no materials are suitable for dyes except those which are soluble in either water or spirits. If the coloured bodies are insoluble they may be used as pigments, but not as dyes, because whatever may be the nature of the process by means of which the reagents are introduced into the fibres, it is quite clear that the state of division must be so small that the molecules can pass through the openings in the cell walls, and we cannot conceive of any mere mechanical division, even though this is obtained by chemical precipitation, being small enough to enable this to be accomplished. Such a molecular state would only be available to give a surface colouration by entanglement within the mechanical structure of the fibre, and could therefore be removed by mechanical means alone. The relation of the various dyeing materials to the wool fibre, so far as their union with it as permanent tinctorial agents is concerned, is similar to that of dyeing materials to cotton, except that there is a considerably larger number of these substances available in the case of wool, and that the majority of these belong to a different class from those which are most largely used in cotton dyeing.

These dyeing materials may be looked upon as of three kinds:—

(1) Those which are coloured in themselves, and which we may term simple or substantive dyes, because they appear to have a direct affinity and action upon the fibre, and without the intervention of any other body give a permanent colour to the fibre. Of this class the aniline dyes are a remarkable example.

(2) Those colours which are true chemical precipitates, formed within the fibre walls, in which the action of the fibre seems to be only mechanical, and does not undergo any change in itself. Of this class Prussian blue is the most striking example, and almost the only mineral colour used in dyeing wool.

(3) Those colours where the use of an intermediate agent or mordant is necessary, and the colour is produced not by the simple union of the colour with the

fibre but by the reaction of the various dyes with the mordant which is united with the fibre, and thus fixes the colour. As an example of these we may take the colours produced from logwood with such metallic salts as copperas or bichromate of potash as the mordant. We may term these adjective colours.

In this class we may also include those colours which are sometimes dyed with such colouring matter as extract of madder or camwood, and afterwards developed to the colour required by boiling with the mordant, and also those where the method is employed of dyeing direct with the mordant and colouring matter in one bath. I think, however, that as a rule it is much better to dye with the mordant and colour separate, for we always lose in effect what we gain in time if the other plan is adopted.

In looking at these three classes of reactions with dyestuffs, you will remember that in the case of cotton, as we might expect from its chemically inert character, by far the largest number of our dyeing processes depended upon the reactions included in the third group, and many in the second, while with the exception of such a dye as turmeric yellow very few belonged to the first. The aniline dyes which in relation to wool belong to the first group in their relation to cotton belong to the third, since they cannot be fixed upon cotton until the yarn has first been mordanted with some such substance as tannic acid.

Even in the dyeing of wool, no very definite lines of demarkation exist between these various classes of dyeing material, because they seem to shade into each other by slow gradations; for even those substantive colouring matters which have a direct affinity for the wool fibre, and can therefore be fixed into it without the use of a mordant, are all rendered brighter and faster by the use of one; and hence, especially when permanency is required, even the dyestuffs which come under the first class are practically treated as if they belonged to the third.

We noticed when treating of the dyeing of cotton that the structure of the fibre and its chemical character rendered it particularly suitable for the use of mineral dyes, which are largely used, and from their very nature have a very permanent character, such as Prussian blue, chrome yellow, or manganese brown, etc., which are merely chemical precipitates, differing in no respect from those which we throw down in the glass vessels in our laboratories, entangled within the cell meshes of the fibre; and we pointed out that when it became necessary to produce great permanence and brilliancy of colour, and to use those dyes which were originally obtained from vegetable sources, such as madder reds, formerly used in the production of the famous turkey-red colour, that it became necessary to produce an artificial surface within the cell walls to receive the colour, because it is impossible to dye the cotton fibre with it, so that the cotton fibre became simply a case or envelope to shield the artificially prepared and dyed surface.

One notable exception occurs in the case of indigo,

which is a colour of vegetable origin, and which is more permanent upon cotton than upon wool, but you will remember that I pointed out that a microscopical examination of the indigo-dyed cotton fibres showed that the method in which the colouring matter was united with the fibre showed clearly that in the case of this dye, although of vegetable origin, it deported itself in the same way as the mineral dyes—the union being far more mechanical than chemical, and the colouring matter being thrown down from the colourless indigo by the action of the oxygen, and mechanically entangled in the fibre meshes in the same way as the mineral precipitates.

Wool, on the contrary, has a great affinity for those colouring matters which are derived from the vegetable kingdom, and many of them play by far the largest part in all those dyeing processes where permanence of colour is required.

Wool appears to have a direct affinity, whatever this arises from, for the following colouring matters, and will extract them from their solutions without the use of any mordant, viz., all the aniline dyes, picric acid, indigo extract, cudbear, archil, and to a smaller extent those derived from the red woods such as brazil-wood, etc., and the yellow woods such as fustic.

In all these cases, although the wool will absorb and fix the colouring matter from the solutions it will not do so equally in all parts of the fibre unless the very greatest care has been taken to secure that the wool is thoroughly cleansed from all mechanical and chemical impurities, and indeed it has been forced, times beyond measure, upon my attention while experimenting in the laboratory, how absolutely essential the preparatory processes before dyeing really are, and I believe that the greatest success will always attend those dyers who make the thorough cleansing of the yarn or wool a matter of first importance. Time after time I have seen defects in goods which I believe arose entirely from want of sufficient preparation, so that the dyestuffs, whether requiring a mordant or not, could not either be evenly or permanently fixed, and were either removed or partially discharged in the finishing of the goods. This leads us to call attention once more to the great care in the washing of the wool before spinning, and even before that to the necessity of using only such sheep washes and salves as will not injuriously affect the wool in after chemical processes, because the use of these, and bad soaps, adulterated with all manner of unknown substances, are sure to interfere with the perfect dyeing of the wool, and can often never be entirely removed by the dyer. While speaking on this point I may venture to call your attention to the fact that nearly all wool dyes are applied to the fibre at a high temperature, very frequently at the boiling point, 212° F., and from the nature of the way in which the wool and admitted steam are related in the vat frequently at a higher point than this. In looking at the action of heat upon wool we have already seen how deleterious this is when the lustre of the wool is to be preserved, and how much the sensitive and delicate surface of the epidermal scales are injured by it. The necessity for this seems to arise from the fact that certain of the associated fats are more soluble at a high than a low temperature; that the cell walls being expanded by the heat are rendered more pervious to the colouring matter than when cold, and perhaps most of all by the fact that there is, as every microscopist who has examined fibres knows, a large quantity of air always enclosed within the fibre walls which resists the entrance of any solutions, and until removed prevents the osmotic action of the cell walls, and the heat of the boiling water and the agitation occasioned by it materially assist the disengagement and escape of the air, and thus leave the passage for the entrance of the colouring matter free.

I have found on the small scale in the laboratory that even thoroughly washed wool when placed in a vessel—in a receiver from which the air can be extracted—and then permitted to come in contact with the solution of colouring matter before the air is re-admitted, both absorbs the dyestuff more evenly, and in a shorter time for the same degree of depth of shade, and at a lower temperature than when dyed in an open vessel. This method of dyeing in a vacuum, which permits the more thorough penetration of every part of the constituent cells by the dyeing materials, seems to me to have many important advantages, and has, I believe, been patented and practised on the small scale in Huddersfield. This treatment has the advantage of permeating the fibre with the dyestuff without entangling the fibres, but it presents great difficulties in thoroughly washing the fibre to remove the mordant where a mordant is required, and unless all excess of mordant is removed there can never be the best dyeing results obtained. Dr. Knecht assures me he has seen a good black produced in this manner at a low temperature in ten minutes.

In making an examination of the wool fibres under the microscope dyed with substantive colours, such as the anilines, I have been particularly struck with the same peculiarity in wool which I noticed in cotton with these colours, viz., the very great evenness and diffusion which was manifested in the arrangement of the colouring material. It seems to make little difference what may be the special colour examined, for all the aniline colours seem to penetrate every part of the fibre; and although there are individual fibres which do not seem to absorb an equal amount of colour to the others with which they are associated, if they take any tincture whatever it is evenly diffused when compared with such a colour as indigo.

When examining a number of yarn dyed samples of wool, I found that although the diffusion is wonderfully even on the surface of the fibres it does not always penetrate to the centre of the fibre, and when it does so the depth of shade is not so great as on the surface. I found also that different parts of the same fibre were unequally coloured, but the different parts were not separated from each other by any distinct divisions, but by slow gradations diffusing gradually into the lighter shades. When dyeing the fibres in small samples in the laboratory, I always found that if the wool was thoroughly cleansed and a sufficient length of time allowed to absorb the dye, when the fibres were examined under even the highest powers, the colour was uniformly diffused through every part of the fibres where a cellular structure was distinctly visible, and even where it was not, and the fibres showed indications of kempy structure, the surface of the fibres was sufficiently stained to prevent the difference being noticed when reflected and not transmitted light was used. This seems to me to indicate how important an element time is in the question of dyeing fabrics; and I am quite persuaded that the hurried manner in which goods are now dyed cannot but affect both the nature of the colour and its permanence. There can be no doubt, therefore, but that in the aniline colours we have a class of dyeing materials which are eminently fitted for the dyeing of wool, and that if the process of cleaning the wool and removing any foreign matter from it is thoroughly carried out, the dyeing may be made practically perfect so far as the colour itself will last, but unfortunately, as we know, nearly all these colours are remarkably fugitive, especially when exposed to light and moisture. Within recent years, however, very great improvements have been made in this direction, and some of the aniline yellows, blues, and scarlets are now as permanent as any of the similar shades derived from other sources except those of indigo or cochineal. The very fact that we can produce by them so many shades, and that they are capable of such very easy molecular displacement, renders them equally liable to easy deterioration as reflecting surfaces. When the wool is imperfectly prepared for dyeing even these readily uniting colours will not be absorbed evenly, and indeed when the wool is perfectly prepared the very great affinity of the fibre for the colouring matter becomes a difficulty, because those fibres which are most favourably situated, as when on the outside of the yarn or piece, will take up more than their share from the solution, and thus leave the others with less, and hence in the dyeing of these colours it is best to introduce the colouring matter at several times in those cases where the yarn or goods can be entirely removed from the vat, so as to prevent the acquisition of too deep a shade by those fibres which from various causes are able to absorb it. So great is the affinity of wool for these colours, that when left for a sufficient time in the solution the fibres will remove and fix all the colour, leaving the original solution perfectly uncoloured, and in practice it is usual to introduce sulphate of soda, borax, alum, and various other substances along with the dyestuff so as to modify the action and render it less energetic. The same is the case with indigo extract.

It may not be out of place here to point out the great importance of using pure water for all dyeing purposes, because the impurities in the water, which often are very various, will introduce a series of imperfections into the dyeing of colours which cannot be overlooked when good and perfect work is to be obtained; for while we are not, in the general sense of the term, lecturing upon dyeing, it will be readily seen that with colouring matters which are so readily acted upon as the anilines the presence even of small quantities of the sulphates, chlorides, or carbonates of lime or magnesia, or worse still of iron or the presence of the alkaline carbonates, such as potash or soda, will materially influence not only the shade of the dye but its diffusion and fixation within the fibre.

On no occasion have I ever found the aniline colours to exist in a distinct molecular aggregation within the fibre walls, for whether the tint is dark or light it is always marvellously diffused through the whole cell walls, so that they retain their apparent translucency when subjected to transmitted light.

This remark does not apply to all the substantive colours if we are to include indigo amongst them, because this colouring matter in itself can hardly be said to have a direct affinity for the fibre, since it is not soluble in its coloured condition either in water, alkali, or dilute acids, and hence cannot be introduced into the interior of the fibres, but it can be rendered soluble by the action upon it of nascent hydrogen, two atoms of which unite with two molecules of the coloured indigo, and form a double molecule of a colourless body, which is termed white indigo, and which is soluble in alkaline solutions, such as lime, soda, or potash, and can thus be introduced by diffusion into the interior of the fibres. When fibres which have been impregnated with this colourless indigo are dried out of contact with oxygen they appear to have acquired a yellow tinge, both examined by reflected and transmitted light, and the shade appears to be very uniformly distributed within the fibres, but when the fibres after impregnation with this substance and before drying are permitted to come into contact with oxygen, the double colourless indigo molecule is again broken up by the removal of the two atoms of hydrogen, and the two molecules of coloured indigo are precipitated within the constituent cells of the fibre.

This reaction may be represented by the following equation:—

$$C_{16}H_{12}N_2O_2 + O = 2C_8H_5NO + OH_2$$
$$\text{Colourless indigo.} \quad \text{Oxygen.} \quad \text{Blue indigo.} \quad \text{Water.}$$

In the indigo vat there is always, in consequence of the contact with the air, a quantity of the coloured indigo in a state of mechanical suspension, and always on the surface of the fibres as they are withdrawn from the vat a quantity of the colourless and coloured indigo adhering to the surface of the fibres, and consequently always a large quantity of surface colouration; and when indigo-dyed fibres are examined beneath the microscope, the dark masses of the non-crystalline indigo are seen adhering to all the surfaces of the fibre, and penetrating beneath the overlapping scales which cover them. Even when this surface colouration is removed, the appearance of the dyestuff within the fibre is very different from that of the aniline colours. In some places it seems evenly diffused through the cell walls, but when examined with high powers there is always a grained structure visible, as though the colouring matter itself was not chemically united with the substance of the fibre, but associated along with it in a mechanical form, but so intimately that it is impossible to separate one from the other. The difference between the regular and transparent diffusion of the aniline and indigo is of course much more marked in some fibres than others, and even in the different parts of the same fibre ; but I cannot come to any other conclusion than that we must look upon indigo as more mechanically than chemically associated with the fibre, and it owes its permanence of colour not so much to the chemical stability of its union with the fibre as to its natural fixity of colour as a substance, and thus when enclosed within the fibre walls, by being thrown down as a coloured insoluble precipitate from a colourless solution, it is firmly retained there, and nothing but the destruction of the fibre can destroy it. The union of the indigo with the wool fibre appears, however, to be more intimate than with cotton, notwithstanding which the indigo is more permanent on the cotton ; but this seems to arise from the fact that from the nature of the cotton fibre, which has an internal cavity, except when perfectly ripe, it can retain the coloured indigo in larger masses, and these resist the action of wear and tear better than the smaller molecular aggregations in the more complex wool. I think, therefore, that we must regard the union of indigo with wool in a different light from that of the aniline colours, and consider that it probably stands intermediate between those which require no mordant and those which, like the mineral colours, such as Prussian blue, are only mechanically associated. At the same time I ought to mention that in the case of thoroughly cleansed wool, the same as cotton, I was never able, after once the wool had come in contact with any salt, such as the prussiate of potash, to remove the whole of this salt from the fibre by any means which I employed. This seems to me to indicate that there must be more than a mere mechanical retention within the fibre, for a part of the solubility seems to be lost, and thus the complete removal rendered impossible.

Neglecting the aniline colours, however, the most important class of colouring matters which are used in the dyeing of wool are those which have no direct affinity for the fibre, and therefore require the use of mordants for the purpose of fixing them, while at the same time they exercise no deleterious action upon the colour. When treating of the mordanting of cotton we saw that the mordants in use were very numerous, and consisted of metallic salts and various organic bodies, such as oil or albumen. In the case of wool the latter are never used, and the mordants are exclusively metallic salts, and mostly those of aluminium, chromium, iron, copper, and tin. These salts fulfil all the requirements of good mordants, because they are completely soluble in the water employed as the liquid menstruum, and yield when absorbed within the fibre an insoluble deposit which readily combines with the colouring matter, and which is rendered more brilliant in many cases by their presence, and they are capable of such even distribution through the fibre that they prevent the uneven appearance which always occurs without their use, even when the colouring matter used along with them has an affinity for the wool, by modifying and tempering the action.

The salts of these metals which are used are various, and have mostly been arrived at as the result of practical experience; but as their action has been further investigated, good reasons can now generally be given from a chemical point of view why they should be used. Aluminium is generally used in the form of alum or alum-cake, chromium as the bichromate of potash or soda, iron as the protosulphate or nitrate, and copper as the sulphate. In tin the solutions most in use are the chloride, bichloride, and nitrate.

I need not tell those who are chemists that in looking over this list it will be noticed that most of these salts are of a very unstable character, in which the acid and base are united together by very feeble affinities, so that in the presence of the wool fibre, and especially at a high temperature, they are decomposed and an insoluble deposit is thrown down within the meshes of the fibrous structure, which is generally either a subsalt of the metallic base, as in the case of the iron and tin compounds, or a hydrate, as in the case of the aluminous salts, or a mixture of the two. In the case of the bichromate of potash, which is one of the salts most largely used, the action as a mordant is different to all others because its constitution is different. "The metal which is deposited as a hydrate upon the wool is present in this salt as the acid, and not as the base, which is potash. Bichromate of potash may be represented as being neutral yellow chromate of potash in combination with dry chromic acid, thus:—

$$K_2Cr_2O_7 = K_2CrO_4 + CrO_3$$
Bichromate of potash.   Chromate of potash.   Chromic acid.

To obtain the full effect of the bichromate as a mordant sulphuric acid is usually employed along with it, the whole or major part of the chromic acid is thus set free:—

$$K_2Cr_2O_7 + H_2SO_4 + HO_2 = K_2SO_4 + 2H_2CrO_4$$
Bichromate of potash.   Sulphuric acid.   Water.   Sulphate of potash.   Chromic acid.

Chromic acid is a most powerful oxidiser, and acts energetically upon wool, and should therefore be used with caution. The wool furnishes the reducing agent, probably in the form of hydrogen, which acts upon the chromic acid, thus:—

$$2H_2CrO_4 + 3H_2 = 2OH_2 + Cr_2(HO)_6$$
Chromic acid.   Hydrogen.   Water.   Chromic hydrate.

The chromic hydrate thus produced is deposited upon

the wool as the mordant hydrate. A portion of neutral chromate of potash is also usually present in the fibre."* Mr. Jarmain also adds: "I have ascertained experimentally that it is not safe to use more than 3 per cent. of the weight of the wool of bichromate, for if 4 per cent. be used the colour becomes impaired, and if 12 per cent. be used the wool cannot be dyed at all with logwood, and the curious effects of over-chroming are produced. These effects are due to the oxidising action of the chromic acid upon the wool. When a still larger quantity of bichromate is used along with the sulphuric acid, the wool is dissolved and a solution of chrome alum is obtained."

We have already, in speaking of the dyeing of cotton, noticed the curious reducing action of fibres upon metallic salts, and the same remarks apply also to wool. Whether or not the action is the result of the power of occlusion of a larger quantity of oxygen than is normally present, or the result of a catalictic action between the metallic salt and the fibres, is at present involved in mystery, but it may explain or at any rate may have something to do with the action by means of which some of the mordants are deposited and retained within the fibres, and the investigation of some of these obscure reactions may at some time throw a new light upon some of the operations which at present are very imperfectly understood. In some cases, indeed, in which the mordant is oxidised within the fibre meshes, as when ferrous hydrate is changed

---

* Cantor Lectures on Wool Dyeing. G. Jarmain, F.C.S., etc.

into ferric hydrate by the action of the air, the reducing action of the fibres is sufficiently powerful to prevent or at any rate materially retard an entire change, and as a consequence the ferrous hydrate may be detected in combination with the wool months after the wool has been mordanted.

While we may, however, speculate on what is the cause of the relation between the fibre and the mordant, our chief interest is in the fact itself as modified by the presence of the fibre; and it has often appeared to me that we cannot form any correct judgment in regard to the matter by any study of the reaction between the substances used for mordanting and any decoctions of the dyestuffs, such as is evinced by precipitates obtained by their mixtures, unless we take also into account the modifying action of the presence of the fibre itself.

While, as we have already pointed out, the mordants used in dyeing wool are almost exclusively readily soluble metallic salts, the dyes are almost entirely decoctions of the colouring matters which are extracted from the various kinds of yellow and red woods, such as logwood or brazil-wood, or of some of the colouring matter extracted from lichens, or weeds.

The action of all these colouring matters is somewhat similar so far as their relation to the fibre is concerned, because although they are capable of imparting colour to it, the colour is more or less transient and uneven unless the fibre has been previously mordanted. Of course the colour is varied by the different kinds of mordant and wood used, and since we can obtain red, yellow, and blue, almost any variety of colour can be obtained by varying the proportions of each. As we are not considering the whole subject of dyeing, but only the relation of the fibre to the colouring matter, it may suffice for us to confine ourselves to the examination of the relation of one of these colouring matters alone, which may serve as a type of the rest.

Undoubtedly the most important dyestuff employed in the dyeing of wool is logwood and the colouring matter which is extracted from it. Logwood is principally obtained from Central America and the West Indian Islands, and is the wood of a tree named by Linnæus *Hæmatoxylum Campechianum*. The large logs in which it is imported are ground into chips or raspings, and the colouring matter is extracted by the use of water or spirituous solvents, in the latter of which it is most soluble. The colour of the extract is a fine red, inclining towards violet or purple, and if left exposed to air becoming yellow, and finally black.

Like indigo, the colouring matter of logwood is capable of existing in two forms—hæmatoxylin, which is colourless, and may be represented by the formula $C_{16}H_{14}O_6$; and a coloured body, hæmatëin, which contains two atoms of hydrogen less $C_{16}H_{12}O_6$. By oxidation on exposure to air, the hæmatoxylin is robbed of two of the hydrogen atoms and changed into hæmatëin, and it is this body which is the colouring matter used in dyeing. An almost infinite variety of shades of colour can be produced by logwood alone, but this range is very much extended by combination with other dyestuffs, and by the action of acids and alkalis which produce red and blue or purple colours. When fibres which have been dyed with logwood are examined under the microscope they are usually dyed completely through, especially when well mordanted. If the fibre is broken up, the colour, whatever the shade may be, seems to penetrate into the interior of the constituent cells, so that there is no wonder that it is so largely used not only by itself but also to form a bottom for other colours. I have, however, found that all the fibres in a lock of wool do not seem capable of equally receiving the colour when subjected to exactly the same treatment for the same length of time. In the case of the coarser and more robust fibres, when the external scales are large and few, as generally found on the flanks of the animal, the colouring matter seems to act on the cellular mass within the fibre with greater readiness than the external scales. When the character of the scales is transparent, such as in the case of the bright deep-grown English wools and the mohair wool, this resistance of the external sheath of the fibre to colour is of less importance than when the external scales are more opaque, as in the case of the alpaca fibre, because the coloured light from the deeper layers is transmitted through the outer sheath, and thus the general depth and regularity of the colour is not impaired. When, however, as in alpaca, the scales are more opaque, this resistance of the outer sheath is more important, because the whole structure of the fibre is denser, and as the colouring matter is more topical it is more liable to removal by the application of surface friction or heat, and the goods acquire a shaded or faded appearance, and the less translucency of the scales prevents the transmission of the coloured light from the deeper seated layers. This necessitates a different method of treatment in the dyeing of alpaca from mohair, if the colour is to be made uniform and permanent under the ordinary conditions to which goods are subjected. I have, on more occasions than one, seen cases where the mixture of mohair and bright wool with alpaca has resulted in serious difficulty in regard to the permanence of colour, the alpaca having faded, while the mohair and wool retained its colour.

This structural peculiarity ought always to be taken into account both in the dyeing and finishing of goods, because the colours are less easily fixed, and more easily disturbed, on all those fibres where the epidermal scales are large and dense, than where they are small and transparent. When these two fibres are mixed in the same fabric the treatment must always be in view of the former class.

When fibres of wool which have been dyed with these colouring matters are examined under high powers, it will be found that not only do the separate fibres exhibit great differences in the power which they seem to possess of absorbing the colour, but that the same fibres exhibit considerable differences in their various parts. This, probably, to a certain extent depends upon the nature of the cell contents which are contained within the cells which constitute the fibre. I have seen some of the cells which were almost unaffected by the dye, while those immediately surrounding them have appeared uniformly dyed. When speaking on the nature of "kemps" I pointed out that in some cases this solidity of structure commenced with isolated cells at first, and that these gradually increased until the structure was manifest in the whole thickness of the fibre; and it appears to me that in some fibres at least we have this solidity of structure appearing in isolated cells, and never proceeding beyond them. The better the class of wool the less irregularity there seems to be not only in the mechanical structure of the respective fibres as a whole, but also in that of their component parts, and it cannot be too strongly urged that in all cases where great perfection of dyeing is desired there should be special attention paid to the classification of the wool out of which the goods are made, for the perfection of the whole can only be attained through the perfection of the various parts.

Before passing to the conclusion of our subject it is not inappropriate to refer to the relation of the wool fibre to the finishing process, to which most goods are subjected before being ready for the merchant's counter.

This process, as you all know, varies very much with the class of goods and the nature of the finish which is required, and this difference in requirement necessitates a considerable variation in the mechanical and chemical processes to which the goods are subjected.

As a rule the chief agents employed in finishing are heat, moisture, and pressure, along with a certain and variable amount of stretching or strain, both lateral and longitudinal. Sometimes a milling or fulling process is introduced so as to shrink and mat or felt the fibres, to give increased substance and body to the goods. In addition to this for certain classes of effect it is necessary to crop the surface, so as to remove the superfluous fibre mechanically, or else to singe away this fibre by the passing of the surface over gas flame or heated copper plates.

When speaking of the relation of the wool fibres to longitudinal strains, we might have also considered the action of pressure upon them, but forbore to do so until we had considered the action of heat and chemical reagents, because when subjected to these two influences their behaviour under pressure is modified, and this plays an important part in the finishing process. We have already seen that when a fibre is subjected to the influence of moisture the curl is increased, arising from the unequal expansion of the component cells; but that if subjected to longitudinal strain when in the moist condition, and permitted to dry while thus elongated, the curl is entirely removed, and a permanent set or fixation of the straight fibre occurs, accompanied by a permanent loss in elasticity. In the same way, if the wool fibre is subjected when in the natural condition to lateral pressure, the natural elasticity of the cortical part enables much of the original form of the fibre to be recovered when the pressure is removed. At the same time, if the pressure is long-continued the fibre becomes more or less flattened, so that the section of the fibre changes from a rounded oval to a flattened ellipse. This is always accompanied by an increase in the lustre of the surface of the fibre, because all the component parts are flattened down. Thus, the dispersion of light from the surface is avoided, and the rays are thrown off in sheets as from the surface of glass or polished metal. When fibres are heated, especially along with moisture, the albumenoid cells are softened, and thus rendered non-elastic and plastic, so that they are easily altered in form and flattened by the pressure. If permitted to dry under the pressure the flattening becomes permanent. I examined a number of fibres under the microscope after subjecting to various degrees of pressure between both hot and cold plates, and both when dry and moist. The difference in form was quite apparent. When subjected to cold pressure the time required for alteration in form was very much longer than when hot and moist. In the latter case, the fibres could be changed by sufficient pressure into flattened ribbons, and all traces of the epidermal scales obliterated. This was always accompanied by a considerable increase in the lustre, even when the original lustrous surface of the scales had been impaired by the moisture and heat, before subjecting to pressure—

the heat, moisture, and pressure removing the pitting of the surface, and thus restoring its reflecting power. Upon this action depends the production of lustrous surfaces by the hot-pressing of goods after subjection to moisture, as well as the setting of goods to a certain width and length. It will, however, be easily seen that even in this case, although it is possible partially to restore the lustre of the fibre, it is not possible to do so to the same extent as it can be accomplished when the smooth lustrous surface of the fibres has not been impaired.

I need not point out how absolutely necessary it is to take the greatest care in the cleanliness of all the rollers, plates, and every part of the finishing machinery, because, when the fibres, especially when dyed light and delicate shades, are brought into close contact with the pressing surfaces they are far more easily acted upon than is generally supposed. I have known of many cases where defects in goods have been traced to the effects produced by various reagents which have been left upon the mill boards by the goods for which they had previously been used.

It may seem to some of you who have followed me through the whole of these lectures, that many of the conclusions at which I have arrived were those which might almost have been anticipated beforehand, but you must remember that there is a great difference between surmise and proof. Keplar and Pascal pointed out the high probability that the planets were kept in their orbits and the stability of the universe preserved by the attraction of the different masses of matter for each other, but it was reserved for our own immortal Newton to prove it and demonstrate the universal sway of gravitation. In the same way we may have known for many years, as the result of practice, many of the conclusions to which I have arrived, but I have endeavoured to point out the reasons for these results, and the causes which have led to them, and a wider knowledge of the structure of our raw materials, and the relation of this structure to our mechanical and chemical processes must be of benefit in enabling us to select and modify both to our advantage. As I have already remarked elsewhere, the general principles upon which all our manufacturing processes, which depend upon the transforming power of machinery are based, are now probably fixed for all time. Any advance which we can make will depend far more upon attention and improvement in small details than in a complete revolution of the method of manufacture. We can only be guided in our search after these improvements by a much more thorough knowledge of the exact nature of the materials with which we have to deal than we at present possess, and I shall at least feel that my efforts and time have not been wasted if they have in any measure contributed to this end. We have probably more to learn chemically than mechanically, but this knowledge is more difficult to acquire. It cannot now be obtained by lucky guesses. The surface soil of the chemical field which lies open to the light of heaven has been well surveyed, and yielded rich results; but the knowledge now to be obtained lies beneath, and nothing but a thorough acquaintance with the great laws of chemical and organic structure will enable us to penetrate the great secrets of nature. These lectures have been delivered to the students of a technical college, and while undoubtedly the primary object of these institutions is to fit the students for the pursuit of the various industries which are based on scientific principles, I believe the time will come when the scope of their work will be enlarged. Is it too much to expect that some of the students, at least, will, when the term of their ordinary course is concluded, still retain their connection with the college and occupy themselves with original research, investigating some of those subjects which are at present involved in difficulties, but which are of supreme industrial importance as well as scientific interest?

These colleges are better fitted for this work than the ordinary university laboratories, which have no industrial section attached to them. Here, the instructors are mostly men who have been engaged in the actual work of manufacturing, dyeing, and finishing, and they know the practical as well as scientific difficulties, and can thus guide the student with practical advice and suggestion.

Perhaps the time may come when there may be endowments specially for original research, so that those best fitted for the work may obtain working fellowships, and thus be enabled to engage in some special investigations in regions where at present there is great lack of knowledge. Let no young man imagine that research and reward in this deeper field will be easy, for, like the syntheses of alizarine or indigo, it will only yield itself up to those who have a profound theoretical as well as practical knowledge, and the future of the world of industry will be for those who unite the skilful hand with the well-trained brain. If as a nation we possess these, our future is assured, and I at least cherish the hope that in this district we may be found, as heretofore, in the foremost ranks of the industrial army—with patience and perseverance ever pressing onward to new fields and new triumphs.

GLOSSARY:

OR,

Explanation of some of the terms used in this work.

Abnormal. An irregular growth or occurrence.

Absorption bands. The dark bands observed with the spectroscope when light is passed through any medium which destroys or absorbs a portion of the vibrations.

Albumen. Matter possessing the same properties as the white of an egg.

Albumenoid. Matter similar to albumen, but slightly differing from it in some of its reactions, such as casein and fibrin.

Aldehyde. A class of organic compounds intermediate between alcohols and acids.

Alizarine. The red colouring matter of the madder root; now prepared from coal-tar.

Alkaline-ley. A solution of an alkaline salt.

Alpaca. The hair of the Alpaca goat.

Analysis. The breaking-up of a substance into its simplest constituents, so as to determine their qualitative or quantitative relation.

Anastomosing. Crossing and re-entering at irregular intervals.

Anhydrous. Containing no water or elements of water in combination.

Aniline. One of the substances derived from the fractional distillation of coal-tar.

Archil. A purple colouring matter obtained from certain species of lichens.

Areolo-fibrous. Fibrous tissue with large irregular meshes.

Aromatic. Possessing a pleasant odour.

Bombycidæ. The family of insects of which the silk-worm is the early stage.

Britch. The extremity of the fleece at the tail end of the sheep or goat.

Brokes. Short locks of wool found on the edge of the fleece in the region of the neck and belly.

Callosities. Hard hoofs on the surface of the skin.

Cap spinning. Spinning by means of a steel cap placed mouth downwards over the spindle instead of a flyer.

Carding. The process of drawing the wool through fine wire teeth fixed upon rollers revolving at different speeds.

Case. To separate fleeces of wool into their various qualities.

Cellulose. The chemical substance of which the cell wall in plants is composed.

Chromatic. Relating to coloured light.

Cocoon. The envelope of silk thread in which the silk-worm encloses itself when in the pupa state.

Colloid. A substance which will not crystallize.

Colloidal. Possessing the property of a colloid.

Combing. The process of drawing wool through the teeth of a comb either by hand or machine.

Convex. Curved outward like a bow.

Corium. The lowest layer of which the skin is composed.

Cortical. The cellulo-fibrous part of the hair structure.

Cots. Matted locks of wool forming a hard felt in the fleece.

Cow-tail. The coarsest hair at the tail end of the fleece.

Counts. The number given to any yarn according to the number of hanks in a pound.

Cross. To mix the breed by coupling two sheep possessing different properties.

Crystalloid. A metallic or organic substance which has the power of crystallizing.

Cudbear. A colouring matter obtained from certain species of lichens.

Cuticle. The scarf skin or outermost layer of the skin; also any thin membrane.

Denticulated. Having teeth like a saw.

Dermis or derma. The deeper skin lying beneath the *Rete mucosum*.

Desiderata. Some things specially to be desired.

Dialyser. A membrane which possesses the power of allowing certain substances to pass through it while it rejects other substances in the same solution.

Dialysis. The method of analysis by means of a dialysing membrane.

Diameters. When applied to microscopy signifies the number of times that a linear inch is magnified by the eye-piece and object-glass in use.

Differentiation. The setting apart of separate organs for the performance of specific functions.

Diffraction grating. A set of closely ruled lines for the purpose of decomposing white into coloured light.

Dissociation. The breaking-up of compounds into their constituents.

Drawing. A process which arranges the fibres in parallel lines by passing through rollers running at different speeds.

Electric arc. The space occupied by the light between the poles of an electric light or battery.

Eliminate. To separate from or remove out of anything.

Empyreumatic. A pleasant pungent odorous smell of burning.

Emulsion. A thick solution as of soap in water.

Z

Endochrome. The coloured substance within animal or vegetable cells.

Environment. The surrounding of any creature or thing.

Epidermal. Relating to the outer skin.

Epidermis. The outer layer or skin.

Epithelial. The lining membrane of any cavities within the animal body.

Excrescence. A growth upon the surface of any body.

Eye-piece. The top part of the microscope to which the eye is applied, and which can be removed to increase or decrease the magnifying power.

Ewe. A female sheep or goat.

Fellmonger. One who deals in skin wool, or removes the wool from the hides or skins before tanning.

Felting. Matting or entangling by motion and pressure.

Fenestrated. Having regular lozenge-shaped openings like the woodwork of a veranda or glass in a cathedral window.

Fibrillæ. Small fibres which build up the larger fibrous tissues.

Fibroine. The substance of which silk is composed.

Finishing. The process of setting and giving a proper surface to goods after the manufacture and dyeing are concluded.

Fleece. The pelt or mass of wool removed from the sheep by the process of shearing.

Fly spinning. The process of spinning on to a bobbin by means of a flyer.

Fœtal. Relating to the fœtus.

Fœtus. The young of a mammal before birth.

Follicle. The involuted sac or bag which contains the hair or wool within the skin.

Frame. A machine which carries the rollers and accessories for spinning or doubling by means of a flyer, cap, or ring and traveller.

Fulling. The process of cleansing and shrinking cloth by means of moist heat and pressure.

Fundamental. That which lies at the base of any object or operation.

Fustic. The wood of the *Morus tinctora*, a tree growing in the West Indies, and which yields a yellow dye.

Gelatine. A substance allied to albumen, which forms the basis of animal tissues.

Gossypium. The generic name for the cotton plant.

Graduated. Having regular divisions like the dial of a clock or the surface of a measuring rule.

Half-bred. A cross between two different classes of sheep.

Halogen. A substance which by combination with a metal forms a haloid salt, such as common salt.

Hank. In worsted, 560 yards wound on to a 36in. reel; in cotton and silk, 840 yards on a 54in. reel.

Hask. Dry and hard, or unpliable.

Histology. The science which treats of the structure of organic tissues.

Hog or hogget. A sheep before its first shearing.

Homogeneous. Uniform in structure throughout.

Imbricated. Lying over each other like tiles or slates on a roof.

Incinerated. Burnt to ashes.

Infra-red. Beyond the red portion of the spectrum.

Inspissated. Dried up.

Iridescence. A play of colours like those seen on mother-of-pearl.

Kemps. Fibres of wool possessing no cellular structure.

Lachrymal sinuses. Glands in the corner of the eyes.

Laminated. Built up in layers like leaves of a book.

Lea. The seventh part of a hank; in worsted, 80 yards; in cotton and silk, 120 yards.

Ley. A solution of any substance, but specially used for alkaline solutions.

Linaceæ. The generic name for the class of plant from which linen is derived.

Litmus. A blue pigment derived from various species of lichens which changes to blue on the application of acids.

Lixiviated. Dissolved out in water.

Logwood. The wood of the tree *Hæmatoxylon Campechianum*.

Lorications. Having a scaly structure like the back of a crocodile.

Luminiferous ether. The ether which forms the physical basis or mechanism of light.

Lymphatic vessels. The vessels which convey a colourless fluid called lymph within the animal body.

Madder. The plant from the root of which alizarine was formerly derived.

Malpighii. Named after Malpighus the discoverer.

Malvaceæ. The generic name for the class of plants to which the marsh mallow belongs.

Matching. A quality of wool in the best part of the fleece.

Medulla. The pith or central axis of a stem or fibre.

Merino. A breed of sheep originally confined to Spain.

Meteorological. Changes dependent on the atmosphere, such as rain, snow, or wind.

Micrometer. A machine for measuring minute quantities of linear space.

Microscope. An instrument for magnifying objects.

Middle-woolled. Intermediate between long and short woolled sheep.

Millimetre. The thousandth part of a metre, ·03939 of an inch.

Milling. The process of thickening cloth by beating or pressure.

Modification. Changes produced in an animal or plant by slow degrees.

Mohair. The hair of the Angora goat.

Molecule. The smallest portion of a compound substance in which its properties can inhere.

Monochromatic. Only possessing one colour.

Mordant. A substance used to fix or intensify the colour of a dye.

Mousseline-de-laine. A fine fabric produced from wool.

GLOSSARY.

Mule. A machine in which the spindles are placed upon a carriage which draws out from the rollers when the yarn is spinning and returns to them when the yarn is being wound on to the cop.

Mule spinning. Spinning yarn on a mule in place of a spinning frame.

Nascent. The state of activity of a substance when first set free from combination.

Nitrogenized. United or associated with nitrogen.

Normal. The usual or ordinary condition of anything.

Nucleated. Possessing a nucleus.

Nucleus. The centre from which germination commences.

Object-glass. The small compound lens which first receives the light in a microscope.

Objective. A short name for the object-glass.

Pack. A measure of weight in wool, usually 240lbs.

Papillæ. Small raised paps or protuberances.

Papillary layer. The third layer of which the skin is composed, forming the highest layer of the dermis.

Pellucid. Clear or translucent.

Picric acid. Called also trinitrophenic acid. An organic acid produced by the action of nitric acid on phenol and other organic substances.

Pigment. A coloured paint, as distinguished from a dye.

Polarized light. A ray or rays of light in which all the luminous vibrations are either in one plane or in two planes at right angles to each other. Circular or elliptical polarized light is where the plane or planes of polarization are rotating round the axis of the ray in a circular or elliptical form.

Polygonal. A figure having many sides.

Precipitated. Thrown down in a floculent manner from solution by a chemical reagent.

Prism. A triangular-shaped piece of glass used to analyse light into its constituent colours.

Protein. A nitrogenous compound, formerly supposed to be the base of albumen and other allied bodies.

Protoplasm. The primitive matter which forms the structure of cells, and is the physical basis of life.

Ram. A male sheep.

Rationale. The reason or cause why.

Reagents. Chemical substances used to act upon other substances as tests for their nature.

Reducing agent. Any agent which deprives another of oxygen.

Refrangibility. The degree of bending which any ray undergoes in passing through a prism.

Reflex action. The action caused on one part of the system by a change produced in another part which acts on the nervous system.

Rete mucosum. The second layer of which the skin is composed, lying immediately below the scarf skin.

Retina. The sensitive part at the back of the eye upon which the impression of objects is received.

Ring spinning. Spinning by means of a ring and traveller in place of a fly or a cap.

Rules of thumb. Rules acquired by experience only.

Say cast. The coarsest part of the fleece at the tail end of the sheep.

Serrated. Possessing teeth like a saw.

Sericin. The chemical substance of which silk is composed.

Single yarn. Yarn with only one strand or thread.

Sorter. One who sorts or divides wool into its various qualities.

Sorting. Dividing wool into its various qualities.

Sorting-board. The table on which wool is sorted.

Specialist. One who devotes attention to one subject or branch of knowledge alone.

Spectroscope. An instrument for examining light when passed through a prism.

Spectrum. The coloured band of light produced by passing white light through a prism or reflecting it from a fine ruled surface.

Spinnaret. The gland or opening in the body of a silk-worm through which the silk gum is exuded.

Staple. The lock of wool or hair which is formed by the aggregation of fibres in the fleece.

Stapler. A merchant who buys wool from the farmer and sorts it into its various qualities for the manufacturer.

Sudoriparous. Relating to the glands which exude the sweat or perspiration from the skin.

Suint or yolk. The fatty secretion from the skin of the sheep which is always associated with the wool.

Tannin. An astringent substance found in oak and other barks.

Technology. The science of the application of science or art to manufacturing industry.

Toppings. The dirt and accumulation of clay, etc., found on the skirts of the fleece.

Translucency. Partial transparency, as in the case of horn.

Tubercule. A small tube or duct.

Tumefied. Shrivelled into a carbonaceous mass by the action of heat.

Turmeric. A yellow colouring matter obtained from the root of *Amomum Curcuma*, a plant found in India and Java.

Twiner. A machine for doubling similar to a mule, as distinguished from a frame.

Twist. The turns or revolutions round the axis put into thread.

Twofold yarn. Yarn having two strands or threads.

Ultra-violet. Beyond the violet rays in the spectrum.

Water of hydration. The water which forms an integral part of the structure of a body.

Wether. A sheep after the first shearing.

Woollen. Made of woollen, as distinguished from worsted.

Woolstapler. A wool merchant.

Worsted. Yarn in which the fibres of the wool are laid in a parallel direction before twisting.

Wrap reel. A machine for winding yarn off cops or bobbins or hanks, and measuring the length of the yarn.

Yarn. Fibre when spun into thread.

Yarn tester. A machine for testing the strength of yarn.

Yolk or suint. The fatty secretion from the skin of the sheep which is always associated with the wool.

INDEX.

A

Abney's researches, 317
Acids, action of, 196
Adjective colours, 325
Affinity, retardation of, 332
African sheep, 115
Air, elimination of, 329
Albanian sheep, 109
Albumen, 167
Albumenoids, 165
,, composition of, 166
,, detection of, 167
Alkalis, action of, 137, 191
Alpaca, 124
,, fibres, 245
,, goat, 123
American sheep, 121
Ammotragus tragelaphus, 62
Analysis, ash of wool, 183
,, spectrum, 312
,, of wool, chemical, 170, 177
,, ,, mechanical, 229
Ancient Upland sheep, 79
Angora goat, 125
Aniline black, 200
,, colours, distribution of, 333
,, colours, spectroscopic examination of, 314
Animal cells, composition of, 10
,, kingdom, division of, 59
Aoudad, 62
Argali, 63, 66
,, American, 64, 67
Ash of wool, 182

Ashenhurst, treatise on weaving, 257
Asiatic sheep, 111
Australasian sheep, 119
Australian Merino, 120
Austrian Merino, 98

B

Baker's researches, 134
Bampton Notts sheep, 89
Barlow, history of weaving, 257
Bast fibres, 17
Bed hair, 49
Belgian sheep, 106
Berkshire sheep, 81
Bichromate of potash, 338
Big horn goat, 64, 67
Black-faced heath sheep, 75
Bleaching of wool, 200
Bolley's experiments, 204
Botany sheep, 120
,, wool fibres, 253
Bovidæ, 61
Britch, 219
Brokes, 220
Bunsen's researches, 316
Burgess' researches, 150, 225

C

Camels' hair, 58
Cape sheep, 118
Capridæ, 61
Carbon disulphide, action of, 191
Carbon disulphide process, 260
Casein, 165

362   INDEX.

Cashmere wool, 114, 249
Casing wool, 221
Cellulose, 10
Cheviot sheep, 77
Chevreul's experiments, 202
  ,, theory of dyeing, 322
Chinese sheep, 115
  ,, wool, 247
Chlorine, action of, 199, 200
Cholesterin, 180
Cholesterylamine, 180
Chromic acid, 338
Chunah sheep, 95
Classification of dyeing materials, 324
  ,, sheep, 64
  ,, wools, 244
Cleanliness, necessity for, 347
Cloth, felting of, 156
Colloids, 323
Colour, nature of, 309
Colouring matters, 324
  ,, matter in wool, 187
Co-ordination of processes in manufacture, 6
Corium, 30
Cortical cells, size of, 37
Cots, 155
  ,, cause of, 156
Cotswold sheep, 90
Cotton, botanical relations of, 14
  ,, chemical composition of, 17
  ,, classification of, 16
  ,, fibre, length and diameter of, 16
  ,, kemps in, 16
  ,, manufacture, extent of, 13
  ,, microscopical structure, 15
Counts and quality, relation between, 264
Crum's theory of dyeing, 307
Crystalloids, 323
Cultivation, advantages of, 225
Curls or curves in wool, 56
  ,, relation to diameter, 57
Cuticle or scarf skin, 29

D

Danubian sheep, 108
Dartmoor sheep, 75
Defects in goods, 328
Defective preparation, 7
Denmark sheep, 110
Devonshire sheep, 90
Dialysis, 323
Diameter of wool fibres, 225
Diseased wool, 237

Distinction between fibres from the same sheep, 214
Disulphide of carbon process, 260
Dorset sheep, 80
Double follicles, 221
Drawing, 219
Dry working of wool, 6
Dyed fibres, microscopic examination of, 330
Dyeing, influence of pure water, 332
  ,, influence of time in, 331
  ,, in vacuo, 329
  ,, materials, 324
  ,, of Alpaca, 343
  ,, of Mohair, 343
  ,, theories of, 319, 322
  ,, with logwood, 341
Dyewoods, 325

E

Early processes, importance of, 5
Egyptian sheep, 115
Elairerin, 181
Elasticity of fibres, 146
English Merino sheep, 100
English wools, 71
  ,, analysis of, 237
Epidermal scales, arrangement of, 38
  ,, number & size of, 39
  ,, variation in, 39
Epidermis, 28
European sheep, 70
Exmoor sheep, 75

F

Fat-rumped sheep, 112
Fat-tailed sheep, 112
Felting of wool, 51, 152
Festing's researches, 317
Fibre, typical wool, 52
Fibres, diameter of, 225
  ,, elasticity of, 145
  ,, felting of, 51
  ,, of Alpaca, 244
  ,, of Australian wool, 253
  ,, of Chinese wool, 248
  ,, of cotton, 16
  ,, of diseased wool, 238
  ,, of flax, 20
  ,, of kempy wool, 162
  ,, of Lincoln wool (coarse), 224
  ,, of Lincoln wool (fine), 224
  ,, of Merino wool, 253
  ,, of Mohair, 248
  ,, of Mohair (half-bred), 250
  ,, of Pacpathian wool, 247
  ,, of silk, 22

INDEX.

Fibres of Southdown wool, 251
,, relation to mordants, 340
,, relation to pressure, 345
,, strength of, 145
,, testing machine for, 142
,, variation in diameter of, 227
Fibrine, 165
Fibroïne, 23
Finishing, 345
Flax, botanical relations, 18
,, chemical composition, 20
,, chemical detection of, 21
,, microscopical structure of, 19
,, preparation of, 18
Fœtal hair, growth of, 44
Forest and mountain sheep, 74
French sheep, 101

G
Gases, absorption of by wool, 199
,, condensation of by wool, 199
Gelatine, 10, 168
German sheep, 105
Gladstone's researches, 316
Glands, sudoriparous, 32
Goat, Alpaca, 123
,, Angora, 125
,, Cashmere, 114, 249
,, characteristics of, 61
,, Rocky Mountain, 64, 121
Grecian sheep, 109

H
Hæmatein, 341
Hæmatoxylin, 341
Hair and wool, 127, 130
,, arrangement of, 42
,, component parts of, 35
,, connection with nervous system, 27
,, curl in, 50
,, difference in structure of, 58
,, diseases of, 27
,, early growth of, 48
,, fœtal, 44
,, follicles, 40
,, follicles, structure of, 40
,, growth of, 27
,, hygrometer, 158
,, longitudinal section of, 35
,, modifications of, 49
,, number of cells in, 36
,, papillary, 47
,, rudiments of, 44
,, transverse section of, 35
Half-shades in colours, 312
Hampshire sheep, 81

Hartley's researches, 316
Havrez's experiments, 206
Heat, effect on lustre of wool, 189
Herdwick sheep, 78
Highland sheep, 72
Hogs and wethers, 215
Hooke's researches, 134
Horny tissue, 169
Hot pressing, 346
Hydrochloric acid, action of on wool, 198
Hypochlorous acid, action of on wool, 200

I
Iceland sheep, 109
Impurities in water, 193
Indian sheep, 114
Indigo, distribution of in fibre, 335
,, dyeing, 326
,, reactions of, 334
Injury to lustre in wool, 7
Irish hogs, analysis of, 233
,, sheep, 73
,, wethers, analysis of, 234
Irregularities in yarn, cause of, 302
Italian sheep, 103

J
Jarmain's researches, 339

K
Kangaroo hair, 58
Kemps, 160
,, cause of, 161
,, structure of, 162
,, variation in, 161

L
Lakes, 321
Languinic acid, 195
Lectures, division of, 25
Leicester botany, 258
Leicester hogs, analysis of, 231
,, (half-bred), analysis of, 235
Leicester sheep, 91
Lightfoot's patent, 200
Lincoln hogs, analysis of, 229
,, sheep, 87
,, wool fibre, section of, 132
,, wool fibres, 224
Logwood, 341
Long-woolled sheep, 86

M
Machine for testing strength of fibres, 142

Manufacture, difficulties in, 255
Matching, 218
McLaren, work on spinning, 257
Mercerizing process, 194
Merino, American, 252
,, Australian, 253
,, English, 100
,, fibres, 252
,, German, 105
,, sheep, 94
,, Spanish, 94
Microscopic power employed, 11
Migratory Merino sheep, 96
Mills' researches, 172, 208
Mineral constituents of wool, 182, 321
Mohair, 125
,, fibres, 248
,, half-bred, 250
Moisture in wool, 174
Monochromatic colour, 312
Montenegrian sheep, 109
Mordants, action of, 337
,, nature of, 336
,, necessity for, 336
Moufflon, 63, 68

N

New Oxford sheep, 91
Nitric acid, action of on wool, 198
Norfolk sheep, 79
Northumberland hogs, analysis of, 232
Norway sheep, 110

O

Oil, use of, 6
Original research in technical colleges, 349
Ornithornycus paradoxus, 58
Ovidæ, 62
Ovis ammon, 63
,, aries, 64
,, montana, 64
,, musmon, 63, 68
Oxford sheep, 91

P

Pacpathian wool, 247
Papillary layer, 30
Penistone sheep, 78
Perkin's researches, 317
Persian sheep, 113
Pigment cells, 139
,, granules, 37
Portland sheep, 81
Potassic bichromate, action of, 338
Protein, 165
Protoplasm, 29

Pure water, importance of in dyeing, 332
,, importance of in washing, 193

Q

Qualities of wool, 217
Qualities of wool, relation of, 222
Quality and counts, relation between, 264

R

Rabbits' hair, 58
Relation of qualities, 222
Rete mucosum, 29
Roard's experiments, 205
Rocky Mountain sheep, 67
Romney Marsh sheep, 89
Ruminantia, 59
,, divisions of, 61
Russell's researches, 316
Russian sheep, 106
Ryeland sheep, 85

S

Samples of yarn tested for regularity of twist, 293
Samples of yarn tested for strength and counts, 273
Say cast, 219
Scales, structure of, 138
Scheme of lectures, 8
Schützenberger's researches, 320
Shedding of wool, 128
Sheep, African, 115
,, Albanian, 109
,, ancient upland, 79
,, Asiatic, 111
,, Australasian, 119
,, Australian Merino, 120
,, Austrian, 98
,, Bampton Nott, 89
,, Belgian, 106
,, Berkshire, 81
,, black-faced heath, 75
,, British, 70
,, British, classification of, 71
,, Cape Colony, 118
,, Cheviot, 77
,, Chinese, 115
,, Chunah, 95
,, classification of, 61, 64
,, Cotswold, 90
,, Danubian, 108
,, Dartmoor, 75
,, Denmark, 110
,, Devonshire, 90

INDEX.

Sheep, Dorset, 80
,, early history of, 60
,, Egyptian, 115
,, English, 70
,, English Merino, 100
,, European, 70
,, Exmoor, 75
,, fat-rumped, 112
,, fat-tailed, 112
,, forest and mountain, 74
,, French, 101
,, German, 105
,, Grecian, 109
,, Hampshire, 81
,, Herdwick, 78
,, Highland, 72
,, Hungarian, 108
,, Icelandic, 109
,, Indian, 114
,, industrial classification of, 64
,, Irish, 73
,, Italian, 103
,, Leicester, 91
,, Leicester Botany, 253
,, Lincoln, 87
,, long-woolled breed, 86
,, Merino, 94
,, migratory Merino, 96
,, Montenegrian, 109
,, Norfolk, 79
,, Norway, 110
,, origin of, 60
,, Oxford, 91
,, Penistone, 78
,, Persian, 113
,, Portland, 81
,, Romney Marsh, 89
,, Russian, 106
,, Ryeland, 85
,, Saxon Merino, 98
,, Shropshire, 85
,, Somerset, 80
,, Southam, 90
,, South American, 123
,, Southdown, 82
,, Spanish Merino, 94
,, stationary Merino, 96
,, Swedish, 110
,, Swiss, 103
,, Tees-Water, 89
,, Thibet, 113
,, Tunis, 116
,, Turkish, 109
,, United States, 121
,, Wallachian, 108
,, Warwickshire, 89
,, wash, effects of, 255

Sheep, Welsh, 73
,, wild, 63, 69
,, Wiltshire, 81
Silk, chemical composition of, 23
,, and wool, chemical means of distinguishing, 209
,, origin of, 21
,, structure of, 22
Single yarns, experiments with, 273
Skin, appendages of, 26
,, structure of, 28
Small differences in composition, importance of, 11
Smears for sheep, 178
Soap, action of, 137
Sorting, 216
Southdown fibres, 251
Specialist, 256
Spectrum, 312
,, analysis, 312
Stearerin, 181
Strength of fibres, 146
,, of yarns, 273
Substantive colours, 324
Sudorate of potash, 180
Suint, 155, 178
,, composition of, 179
Sulphur in wool, 185
Sulphuric acid, action of, 197
Sulphurous acid, action of, 201

T

Table of counts and weight, 268
,, of strength and elasticity, 146
,, of wool and counts into which it can be spun, 265
Takamine's experiments, 208
Technical education, 3
Tees-Water sheep, 89
Temperature, influence of, 5
,, in relation to dyeing, 328
Testing houses, 176
Textile materials, 9
,, processes, errors in, 5
Thénard's experiments, 205
Theories of dyeing, 319, 322
Thermometer, use of, 5
Thibet sheep, 113
Time, influence in dyeing, 331
Toppings, 220
Transhumantes, 96
Turkey-red dyeing, 326
Turkish sheep, 109
Twist, variation in, 293
Twofold yarns, experiments on, 282

U

Ultimate structure of wool, 132, 140
United States, sheep of, 121

V

Van Laer's experiments, 198
Variation in counts, 290
,, in different countries, 244
,, in different years, 239
,, in strength of yarn, 290
,, in twist in yarn, 293
,, through environment, 240
Vegetable cells, composition of, 10
Vicaneer wool, 247
Vicugna, 124

W

Wallachian sheep, 108
Warwickshire sheep, 89
Washing of wool, 192
,, ,, rules for, 258
Water of hydration, 174
Weight of various counts, 268
Welsh sheep, 73
Wethers and hogs, 215
Wiltshire sheep, 81
Wool, action of acids on, 196
,, ,, alkalis on, 190
,, ,, chlorine on, 199
,, ,, gases on, 199
,, ,, heat on, 189
,, ,, water on, 158, 190
,, analysis, chemical method, 171
,, and hair, 127, 130
,, and silk, 209
,, ash, 182
,, bleaching of, 200
,, chemical analysis of, 170, 177
,, ,, composition of, 164
,, classification of, 244
,, colouring matter in, 187

Wool, curling of, 56, 149
,, decomposition of, 173
,, diseased, 237
,, early microscopic examination of, 134
,, felting of, 152
,, fibres, epidermal scales on, 136
,, ,, fracture of, 144
,, ,, mineral constituents of, 182, 321
,, ,, reducing action of, 339
,, ,, section of, 132
,, ,, typical structure of, 52, 130
,, general observations on, 24
,, lustre of, 138
,, manufacture of, 13
,, mechanical analysis of, 229
,, milling of, 157
,, moisture in, 174
,, molecule of, 172
,, number of fibres on sheep, 221
,, shedding of, 128
,, sulphur in, 185
,, ultimate structure of, 133, 140
,, variation in different climates, 241
,, variation in different seasons, 239
,, ,, structure, 159
,, washing of, 192, 258
Woollen and worsted, difference between, 262
Working fellowships, 350
Worsted counts, 267
,, table, 266
,, yarns, experiments with, 266

Y

Yolk, 155, 178
Youatt's researches, 134

Palmer and Howe, Printers, 73, 75, & 77, Princess Street, Manchester.

Second Edition, 1 Vol. Demy 8vo., 228 pp., Price 10/0

THE STRUCTURE OF THE COTTON FIBRE
IN RELATION TO THE USE OF COTTON FOR TECHNICAL PURPOSES.
BY DR. F. H. BOWMAN.

Manchester: PALMER & HOWE, Publishers, 73, 75, & 77, Princess-St.

Opinions of the Press.

"A very interesting and elaborate monograph, valuable both from a scientific and an industrial point of view. . . . A most valuable contribution to tinctorial literature."—*Chemical News.*

"The author possesses the unusual advantage of having both a scientific and a practical acquaintance with his subject. We must pronounce the book valuable not merely to the student, but also to the experienced practical man."—*Chemical Review.*

"It is rather singular that Yorkshire, the county most thoroughly identified with wool, should send forth a good scientific essay dealing with the structure of the cotton fibre, the speciality of Lancashire. We are afraid the County Palatine will not be able to return the compliment. Be that as it may, everyone will be quite satisfied to accept a gift from any good source. It is probably owing to the accident that Dr. Bowman, whose many scientific acquirements peculiarly fit him for the task, though a resident of Yorkshire is a cotton spinner of high repute. . . . We cordially advise that all our readers interested in the subject dealt with should procure the work at once, as its perusal will be found highly gratifying."—*Textile Manufacturer.*

"Dr. Bowman is a practical cotton spinner as well as a scientific man. We have probably said enough to show those of our readers who are interested in cotton spinning that the volume is worth their attention. Apart from the learning and labour involved in the production of the work, few readers will fail to be struck with the enthusiasm of thoroughness that possesses the author, whose inculcation of conscientiousness in technical industry is enforced even more by example than by precept."—*Manchester Examiner and Times.*

"In this elaborate monograph Dr. Bowman gives, with additions, the substance of three lectures delivered by him before the Council of the Bradford Technical School. His work is a guarantee that in the matter of technical education nothing is likely to be wanting. . . . A highly meritorious attempt to bring wide scientific and general knowledge to bear upon a trade question of the highest importance."—*Manchester Courier.*

"Dr. Bowman may be congratulated on having produced a work which is likely to be useful, not merely for the technical information which it conveys, but because of its suggestiveness and the intelligent interest in the materials and process of the cotton manufacture which it may awaken."—*Manchester Guardian.*

"Those who are connected with the cotton manufacture, however wide may be their knowledge of the material in which they are working, will no doubt learn something from the teachings of Dr. Bowman, who goes over a wide field, and who works with the idea of stimulating those who are young and energetic, and who have life before them, to give their attention to the first principles of the processes in which they are engaged, so as to find out the best means of giving perfection to the most minute parts of the raw material."—*Glasgow Herald.*

"Undoubtedly the very best yarns which can be produced are a long way from anything like perfection, and our cotton manufacturers have been too much inclined to neglect the scientific side of their business. Dr. Bowman's work, which by the way is illustrated with some really excellent diagrams, will serve a useful purpose if it has the effect of drawing their attention to this fact."—*British Trade Journal.*

"The book is a valuable contribution to the literature of cotton, and no spinner can read it without profit and pleasure."—*Manchester City News.*

"The author of this treatise on cotton has not only mastered the practice and the theory of what he manufactures, but has also conscientiously discharged the duty of helping forward the cause of technical education by imparting his knowledge to the world. The fact that Dr. Bowman puts the principles he here enunciates to every-day use in one of the largest cotton spinning mills out of Lancashire adds weight to what he has got to say on the subject. Nothing but life-long research could have produced such an essay as this, for it embraces, in the form of an entertaining narrative, everything that may be told about cotton, from the plant to the finest yarn."—*Yorkshire Post.*

"Few persons have more actively contributed, either in the laboratory or in the workshop, to the advancement of science, as applied to cotton spinning and its cognate industries, than the author of the work referred to. It is well worth study, and as a work of reference it should find a place in every establishment where the manufacture of cotton is carried on."—*Yorkshire Inventor and Manufacturer.*

"All who take an interest in the progress of our two leading manufactures will join us in the hope that the present volume is but number one, and that in due course a similar work on the wool fibre will follow, as volume two, from the same talented pen. The work will form a valuable addition to the library, and a most useful adjunct to the cause of technical education. . . . The work is most beautifully got up, and it is at once a credit to the author, and an evidence of his zeal in the cause of technical education."—*Halifax Guardian.*

"Not slothful in business we knew was Mr. Bowman's characteristic, but this work on the cotton fibre indicates a rare devotion; he has endeavoured to master his calling in all its details, and has striven to solve difficulties which, once mastered, will give fresh impetus to this gigantic and ever increasing industry. . . . The book is admirably printed, and the illustrations are excellent. It deserves a large sale amongst cotton manufacturers, dyers, and other technologists."—*Halifax Courier.*

"La recherche toujours croissante de connaissances techniques dans les différentes branches des arts et manufactures a provoqué dans ces derniers temps l'apparition d'ouvrages spéciaux sur les multiples genres de l'industrie textile. Le plus récent est le volume que nous annonçons du docteur Bowman, qui est une monographie complète de l'état de nos connaissances actuelles touchant la fibre du coton, considérée comme matière première des produits manufacturés. La haute situation scientifique de l'auteur, sa collaboration à une des plus grandes manufactures de coton d'Angleterre, dont il est le chef, l'ont tout particulièrement mis à même de traiter ce sujet au double point de vue scientifique et pratique. . . . En Angleterre, on apporte une attention croissante aux sciences, qui sont la base de tous les procédés manufacturiers. Seule, cette connaissance peut permettre de lutter avantageusement sur tous les marchés du globe. Rien ne pouvait paraître plus à propos que cet ouvrage d'un homme qui est une autorité comme le docteur Bowman : tous devraient l'avoir, tous devraient le lire, y compris les écoles techniques, qui doivent l'adopter partout où elles existent."—*Moniteur Scientifique.*—Quesneville.

"Cet ouvrage est celui d'un practicien et d'un savant; c'est l'exposé le plus complet de nos connaissances actuelles sur le coton. Nous lui avons fait de nombreux emprunts, et nous le considérons comme un livre classique."—*Etudes élémentaires sur le Coton.*—Louis Deschamps.

Palmer & Howe's

ECHNICAL & SCIENTIFIC PUBLICATIONS

✤ ✤ ✤ ✤ ✤ ✤ ✤

COTTON SPINNING.—The Science of Modern Cotton Spinning. Embracing mill architecture; machinery for cotton ginning, opening, scutching, preparing, and spinning, with all the latest improvements; also articles on steam and water power; shafting, gearing, and the American system of belting compared; generation and application of steam criticised and explained; boilers, boiler explosions, etc.; all tending to show where the outlay of capital may be economized and production cheapened. By EVAN LEIGH, C.E. Fifth edition, illustrated with 259 cuts and 29 plates. Two vols. large 4to, strongly bound in cloth, price £4. 4s.

COTTON FIBRE.—The Structure of the Cotton Fibre in its Relation to Technical Applications. Second edition, illustrated with numerous engravings and coloured plates. By Dr. F. H. BOWMAN, F.R.A.S., F.L.S. One vol. demy 8vo, price 10s.

CALICO PRINTING.—The Practice and Principles of Calico Printing, Bleaching, Dyeing, Etc. By CHARLES O'NEILL, F.C.S. Two vols. demy 8vo.

PALMER & HOWE, Publishers and Booksellers,
73, 75, and 77, Princess Street, Manchester.

TECHNICAL & SCIENTIFIC PUBLICATIONS.

CHEMISTRY OF BAST FIBRES.—Contributions to the Chemistry of Bast Fibres. By E. J. BEVAN and C. F. CROSS (read before the Owens College Chemical Society, Prof. Schorlemmer, F.R.S., in the chair), with engravings of the authors' micro-photographs. Price 1s.

DYEING AND CALICO PRINTING; Including an account of the most recent improvements in the manufacture and use of aniline colours. Illustrated with wood engravings and numerous specimens of printed and dyed fabrics. By the late DR. F. CRACE-CALVERT, F.R.S., F.C.S., etc. Edited by JOHN STENHOUSE, LL.D., F.R.S., and CHARLES EDWARD GROVES, F.C.S. Third edition, demy 8vo, price 25s. net. (Nearly out of print.)

DYEING AND CALICO PRINTING; Containing eleven page-plates, 47 specimens of dyed and printed fabrics, and 38 woodcuts. By WILLIAM CROOKES, F.R.S., etc. This important and practical handbook is nearly out of print; a few copies only for sale.

ENGLISH DYER.—The English Dyer, with instructions showing how to dye—

150 Shades on		Cotton Yarns in the Hank,
50	,,	Cotton Wool,
150	,,	Worsted Yarns,
100	,,	Animal Wool,
50	,,	Silk in the Skein,

to which is added most valuable information for the use of dyers, manufacturers, merchants, etc. With each of these shades a dyed pattern (500 in all) and a genuine receipt is given; also receipts for making all the dye spirits referred to in the work, and the best mode of extracting burrs from wool, and cotton from rags. By DAVID SMITH. One thick 8vo vol., half morocco, price £4. 4s.

PALMER & HOWE, Publishers and Booksellers,
73, 75, and 77, Princess Street, Manchester.

TECHNICAL & SCIENTIFIC PUBLICATIONS.

DYER'S GUIDE.—The Practical Dyer's Guide; containing five hundred dyed patterns, to each of which a genuine receipt is given. The work comprises practical instructions in the dyeing of Silk, Cotton, and Wool in a raw and manufactured state, and instructions for Dyeing Plain and Mixed Fabrics in single and two colours, and a great variety of Bronzes; also receipts for making all the dye spirits with which to dye every colour in the work. By DAVID SMITH. Second edition, half morocco, price £3. 3s.

THE HESSIAN CALCULATOR.—A new edition in preparation.

MANUFACTURER'S COMPENDIUM.—A most valuable series of TABLES, compiled for the use of manufacturers, cloth agents, managers, putters-out, and others, for all kinds of Plain and Fancy Fabrics, in which Cotton, Worsted, Woollen, Linen, and Silk are required. Arranged on an entirely new plan, with a variety of calculations for Plain Cloths, Ginghams, and Mixed Goods, giving the pattern of cloth for each calculation. By JOHN S. BUCKLE. One large 8vo vol., price 40s.

SIZING AND MILDEW IN COTTON GOODS.—An exhaustive inquiry into the Chemistry of Sizing, and the origin of mildew and other discolorations in Cotton Goods. By GEORGE E. DAVIS, F.C.S., CHARLES DREYFUS, Ph.D., and PHILIP HOLLAND, F.C.S. One vol. 8vo, illustrated, price 15s.

TEXTILE COLOURIST.—A Journal of Bleaching, Printing, Dyeing, and Finishing Textile Fabrics, and the Manufacture and Application of Colouring Matters. Edited by CHARLES O'NEILL, F.C.S. 4 vols. demy 8vo, with numerous illustrations and dyed patterns.

PALMER & HOWE, Publishers and Booksellers,
73, 75, and 77, Princess Street, Manchester.

Palmer & Howe's New List

OF

TELEGRAPH CODES.

THE

TELEGRAPH CYPHERS WITH TERMINATIONAL ORDER.

NEW AND IMPORTANT WORK. FOR PHRASES, &c.

JUST PUBLISHED.

22,500 English Words, 900 pages, printed 25 words to the page, on hand-made paper, ruled with blue lines, with the full width of the quarto page for filling in phrases; containing also two systems of numbering, a preface fully explanatory of the work and of the figure system of telegraphing, and a terminational order.

Specimen Sheet sent on application.

Price : Two or more Copies, 60/- each ; Six Copies for the price of Five.

PALMER & HOWE, Publishers and Booksellers,
73, 75, and 77, Princess Street, Manchester.

THE TELEGRAPH CYPHER OFFICE.

WHITELAW'S TELEGRAPH CYPHERS.
FINAL REVISED EDITIONS.

Two or more Copies.
25,000 English Words ... ... 40*s*. each.
42,600 German Words ... ... 50*s*. ,,
68,400 Latin, Italian, French, Spanish, Portuguese Words 60*s*. ,,

136,000 Words in all.   Six Copies for the price of Five.

The new final revised editions of the above works contain the improvements and alterations suggested after four years' experience and careful watching, in several quarters, of their actual use in daily long and important extra-European telegrams received and despatched.

14,400 **Latin Words** arranged so as to represent any three-letter group, or any three two-figure groups not exceeding twenty-four. Price, two or more copies, **15***s*. each; six copies for the price of five.

All the above works contain only words not exceeding ten letters, arranged both in alphabetical and terminational order, the terminational order being now acknowledged to be the best and readiest detector of words mangled in transmission; arranged also so as to represent any figure-groups, and are compiled on the principle that there shall be at least two letters difference between each of the words, and that no one of the words shall be telegraphically convertible with any other.

Quantity and Quotation Tables for use with the foregoing works, and containing an introduction fully explanatory of figure arrangements of all kinds. Price **20***s*. per copy.

Telegraph Detector, extending to all two-letter groups. Price **2***s*. **6***d*. per copy.

This work often leads to the detection of a mutilated word, and saves the time lost in repetition.

PALMER & HOWE, Publishers and Booksellers,

73, 75, and 77, Princess Street, Manchester.

THE TELEGRAPH CYPHER OFFICE.

Macgregor's Variation Tables (for Indexing, etc.), by which the whole or any part of Whitelaw's **136,000** words (and any other range of words expressing numbers) can be applied to each of any number of different codes or transactions referred to in the same telegram; thus by means of an Index Word at the commencement of a telegram, multiplying indefinitely the number of words available for telegraphing; and giving other advantages, as (*e.g.*) a check to the general tenor of a message, etc.

Mackay's One-Word Telegraph Code. Price **21***s*.; two copies for **31***s*. **6***d*.; additional copies, **10***s*. **6***d*. each.

Adapted to the India, China, Japan, etc. Markets. The object of this Code is to wire in one word **Purchases** or **Sales, Quotations, Firm Offers,** and **Recommendations.**

Parker's Combination Telegraph Code. Single copy, **21***s*.; two or more copies, **15***s*. each.

In publishing this Combination Code, the author has had in view three special objects—**Economy, Simplicity,** and **Comprehensiveness.**

"A B C" Universal Commercial Electric Telegraphic Code. By W. CLAUSON-THUE. Price **15***s*., or interleaved with plain paper, **20***s*.

Specially adapted for the use of **Financiers, Merchants, Shipowners, Brokers, Agents,** etc.

Hawke's Sequence Indicator and **Combination Figure Codes,** accompanied by various useful Telegraphic Tables.

This "Indicator" has been published to supply a want long felt by many firms having telegraphic communications of an extensive nature; is particularly suitable to the requirements of the Manchester Trade, and adapted to all Number Codes. Price **42***s*.

The Special Telegraph Code. Compiled by JOHN DUXBURY. Is adapted to the Eastern Trade, and may be used in connection with Whitelaw's, Ager's, or any Code with 100,000 words. Price **30***s*. net; six copies for the price of five.

PALMER & HOWE, Publishers and Booksellers,

73, 75, and 77, Princess Street, Manchester.

THE TELEGRAPH CYPHER OFFICE.

Dr. Ager's Telegraphic Codes comprise—
  The Standard Telegraph Code, 100,000 words. Price £5. 5s.
  The Standard Supplementary Code for General Merchants, used in connection with Dr. Ager's Standard Code. Price 21s.
  The 10,250 Extra Code Words following in Alphabetical and Numeral Sequence those in the Standard Code. Price 15s.
  The Telegraphic Code. Price £2. 15s. Contains 56,000 Code words. Alternate pages have blank Code words throughout the greater part of the book, giving about 20,000 words available for special telegrams.
  The Telegraph Primer. Price 12s. 6d.
  The Shipping Telegraph Code. Price 21s.
  The Tabular Code. Price £2. 2s.
  The Social Code. Price 12s. 6d.
  The Corn, Seed, and General Merchants' Telegram Code. Price 31s. 6d.

Meyer's Telegraph Codes comprise—
  The International Telegraph Code. Price 25s.
  The General Telegraph Code. Price 21s.
  The Liverpool Cotton Code. Price 63s.
  Appendix Telegraph Code. Price 25s.
  The Commercial Code. Price 25s.
  The Anglo-American Cotton Code. Price 42s.
  The Anglo-American Cotton Code, with Supplement. Price 50s.

Watt's International Telegraph Code. Price 84s. Etc. etc.

ALL NEW CODES MAY BE SEEN AS SOON AS PUBLISHED.

TELEGRAPH CODES FOR BUSINESS AND PRIVATE USE
PRINTED WITH CARE AND DESPATCH.

PALMER & HOWE,

MANUFACTURING AND EXPORT STATIONERS,

Letterpress and Lithographic Printers,

BOOKSELLERS AND PUBLISHERS,

73, 75, & 77, PRINCESS STREET, MANCHESTER.

NEW AND IMPORTANT WORK ON THE WOOL FIBRE.

Just Published, in One Thick 8vo Vol., Bound in Cloth, Price 16s.,
Profusely Illustrated with Engravings and Coloured Plates.

THE STRUCTURE OF THE WOOL FIBRE in Relation to the Use of Wool for Technical Purposes, being the Substance, with Additions, of Five Lectures delivered at the request of the Council to the Members of the Bradford Technical College and the Society of Dyers and Colourists. By F. H. BOWMAN, D.Sc., F.R.S.E., F.L.S.

Just Published, in One Vol., Demy 8vo, Price 10s.

TABLES OF MARINE INSURANCE PREMIUMS, on Sums ranging from £5 to £10,000, at Rates from 2s. 6d. to 50s. per cent. By C. H. PEARSON.

WORKS BY LEO. H. GRINDON.

MANCHESTER BANKS AND BANKERS: Historical, Biographical, and Anecdotal. Few copies now for sale.

COUNTRY RAMBLES, and Manchester Walks and Wild Flowers; being Rural Wanderings in Cheshire, Lancashire, Derbyshire, and Yorkshire. Price 6s.

THE SHAKSPERE FLORA: A Guide to all the principal Passages in which mention is made of Trees, Plants, Flowers, and Vegetable Productions; with Comments and Botanical Particulars. Price 6s. A limited edition, printed on large paper, price 18s.; a few copies only for sale.

New Work in the Press.

FRUITS AND FRUIT-TREES, Home and Foreign; being an Index to the Kinds Valued in Britain, with Descriptions, Histories, and other Particulars. By LEO. H. GRINDON. A small and strictly limited number of copies will be printed on large paper, and elegantly bound in half morocco, gilt top, Roxburghe style, price 12s. 6d., for which *immediate application* should be made.

PALMER & HOWE, Publishers and Booksellers,
73, 75, and 77, *Princess Street, Manchester.*

www.ingramcontent.com/pod-product-compliance
Lightning Source LLC
Chambersburg PA
CBHW031958300426
44117CB00008B/812